JOURNEY

to

THE UNITED STATES
OF NORTH AMERICA

Portrait of Lorenzo de Zavala which hangs in the
Texas State Capitol. (Courtesy Texas State Archives.)

JOURNEY

to

THE UNITED STATES OF NORTH AMERICA

By

LORENZO DE ZAVALA

Translated from the Spanish by

Wallace Woolsey
Professor Emeritus
Texas Women's University

Jacket by Vic Blackburn

SHOAL CREEK PUBLISHERS, INC.
P.O. BOX 9737   AUSTIN, TEXAS 78766

First Edition

Lithographed and Bound in the United States of America

Library of Congress Cataloging in Publication Data

Zavala, Lorenzo de, 1788–1836.
    Journey to the United States of North America.

    Translation of Viage a los Estados-Unidos del Norte de America.
    Includes index.
    1. United States—Description and travel—1783–1848.
    2. Zavala, Lorenzo de, 1788–1836.
I.   Title.
E165.Z3913   973   80–11735
ISBN O–88319–050–8

CONTENTS

*Translator's note: An abbreviated form of Zavala's table of contents is included
in this volume. The lengthy original has been omitted because the entries are
repeated at the beginning of each chapter.

ILLUSTRATIONS

FOREWORD

In a number of ways Lorenzo de Zavala has earned a permanent place in our history. Known as an advocate of democratic reforms in Mexico, de Zavala served his native country—and later Texas—in a number of high government positions. He was well educated and studied religion, medicine and the English language. Among his lasting contributions was the authorship of books, "the most remarkable creation of man," in the words of Clarence Day.

As a writer, de Zavala made valuable contributions to the history of Mexico, Texas, and the United States. His two-volume *Ensayo Histórico de las Revoluciones de Méjico, desde 1808 hasta 1830* was printed in Paris in 1831–1832 and reprinted in 1845 and 1918. The present work *Viage a los Estados-Unidos del Norte de America* was published in Paris in 1834. Long out of print and available in only a few libraries, the present translation by Professor Wallace Woolsey will be applauded by interested historians and others on both sides of the Great River.

When I hear the name of Lorenzo de Zavala I am always reminded of his granddaughter Adina de Zavala. She was the eldest of six children of Augustine and Julia (Tyrell) de Zavala. Augustine was Lorenzo's son by his second marraige to Emily West.

In 1946 when I became a student at the University of Texas and had part-time employment with the Texas State Historical Association, I came across the name of Adina de Zavala as an honorary life member of the organization. "Miss Adina," as she was known at the time, was an active member of the Association, attended the annual meetings, and always contributed a book for the annual book auction. I had the very pleasant assignment to "look after" Miss Adina when she came to the Association meetings in Austin. She was in her eighties then, having been born on November 28, 1861, in Harris County. We became friends and met at least yearly so long as her health permitted her to attend the Association meetings before her death on March 1, 1955, at the age of ninety-three. In her presence I was always a little awed. At the same time I felt I had direct contact with the past, for she was a true living link to the patriot of both the Mexican and Texas revolutionary periods.

My employment brought me in contact with the name of Lorenzo de Zavala a second time when on June 14, 1973, by an act of the 63rd Texas Legislature, the name of the Archives and Library Building in Austin was changed to the Lorenzo de Zavala State Archives and Library Building. The name is now incised on the west facade of the building and pays appropriate honor to the vice-president *ad interim* of the Republic of Texas and signer of the Texas Declaration of Independence. As permanent as the name is on the building so is de Zavala perpetually identified with Texas and Mexican history as ardent liberal, revolutionary, *empresario,* and government official.

Dorman H. Winfrey
Director and Librarian
Texas State Library

PREFACE

The burgeoning new nation—the United States of America—was attracting widespread attention in the early years of the nineteenth century, and domestic and foreign writers were busy touring the country and writing their impressions. One of these was Lorenzo de Zavala who wrote for the benefit of his fellow citizens in Mexico; he hoped to transmit to them his great admiration for the democratic principles that he saw operating here—often overlooking some of the less praiseworthy aspects of nineteenth-century American life. Naturally he wrote his work in Spanish, and one hundred forty-five years later it has never been made available to the English-speaking American public. This has seemed to me to be a bit of Americana that deserves to be known here, and it is for this reason that I have undertaken the translation of the Zavala travelogue.

Here I should like to acknowledge my gratitude and appreciation to those who have been helpful to me in this undertaking:

Dr. Dorman H. Winfrey, Director and Librarian of the Texas State Library, for most graciously consenting to write a brief introduction for the translation. This seemed especially appropriate since the building which houses the Texas State Library bears the name of Lorenzo de Zavala, and Dr. Winfrey is so knowledgeable concerning the author and his life.

Miss Jean Carefoot, a former student of mine at Texas Woman's University and at present Archivist in the Texas State Library, for calling my attention to this particular Zavala work and suggesting that the translation would be a worthwhile project.

Mrs. Mildred Nelson, formerly a member of the Department of English of Texas Woman's University, for her time and effort in reading the manuscript and giving valuable suggestions as to form and style.

The Reference Staff of the Library of Texas Woman's University for their cooperation and aid in running down books and materials.

Ruth Steyn for her many helpful editorial suggestions.

My wife Elizabeth for reading the final draft of the manuscripts in search of those elusive errors that will slip by.

LORENZO DE ZAVALA
Biographical Sketch

Lorenzo de Zavala was born in the small village of Tenoch near Merida in the state of Yucatan, Mexico, October 3, 1788. His parents were Don Anastasio de Zavala and Doña María Barbara Saenz, both of whom were from well-known families of moderate means. He attended the seminary of Ildefonso, which was in the city of Merida and under the direction of the Franciscans. Here he studied Latin, morals, theology and classical philosophy.

When he completed his studies, he came out a very active liberal and a staunch advocate of democratic reforms; with these ideas he went into politics. Because of his political activities and his liberal tendencies he was arrested in May of 1814 and was imprisoned in the castle of San Juan de Ulua for three years. He took advantage of his time there to study medicine as well as English, in which he became very proficient. When he was released in 1817, he returned to Yucatan, where in 1821 he was elected to represent Yucatan in the Spanish Cortes in Madrid. He spent a short time in Spain, but as soon as he learned that Mexico had declared her independence, he returned to Yucatan and was elected to represent the state in the National Congress in Mexico City.

Zavala was chosen president of the Chamber of Deputies, and because of his office he was the first to sign the Federal Constitution when it was adopted October 5, 1824. He was elected governor of the State of Mexico in March of 1827 as a Federalist. However, because of persecution of the Federalists by the army he was forced to flee from the capital and hide in the hills for about a month. Back in Mexico City he became a member of the cabinet of the newly elected President Vicente Guerrero, at the same time retaining his position as governor of the State of Mexico. When he was later forced to resign from the cabinet, he was told that he was no longer qualified to serve as governor and was forced to resign.

After his forced resignation as governor in 1829 Zavala made his way to Veracruz, and from there he went to New Orleans. He did this rather hastily since his friends were convinced that his life would be in danger if he remained in Mexico; this is discussed in the book. In New Orleans he began the travels which he recounts in his *Journey*. After he arrived in New York, and before proceeding on to Philadelphia and Washington, he made a trip to Europe in connection with the business of the Galveston Bay and Texas Land Company. He makes reference to this also in his travelogue, although he gives no details of his stay in Paris.

From 1826 to 1828 Joseph Vehlein, a German merchant of Mexico City, David G. Burnet of New Jersey and Zavala had been granted empresario contracts for settling a total of twelve hundred families in Texas. In October of 1830 these contracts were transferred to the Galveston Bay and Texas Land Company. The policy of this company resembled closely the methods of a modern real estate firm, and any news favorable to the company's prospects was published. Thus when Zavala sailed for Europe the company saw to it that this fact was published.

During his spare time in Paris he wrote his most important historical work entitled *Essay on the Revolutions of Mexico,* which was published in Paris and New York.

Zavala was first married to Teresa Correa with whom he had three children—Lorenzo, Jr., Manuela and a daughter who died in infancy. Teresa died in the spring of 1831 while Zavala was in Paris, and on November 12, 1831, he married Emily West in the Roman Catholic Church of the Transfiguration in New York City. From this marriage also three children were born—Agustin, Emily and Ricardo. Zavala mentions his second wife's birthplace in upper New York state in his travelogue.

In 1832 he returned to Toluca, which had by that time been made the capital of the State of Mexico, and he was again elected governor of the state. In October of 1833 President Santa Anna appointed him minister to France, but by the summer of 1834 Lorenzo de Zavala saw clearly that Santa Anna did not intend to follow the Constitution of 1824 and had in fact made himself a dictator. Because Zavala was an idealist and a staunch defender of democracy, he decided to resign rather than support Santa Anna and his administration. This he did in a letter to the Mexican Government in August 1834. However, he did not leave Paris until April 1835. Zavala arrived in Texas in July 1835 and was joined later by his wife and younger children. He purchased a home just across Buffalo Bayou from what was later to be the site of the Battle of San Jacinto.

Lorenzo de Zavala was only one among many liberals who had fled from Mexico to escape the despotism of Santa Anna. He cast his lot with the growing movement in Texas against the central government. At first, Zavala and many others did not consider separation from Mexico. But the cry for independence began to be heard, and he eventually joined in that also. Zavala represented the Harrisburg Municipality at the Consultation at San Felipe de Austin in 1835. Later, as one of the representatives from Harrisburg to the Constitutional Convention he became one of the signers of the Texas Declaration of Independence. On March 17, 1836, Zavala was unanimously elected provisional vice-president of the Republic of Texas and his colleague David G. Burnet was elected provisional president. After the Battle of San Jacinto, Zavala was also one of those commissioned to accompany Santa Anna to Mexico to negotiate a treaty. For various reasons there were several delays, and as a consequence the trip was never made by Zavala.

During September and October he was too ill to take an active part in the government. In order that the executive and legislative branches of government might take up their functions at the same time, Burnet suggested to Zavala that both of them resign from their respective offices. This they did, and Zavala's letter of resignation is dated October 21, 1836.

He had been in bad health for some time, and when a boat capsized with him and his son in the cold waters of Buffalo Bayou he contracted pneumonia. He died on November 19, 1836, and was buried in the family cemetery on Buffalo Bayou opposite the San Jacinto battlefield. The cemetery is now a part of the San Jacinto State Park, and the State of Texas erected a monument at Zavala's grave in 1931.

Always a great admirer of the American Union, Zavala wrote *Journey to the United States* in order to inform and instruct the Mexican people concerning the manners, customs and, most of all, the political philosophy of their neighbor to the north. Examples of his remarkable liberalism are to be found throughout the book, and he lost no opportunity to point out customs and laws of our country that he felt would be highly beneficial to his native land if adopted there.

In 1838 the town of Zavalla (spelled with double *l*) was incorporated. It is located in the original Lorenzo de Zavala grant, in what is today Angelina County, about thirty miles southeast of Lufkin, Texas. In 1858 Zavala County, whose county seat is Crystal City, was created by the Texas legislature. Originally the spelling for the county was also Zavalla, but towards the middle of this century it was changed to Zavala. The State Archives Building in Austin is named for this early Texas patriot, and an oil painting of the first vice-president of the Republic of Texas hangs in the Senate chamber of the Texas State Capitol in Austin.

Taking into consideration that the present government of Texas had lost the moral confidence of the People and is therefore no longer able to carry into effect their measures I have to tender my resignation as Vice President of the Republic Vic of Texas.

Quintana 3rd June 1836.

Lorenzo de Zavala

After his election as ad interim vice-president of the Republic of Texas, Zavala was disappointed with the government's ineffectual leadership under President Burnet. This, plus his poor health and the controversy over what to do with the captured Santa Anna, probably caused Zavala to tender his resignation on several occasions. However, he continued to serve as vice-president until October 1836. (Courtesy Texas State Archives.)

Zavala wrote in a thoroughly romantic style as evidenced by his intense interest in the manners and customs of the American people—what the Spanish would call *costumbrismo*. His nature descriptions also are most eloquent and romantic—witness his superb word-pictures of the Mississippi River, Niagara Falls and other spots that he described in great detail.

A brief summary of Zavala's life may be found in Louis Wiltz Kemp's book *The Signers of the Texas Declaration of Independence*, The Anson Jones Press, Houston, Texas, 1944, pp.371–380. A detailed and well-researched biography is the unpublished doctoral dissertation of Raymond Estep, ''The Life of Lorenzo de Zavala,'' The University of Texas, Austin, Texas, 1942. This contains excellent and informative footnotes and an extensive bibliography.

Wallace Woolsey
Denton, Texas

The translation by Wallace Woolsey of Lorenzo de Zavala's *Viage a los Estados-Unidos del Norte de America* begins on page 1. The illustrations, index, and front matter contained in this volume have been added by the publisher and do not appear in the original text.

VIAGE

A LOS

ESTADOS-UNIDOS

DEL NORTE DE AMERICA,

Por D. Lorenzo de Zavala.

PARIS,

IMPRENTA DE DECOURCHANT,

CALLE D'ERFURTH, N° I, JUNTO A LA ABADIA.

—

1834

Title page of Zavala's *Viage a los Estados-Unidos del Norte de America* published in Paris in 1834. A copy of the original edition in Spanish is housed in the Texas State Archives. (Courtesy Texas State Archives.)

PROLOGUE

Two things have caused me to write of this journey. The first is that I have believed that nothing can give more useful lessons in politics to my fellow citizens than the knowledge of the manners, customs, habits and government of the United States, whose institutions they have copied so servilely. Secondly, because since I offered in my *Historical Essay* to publish my memoirs, it is now time that I begin, although it may be in incoherent bits and pieces as circumstances permit.

Because a book written by me in which I criticized more or less severely the conduct of the rulers of the Republic in accordance with my conscience, in my capacity as minister of the Mexican Government in France, would not be in keeping with public policy, I have not been able to continue the *History of Mexico* beyond the year 1830, nor to publish the part of my memoirs prior to that period. On the other hand, I was not going to publish a partisan work, much less a collection of panegyrics. The historical truth must come out of the official documents, the press of the period, and the conscientious publications of the few men who divest themselves of personal and party feelings to transmit to posterity events as they are revealed to their understanding by a critical examination. Now that we have committed so many errors that have been so fatal to our fellow citizens, let us at least do the service of confessing them and of presenting ourselves as we have been. Coming generations will profit by these terrible lessons.

This book has no merit as far as originality is concerned. I can say that it has been no great mental effort for me because most of the descriptions, documents, and even many of the reflections, I have taken from others or from my own notes made concerning the places. I have added at the time of coordinating it some considerations that grew out

Zavala's Itinerary

Vera Cruz to New Orleans by steamship.

New Orleans to Pittsburg by steamboat on the Mississippi and Ohio Rivers. Stops at Baton Rouge, Memphis, Louisville, Cincinnati, and Wheeling.

Pittsburgh to Erie by stagecoach.

Erie to Buffalo by steamer on Lake Erie.

Buffalo to Niagara by stagecoach.

Niagara to Quebec and back to Montreal by steamer on Lake Ontario and the St. Lawrence River.

Montreal to St. Jean (Canada) by stagecoach.

St. Jean to Albany by steamboat on Lakes Champlain and George. Stops at Black Island (New York), Plattsburg, Ticonderoga, Whitehall, Glens Falls, and Saratoga.

Albany to New York City by steamboat on the Hudson River.

New York to Philadelphia by steamboat on the Raritan Bay and Raritan River. Stop at Trenton (New Jersey).

Philadelphia to Baltimore by steamboat on the Delaware River and Chesapeake Bay.

Baltimore to Washington, D.C. and Mount Vernon and back to Washington, D.C. by stagecoach.

Return trip from Washington, D.C. to New York City by stagecoach and steamboat.

New York City to Albany by steamboat on the Hudson River.

Albany to Boston by stagecoach. Stops in New Lebanon (New York), Northampton (Massachusetts), Mount Holyoke (Massachusetts), and Lowell.

Boston to New York by stagecoach. Stops in Providence, Hartford, and New Haven.

New York City to West Point and return by steamboat on the Hudson River.

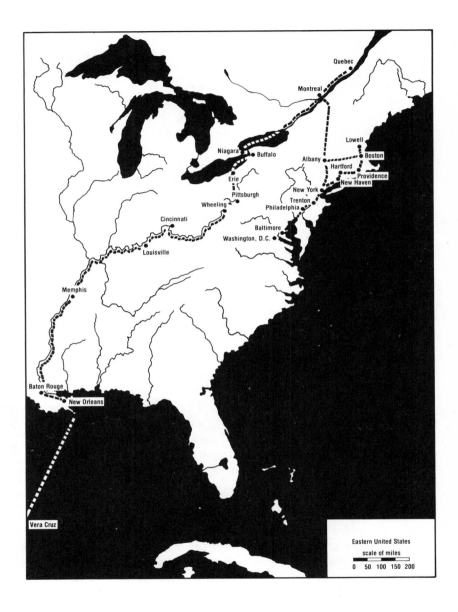

Quebec

Montreal

Lowell

Niagara • Buffalo
Albany • • Boston
Hartford
Erie • Providence
Pittsburgh New Haven
New York
Wheeling Trenton
Cincinnati Philadelphia •
Baltimore
Washington, D.C.
Louisville

Memphis

Baton Rouge
New Orleans

Vera Cruz

Eastern United States
scale of miles
0   50 100 150 200

3

of the circumstances or events that I was relating. However, it should be very useful to Mexicans, for it is to them that I dedicate it. In it they will find a true description of the people whom their legislators have tried to imitate—a people that is hard working, active, reflective, circumspect, religious in the midst of a multiplicity of sects, tolerant, thrifty, free, proud and perservering.

The Mexican is easygoing, lazy, intolerant, generous almost to prodigality, vain, belligerent, superstitious, ignorant and an enemy of all restraint. The North American works, the Mexican has a good time; the first spends less than he has, the second even that which he does not have; the former carries out the most arduous enterprises to their conclusion, the latter abandons them in the early stages; the one lives in his house, decorates it, furnishes it, preserves it against the inclement weather; the other spends his time in the street, flees from his home, and in a land where there are no seasons he worries little about a place to rest. In the United States all men are property owners and tend to increase their fortune; in Mexico the few who have anything are careless with it and fritter it away.

As I say these things it must be understood that there are honorable exceptions, and that especially among educated people are to be found very commendable social and domestic virtues. There are also in the United States people who are prodigal, lazy, and despicable. But that is not the general rule.

I seem to hear some of my fellow countrymen yelling: "How awful! See how that unworthy Mexican belittles and exposes us to the view of civilized peoples." Just calm down, gentlemen, for others have already said that and much more about us and about our forefathers, the Spaniards. Do you not want it said? Then mend your ways. Get rid of those eighty-seven holidays during the year that you dedicate to play, drunkenness and pleasure. Save up capital for the decent support of yourselves and your families in order to give guarantees of your concern for the preservation of the social order. Tolerate the opinions of other people; be indulgent with those who do not think as you do; allow the people of your country to exercise freely their trade, whatever it may be, and to worship the supreme Author of the Universe in accordance with their own consciences. Repair your roads; raise up houses in order to live like rational beings; dress your children and your wives with decency; don't incite riots in order to take what belongs to somebody else. And finally, live on the fruit of your labors, and then you will be worthy of liberty and of the praises of sensible and impartial men.

The people of Mexico are my Maecenas, but I do not follow in the way of others who fill a page with the praises of those persons whose patronage they solicit. The advantage of those who write without expecting a reward is that they say what they feel, and they are believed and respected.

In my writings I have never sought anything other than the truth. Whoever reads what I write, unless he has been badly advised, will find naturalness, frankness, good faith, an unquenchable desire for the public good and an insatiable love of liberty. If passion or affection be mixed in once in a while, surely it has been without my noticing or suspecting it.

You, my dear reader, try to read this book with attention, and I hope that when you have finished it you will have changed many of your ideas—not in prejudice to reason, nor even less to morality, nor to your religion, whatever it may be, but in favor of them.

THE MISSISSIPPI IN TIME OF PEACE

Currier & Ives, 1865

6

CHAPTER I.

After the fall in December of 1829 of General Guerrero, who was ousted from the presidential chair by General Don Anastasio Bustamante, I had remained in Mexico exposed to all the fury of the dominant party. This position was all the more dangerous for me because one of the pretexts that they had alleged against Guerrero's administration was that I was one of the secretaries, and that my abuses and pilferings were carrying the nation to the brink. Neither could they forget that I had had a large part in the popular revolution of Acordada—a revolution covered with ignominy because of the looting that accompanied it and the illegality of its beginning, since it had as its purpose to substitute for the legally elected Don Manuel G. Pedraza another individual who had a smaller number of votes. However, he was more popular, and if the election had been carried out by direct vote, he would have garnered an immense majority in his favor. This is one of the great defects of the present constitution of the United Mexican States.

I was the object then of the hatred of the victorious party, and Don Lucas Alaman kept repeating this to me every day on the visits that he made to observe me. There was no daily paper of the Government or of

7

the party that did not contain some diatribe, some slander, some incitement against me; and I, confined to my house, given over entirely to reading and private work, saw my existence threatened, following several assassinations carried out and the persecution loosed against the partisans of the previous administration. Finally, Minister Alaman made it clear to me that I should leave the country, and that this would be the only means of assuring my safety.

May 25, 1830, four years before the date on which I am beginning to write this book, I left Mexico City in the company of General Don José Antonio Mejía, then colonel and secretary of the Mexican legation to Washington. We had no escort because several friends had told me that I would not be very safe in the hands of people that could get rid of me with very little effort, and we preferred being exposed to attack by bandits, who after all would be satisfied with taking from us what we had, and at the most would give us a beating.

We arrived in Puebla de los Angeles and stopped at the house of Don Domingo Couto, a wealthy man of the city, whose family with every courtesy consoled us somewhat for our suffering in the past. At that time without the line of coaches that exists today linking Mexico City, Puebla, Jalapa and Veracruz, the trip was made in ten or twelve days with the greatest of inconvenience. There was no inn where the traveler could rest—I do not say with decency, but not even with the most common conveniences, such as bed, chairs, tables, glasses, plates, etc. Things have changed a great deal since that time, and it is to be hoped that they will continue to improve from day to day. In Jalapa there was already a French inn with good service, and it is certainly a comfort, after a hard trip, to find a well kept lodging in which are to be found the advantages of civilization.

As he descends to the beaches of Veracruz one begins to feel the blistering air of the low country of the tropics. The broad and vast plains of the plateau do not present, it is true, that vigorous vegetation, that perfumed air, that variety of flowers, fruits, birds and waters that arouse such great emotions in the traveler to the hot country. But a burning atmosphere, clouds of mosquitoes and other flying insects, poisonous reptiles, and the death-dealing yellow fever that threatens those born in cold or temperate climates, are terrible plagues that cause more of an unfavorable impression than they do of the gentler feelings of its advantages. But those who have enjoyed the wonderful evenness of the delightful climate of the Valley of Puebla, the constant salubriousness and uniform freshness of that of Toluca, the gentle and almost divine climate of Queretaro, what strong feelings must they not experience as they come into the hot country which Agustin believed to be uninhabitable, no doubt because he felt the coming of the south winds from the sands of

Africa where his bishopric was? I, since I was born in Yucatan, had no reason to fear yellow fever. We arrived in Veracruz May 30.*

As I was dining at the home of Mr. Stone, the American vice-consul at that time, on the day after my arrival, I received letters and public papers from Mexico City, in which it was announced that in that city Captain Don Mariano Zercero was to be executed, standing accused a few days earlier of having been implicated in a conspiracy. Such was the terror that this news caused us that Señor Mejía and I resolved to give the captain of the schooner *United States* five hundred dollars provided he would leave with us the next day for New Orleans where we had decided to go in order to travel up the Mississippi.

Since a north wind had blown up, the departure of the schooner was delayed until June 2 when we set sail in a boat that offered no type of conveniences, but which was taking me out of a country where at that time there were no guarantees, and even less for me who had been through so many risks and hazards in the bitter days when military power was governing that unfortunate nation.

The sight of the ocean, whose imposing majesty always produces a strong feeling in those who have not seen it, or have not seen it for some time, or contemplate it with the eyes of a philosopher, that grandiose spectacle produced in me profound meditations concerning the events to which I had been witness, and in many of them a participant, since my entrance into Mexico City in April of 1822, when I went there for the first time to discharge my duties as the deputy from the State of Yucatan, my native land, after having fulfilled that same mission in Spain the previous year. Eight years had passed, and I had seen the enactment of the most important historical dramas—a great nation lift itself up from a colonial nonentity, an empire formed, a national assembly convened, a Mexican general crowned, the throne in eclipse and the empire dissolved, the elevation from the embers of the monarchy of a federated republic, this people given a constitution and its states organized sovereign and independent, diplomatic relations established with the leading powers, with this republic taking its place among the nations of the earth. But, ah! What germs of civil dissention!

After six days of sailing—June 7—the captain announced to us that we were approaching the Balize, the New Orleans lighthouse. The first impression that one gets is the remarkable change in the color of the waters of the Gulf of Mexico some leagues before enter-

*Translator's note: Although the dates given for Zavala's departure (May 25) and his arrival (May 30) appear to be inconsistent with his statement that the trip took ten to twelve days, this wording is according to his text.

9

ing the mouth of the mighty Mississippi. This immense river battles against the waters of the ocean and causes them to back up in such a manner that for more than six leagues that water does not have the same taste as the sea water. The beaches are so low that they are seen, even when passing the Balize, as nothing more than mounds of earth at the level of the water, upon which there are a few miserable huts where it is scarcely conceivable that rational beings live. Floating on the current can be seen great pieces of wood, entire trees, that the force of hurricanes pulled loose two or three thousand miles away and which have been dragged along by the roaring currents of the tributaries of the Mississippi. The view of this entrance and even the course of the river as far as Fort Placquemines is unpleasant, for the only thing to be seen are reeds and wretched shrubs, the sight of which appears all the more distasteful because there are only mountains of mud and an endless number of lizards that look like pieces of dried wood.

We were forced to anchor twelve miles from the Balize up the river to await a favorable wind or the passing of some steamer of the type that are used to tow ships that arrive at the port and are willing to pay at the rate of twenty-five cents a ton. During the night the moon rose clear and beautiful, and its light, gently reflected in the turbid waters of the river, made pleasant the night whose silence was interrupted by the buzzing of an infinite number of mosquitoes that sucked our blood. The following day, June 9, we continued as far as Fort Placquemines, where we transferred to the steamboat that was going up to New Orleans towing two brigantines and a schooner. I arrived in New Orleans at seven o'clock in the evening on Thursday, June 10.

In that city a few Spaniards were publishing a newspaper entitled *El Español,* paid for by the government of Ferdinand VII. It was established with the purpose of serving as vanguard to the Barradas expedition, whose success was, as is well known, in accordance with the far-fetched ideas of the project. My arrival in New Orleans was announced by them with gross insults while *La Abeja (The Bee)* and the *Louisiana Advertiser* spoke of me with the praise and respect always due the unfortunate ones. I took lodging in the French inn of Madame Herries, one of the best in the city—good rooms, decent beds, plenty of well-seasoned food, although somewhat expensive, since it was no less than three dollars per day.

New Orleans is a city inhabited by small remnants of old Spanish families, a considerable proportion of French families, one half of the population made up of blacks and those of mixed blood, and the rest of North Americans who are, as is well known, a composite of the sons and descendants of the English, German, Irish and other peoples of Europe. In the city very little Spanish is spoken, much more French, and generally English, in which language are written the public registers of the authorities.

The overall view of the city offers nothing that can please the eyes of the traveler; there are no cupolas, nor towers, nor columns, nor buildings of handsome appearance and exquisite architecture. Its location, lower than the surface of the river and surrounded by lagoons and swamps, makes it gloomy and unhealthful. The character of the people is completely unlike that of the other cities of the United States. The river is at that point nearly a mile wide, and a wall of sand forms a powerful dike that extends for many leagues and is called the Levee; it keeps the waters of the great river from flooding the city and surrounding areas. In New Orleans the tide is hardly perceptible.

The location of New Orleans is ideal for a commercial city. A forest of masts comes into view as one approaches the Levee, and since the river is deep at this point, the ships have ready access to the bank where they can unload easily by means of wooden planks laid to the boats. There is not a city in the world that has the advantage of such extensive internal navigation. There are more than twenty thousand miles of navigable waters not only along the Mississippi, the Missouri, the Ohio and other great tributaries of the Mississippi, but along and through lakes and bays that put it in communication with Florida and other points.

When I arrived, there were more than a thousand boats, large and small, and at least five thousand sailors. When I was in the city in December of 1821, there were at the most forty thousand inhabitants, and today it is estimated that there are at least seventy thousand. Commerce has increased considerably, and the customs duties today amount to more than two million dollars. If yellow fever, intermittent fever, mosquitoes and the unbearable heat of summer did not offer such serious drawbacks to the growth of population, certainly New Orleans would become under the free and popular government that it has today one of the richest and most distinguished cities in the world. In spite of the plagues referred to, it is progressing rapidly and will become one of the leading cities of the New World.

The reader will not find displeasing the description which Mr. Flint gives of the city:

A thousand miles distance from the sources of the Mississippi River, and more than a thousand from those of the Ohio, in a sharp bend upon the east bank of the river is located New Orleans, the great commercial capital of the Mississippi Valley. Its position as a

11

commercial city has no equal in the world, in my opinion. A short distance from the Gulf of Mexico, upon the banks of a river which it might be said waters the universe, six miles from Lake Pontchartrain and connected to it by a navigable canal; with the immense flood of waters that descend from all directions and form pools connected easily by means of natural canals; with hundreds of steamers that frequent the port from fifty different points; with agricultural products from its own state and from others that can compete with the richest of any country in the world. Its location is superior to that of New York. It has, however, one terrible disadvantage—the unhealthfulness of its location. If they could drain the immense swamps that lie between the city and the eternal forests, complete the improvements that the city has undertaken—in short, if they could bring it about so that the climate was not so humid, New Orleans would no doubt become the leading city of the Union.

Many efforts are being made to accomplish these great results. Unfortunately when the constellation of the Dog Star is at its zenith, yellow fever begins to appear in the east. But in spite of the fact that annually, or at least biennially, this pestilential plague visits the city; in spite of the fact that its mortal scythe destroys a multitude of unfortunate beings that are not acclimated and obliges the rich to seek out healthier places at considerable distances; and, finally, in spite of the terror that everywhere accompanies these plagues and to a certain degree is associated with the name of the city, its population is growing considerably.

Everywhere can be seen new buildings that are going up rapidly, and the appearance of the city is improving month by month. Americans come here from all of the states; their purpose is to accumulate wealth and go somewhere else to enjoy it. But death, which they are not disposed to take into account, obliges them to abandon the place before fulfilling their desires.

New Orleans is on an island formed on one side by the Mississippi, and on the others by Lakes Borgne, Pontchartrain and Maurepas, and the Iberville River, which separates from the Mississippi 120 miles above the city and flows into Lake Maurepas.

The market place is well supplied, and things are cheap. During the month that I was there there was a scarcity of vegetables which are abundant in March, April and May. The market is the Tower of Babel, for there one can hear blacks, mulattoes, Frenchmen, Spaniards, Germans, and Americans crying their wares in different languages. The *quadroon* women dress tastefully and neatly, and as they generally have very good figures and are beautiful, they present a striking contrast to the blacks from whom they are descended, and the philosopher cannot help noticing this variety of castes that forms surprising shades.

There are two distinct cities divided not by some river, or district, or other similar object, but by the type of buildings, customs, language and class of society. The fact is that this was a French colony in its beginnings, and it passed for some time into the hands of the Spanish; in the time of Charles IV, the Spanish government ceded it to France in an agreement on the settlement of certain debts and the occupation of the Florida territory. Napoleon sold it to the United States for ten million dollars, and from that time dates the rapid progress of Louisiana. Hence the diversity of customs and manner of living that in that city is one of the peculiar characteristics of its population.

ACROSS THE CONTINENT
Westward the Course of Empire Takes Its Way

Currier & Ives, 1868

14

CHAPTER II.

French expedition and founding of the colony.—Occupation of Canada by the English.—It passes to the hands of the Spaniards.—Returned to the French in the time of the Republic.—North American marine trade.—Negotiations started with this in mind.—Mr. Livingston and Mr. Monroe, ministers for the republic.—M. Barbé-Marbios on the part of the French.—Conclusion of the treaty.—Rapid progress of Louisiana after this agreement.—Arable lands under the control of the United States.—Difficulties in marking the boundaries of that immense territory.—Reflections of M. Barbé-Marbois.—Products and trade of Louisiana.—Its government.—Theater.—The fair sex.—Holidays.—Catholics and Protestants.—Catholic slaves.—Religious consolation.—Father Cedella.—Cemeteries.—Battlefield in 1815.—Strategy of General Jackson.—Attack of English General Pakenham.—Defeat of the English.—Glorious triumph of the Americans.—Confidence and measures of the American general.—Regular troops of this country.—Opinion of the Princes of Saxony-Weimar and Wurtemberg concerning these troops.—Method of replacements.—Brief thoughts on slavery.—General Guerrero's decree that abolished it in Mexico.—Harsh treatment that the slaves in Louisiana experience.—Antiphilosophical laws in the same state concerning this unfortunate class.—Reflections.—Influence of slavery on the progress of civilization.—Brief memoir on the haciendas of the hot lands of the Mexican republic.—An unpleasant happening before my departure from New Orleans.

In 1672 the French, who owned Canada, made an expedition along the Mississippi and descended it as far as the Arkansas River, about latitude 33° north. In 1682 the governor of Canada descended as far as the Gulf of Mexico, and gave the name of Louisiana to the lands through which the river ran in honor of Louis XIV. The French took possession of those areas from the mouth of the Mobile River as far as San Bernardo Bay, a distance of about 120 leagues beyond the mouths of the Mississippi. Louis XIV granted to Crozat, a rich financier, the exclusive trade in these colonies for twelve years. The grant came to an end in 1719, and when the colony was transferred to the West Indies Company, the latter sent a considerable number of colonists.

Father Charlevoix, a well-educated Jesuit who traveled through Louisiana in 1722, made fun of the writers who had praised so highly the mineral wealth of this province, and at the same time he prophesied its future prosperity because of the fertility of its lands and the abundance of waters and rivers. The colony was poorly governed; the company made war on the Indians, and in 1731 trade was declared free. A short time after this period the French government tried to realize the project of uniting Canada and Louisiana, with the purpose of closing off all communication by the English colonists with the western parts of the continent. In that period the English had not yet penetrated to the west of the Allegheny Mountains. Many Frenchmen had moved their families and their fortunes to Illinois, a country of unlimited fertility, watered by several navigable rivers, endowed with one of the mildest climates in the world. The colonists, instead of selecting points that they were able to occupy as their own property, fencing and clearing them to make them secure as they should, scattered themselves indiscriminately without any boundaries or limits.

In the war between France and England in 1754 the latter conquered, and the former agreed to cede all the territory existing on the east bank of the Mississippi, with the sole exception of Louisiana. A line drawn in the middle of the Mississippi separated the English possessions from the French. In 1764 Louisiana passed into the hands of the Spanish government by a secret treaty, but the administration remained in the hands of the French until 1768. After that, the two great revolutions of America and France occurred, and Napoleon, elevated to power and looking out over all points of the globe, had the idea of occupying Louisiana, in order to have a powerful influence in the great transactions of America which was beginning to attract the attention of Europe. By a secret treaty in 1800 he managed to bring about Charles IV's restoration of Louisiana to the French Republic. This agreement was not made public until the peace between Great Britain and France was signed, and it was fully revealed at the time of the Peace of Amiens, March 29, 1802. But when it was announced in England, from all sides came loud outbursts against the cession of Louisiana to France. Lord Hawkesbury said in the House of Commons that France had held Louisiana long enough without having reaped any benefit. On this occasion he came forth with the bold and unwise phrase: "We only wish to make an experimental peace."

General Bernadote, today King of Sweden, was named the first governor of the colony, but he refused the appointment, and in his place General Victor was named; he was on the point of departure to his new post when hostilities began anew between England and France.

During this interval when the Congress of the United States was informed of the cession of Louisiana to France, and the preparations of the latter to take possession, that body did not think it should remain indifferent to seeing established on its borders and in such important places a warlike nation that would not remain as inactive as the Spanish, and that soon would begin to raise questions about navigation on the Mississippi. Alarm was so great in the western part of the United States that President Jefferson had great difficulty in pacifying the inhabitants there, who were ready to resort to force. This would have put obstacles in the way of negotiations that the American government was trying to initiate with France, first for maintaining free navigation on the Mississippi, second that New Orleans would remain a free port for the products of the states of the interior, and finally to conduct matters to the point where they would bring about the transfer of power.

During this time Mr. Livingston, brother of the present minister of the United States in France, and well known as the cooperator with Fulton in the establishment of steamships, exercised the same charge that is today filled by the honorable Edward Livingston. He had made representations to President Jefferson concerning the crisis that would threaten the United States if the French Republic occupied Louisiana, and Jefferson could not deny the consequences of such an occupation. To treat with Napoleon he then gave the mission of envoy extraordinary to Mr. Monroe, instructing him that in case he did not obtain a satisfactory agreement conforming with the interests of the United States, he should communicate with the cabinets of Saint James and Madrid. Mr. Monroe, who was later president of the United States, had been an envoy during the time of the Directory, and his conduct had established for him a considerable reputation in France.

The mission committed to Mr. Monroe and Mr. Livingston was that of obtaining from the French government, by means of the proper indemnification, the cession of New Orleans and all the territory belonging to France on the east bank of the Mississippi, the middle of which was considered to be the dividing line between American and French territories. They had instructions that in the event that they were not able to obtain this, or as a last resort the free navigation of the Mississippi, and the circumstance of New Orleans remaining a free port, they should enter into negotiations with England with the purpose of making common cause with her against France. In the letter written to Mr. Livingston by President Jefferson are found these remarkable words: ''The day that France takes possession of New Orleans she pronounces the sentence of lowered esteem for herself on the part of the United States, and she seals the alliance between two nations that together can maintain the exclusive possession of the ocean. From that moment on we shall link ourselves closely with the English nation, her navy, etc.''

Mr. Monroe left New York March 8, 1803, the same day that there was delivered to the British Parliament the message from the crown that announced the approaching break with France, so that on his arrival Mr. Monroe found the French government well disposed to treat with the United States. Napoleon recognized that since he was at war with England he must change his outlook and his policy with respect to the control of Louisiana. He could not fail to see that since the English were so powerful on the seas they would cut all his trade relations with the colony, and that they would occupy it at the first opportunity in order to sell it to the North Americans. By one of those masterstrokes that were so much a part of his nature he made up his mind to sell the colony to the United States. In this manner not only did he prevent the conquest that the English could make of that region, he also received a considerable amount of money in payment for it, which sum would be of great use to France in the circumstances in which she found herself with her resources exhausted and on the eve of a continental war.

There were two opinions in the cabinet of the first consul. M. Marbois was in favor of the measure for the reasons set forth, and M. Talleyrand felt that the possession of Louisiana should in time indemnify France for her great losses because of the richness and fertility of the soil, its dominant position on the Mississippi and its trade; in case the English should occupy it, the French could do likewise with Hanover, which would be a pawn against its restitution.

The first consul did not change his decision, and the next day he called M. Barbé-Marbois and said to him,

Mr. Minister, I renounce Louisiana. Not only do I want France to get rid of New Orleans, but of the entire colony without reserve. I commission you to handle this delicate subject with the agents of the United States. I need a great deal of money for this war, and I do not wish to begin it with fresh levies. If one were to arrange the terms of the price in view of the advantages that would accrue to the United States from this cession, certainly there would be no sum sufficiently large to cover it. I will be moderate out of the need in which I find myself to make this sale—I want fifty million francs (a little less than nine million dollars), making it clear that I will not enter into any sort of treaty for less. Mr. Monroe will be here soon; begin by making him the proposal without any further preliminaries. You will keep me informed day by day and hour by hour of the progress of the negotiations. The cabinet in London will know the decisions of Washington, but they will not know mine. Maintain the greatest secrecy, and demand it of the American ministers.

The conferences began the following day, and the ministers of both countries, who had an equal interest in a prompt conclusion, carried the negotiations as far as they could in accordance with the instructions and powers of the Americans. But as I have said, they had them only for dealing with the left bank of the river including New Orleans, and not concerning the west side.

It was impossible to confer with their government over so great a distance on a matter that was so delicate when hostilities had already begun or were about to begin between England and France. Consequently the American ministers did not hesitate to take upon themselves the responsibility of dealing with that vast portion of North America belonging to France that extends along the banks of the greatest rivers of the universe. On this basis they signed the treaty. In a letter written by Mr. Jefferson to Mr. Monroe he said to him:

Our project of acquiring by purchase New Orleans and the Florida territory is subject to so many combinations and diverse efforts that we cannot give definite instruction; it was necessary to send a minister extraordinary so that he and the regular minister might work with discretionary powers.

This clause indicates that the American envoys were confident that their conduct would be approved, and indeed it was. The negotiations were concluded on eighty million francs, with twenty million remaining on deposit to cover the claims of the United States against France. The treaty was ratified in Washington, and Louisiana became a province of the United States.

From that time on states have been formed from that territory. The first was Louisiana, which takes in New Orleans and contains forty-eight thousand square miles, and then Missouri, a part of the extensive territory of the Missouri River, on the west side of the Mississippi, the extent of which is sixty-three thousand square miles. A state has not yet been formed from the Arkansas Territory, also a part of what was formerly the French province. It is about 550 miles long and 220 miles wide. The Northwest portion of the Missouri River to the shores of the Pacific is of enormous extension. The river runs for more than two thousand miles.

As one surveys the prodigious extent of these parts and the other possessions of the United States in the Northwest, as well as in Florida and Michigan, which are as yet sparsely populated, the calculation of M. Chateaubriand is not out of line when he says that the population of the United States *as of now occupies an eighteenth part of its territory*. M. de Marbois, employed for a long time in the United States, wrote:

> In these boundless regions the human race can multiply with complete freedom. There *for many centuries* there will be no obstacle to marriages, and parents will not fear that their descendants will lack for lands to feed the fruits of their gentle and honest conjugal union.

This calculation and these reflections are equally applicable to our United Mexican States, where unquestionably nature has been most provident with regard to the fertility of the land and the ease of subsistence.

In the United States there are in effect three hundred million acres of arable lands, not counting the vast stretches of the West and the Northwest. A great portion of these lands remain in the hands of the Government of the Union, and in the course of a few years they will produce for their territory many millions of dollars. There is no way of calculating their value.

All the unoccupied territories became, as a consequence of the treaties made with France and Spain, the property of the United States. The government in Washington had a great deal of difficulty in marking the limits of the territories that they were to occupy in accordance with the treaty made with France, since they are classified in geography only under the designation of unknown lands. The one commissioned to do so was Mr. Jacob Astor of New York, who founded a town on the banks of the Columbia named Astoria after him.

Says M. Marbois:

> Conquerors extend their states by force of arms; they become known for the blood that they spill and the desolation that they inflict in the countries that they occupy. The republic of the United States has extended itself by sending surveyors and wise men up to distances of five hundred leagues. Without force they establish the boundaries of their peaceful conquests, and with good laws they assure the lasting prosperity of the communities for which they were acquired.

When people speak of the city of New Orleans they seem to be filled with pride because of its rapid progress; it had a population in 1803 of only eight thousand persons.

New Orleans, founded in 1707, which has remained unchanged for a century, has become in the short span of twenty-five years one of the most flourishing of cities—as soon as it became a part of the great community of the United States. A few years of good government have produced what many generations could not bring about under the dominion of *prohibitive laws and petty restrictions.* The town, which in the time of those laws stood still, has multiplied five times; its lands produce everything from the most necessary to the most delicate articles of luxury and comfort.

In the states of Louisiana and Mississippi sufficient sugar is manufactured to provide half the consumption of the United States. The other products of those lands are increasing proportionally. There are warehouses of pelts of beaver, ermine, martins, seals and other animals. Lands sold in the time of the French and Spanish governments have risen to an extraordinary price. I knew a former Spanish colonist, Don José Vidal, who made a considerable fortune with the lands that he acquired in Natchez at the time that it was a Spanish colony.

In the state of Louisiana there are two legislative chambers. It is the only state where I have seen the discussions carried on in two languages; the result is that often the Creole representative who speaks French is not understood by the American representative who speaks English. However, in the end the discussions are printed in both languages. Many newspapers are published half in French and the other half in English. There is also an interpreter who translates the speeches into the respective languages to be understood by everyone. Although this has the drawback that it can never be translated exactly as it was said, and much time is lost, there is an advantage, however, in that the interpreter may tone down some personal remarks in the discussion.

In New Orleans there is a French theater and an English one. The first is rather good, and I have seen some *vaudevilles* that were well sung and acted. The English travelers speak very disparagingly of the English theater. I believe indeed that it must not be very good because, generally speaking, the North Americans do not care for this type of entertainment, and as Mrs. Trollope says, they will think a long time before shelling out shillings to pay the price of admission.

The Creole women are pretty and charming. Although they are not as white as the North American women, they have better figures, dress with more charm, carry themselves better, and their manner is more open and pleasant.

As in all Catholic countries, Sunday is a day of fun in New Orleans. Stores of Catholics are open; there are dances, music and parties. During the morning they run to the cathedral to hear mass where people of all colors are gathered. The cathedral is a small temple that has no regular order of architecture and in no way resembles the churches of Mexico. The altars are like those of our small towns, except that the images are much better.

Although Catholics and Protestants agree that all men are children of God, brothers one to another and joint heirs to glory, only the former give practical examples of this profession of faith. In a Catholic church the black and the white, the slave and his master, the noble and the common man kneel before the same altar, and there is a temporary unawareness of all human distinctions; all come in the character of sinners, and there is no rank other than that of the ecclesiastical hierarchy. In this sacred precinct the rich man does not receive incense, no one's pride is flattered, nor does the poor man feel himself put down. The mark of degradation disappears from the brow of the slave as he sees himself admitted together with the free and the rich to lift his songs and prayers to the author of nature. In the Protestant churches such is not the case. All people of color are excluded or separated in one corner by bars or railings, so that even in that moment they have to feel their degraded condition.

The most wretched slave receives from the hands of the Catholic priest all the consolations of religion. He is visited in his sickness, comforted in his afflictions; his dying lips receive the sacred host, and in the final moments of his death agony the last voice that he hears is the sublime apostrophe that the Catholic addresses to the dying person: *Profiscere, anima christiana.* ("Depart in peace, oh Christian soul"). Why shouldn't all the slaves and blacks of Louisiana be Catholics? The congregation of the Protestant church consists of a few well-dressed ladies in the decorated pews, while all the paving stones of the cathedral are filled with people of all colors. I recall as an example that Father Antonio de Cedella, a Capuchin religious, with whom I made friends in 1822, but who is dead now, was the oracle of the colored people and respected by all classes of the city. This Spanish ecclesiastic by his friendliness, his tolerance and other virtues had made himself honored and loved.

In New Orleans, as in Mexico, deep graves cannot be dug without striking water. The cemetery, on a parcel of land not more than half a mile from the city, surrounded by swamps, although of great extent, is scarcely sufficient for the necessities of the population.

A curious traveler interested in the glories of America cannot visit New Orleans without spending some time seeing the field of the famous action of General Andrew Jackson against the English troops who were under the command of General Edward Pakenham,

N. Currier, 1842

THE BATTLE OF NEW ORLEANS, FOUGHT JAN. 8th, 1814

23

in January of 1816. The plain on which the action took place is about four miles from the city; it extends for about a mile, and at the time of the landing of the English it was covered with sugar cane.

Today it is used for pasture land. The Mississippi borders it on the west; on the east there is a thick woods of cypress and pine trees. There still remain the traces of the ditches that the American general ordered to be dug between the river and the swamp. The excavation could not have been deep because in a short time it caved in and filled with water. The trenches that were made were formed from sacks of cotton that were certainly very appropriate for the purpose because of the softness of the cotton which deadened the effect of the bullets. Behind these trenches General Jackson placed his riflemen, putting at the back of each one another to load in a moment so as not to lose time.

A week or two was spent in skirmishes until January 8 when Sir Edward Pakenham began to attack the line. The field in between up to the point of defense was completely open, and thus the English general left his troops unprotected to receive all of the enemy fire without any defense. Exposed to the terrible artillery fire, even at half a cannon shot distance, and then to the sure fire of the rifles, the invaders could not maintain the order of attack and broke ranks. The defenders at some points were six deep and inflicted horrible casualties. The daring Pakenham led the attack in person, struggling to reestablish order, but he was wounded by flack from the artillery that took both his legs, and was then killed by rifle fire. Generals Gibbs and Kean who followed him with the same courage suffered the same fate, and General Lambert, who finally saw the impossibility of gaining any advantage, ordered the retreat and the reembarkation of the troops.

The number of invaders was about 10,000 men, and that of the Americans 3,400. General Jackson reporting on his triumph informed his government: "There is no case in history of a more complete victory, nor one that cost less blood to the victors. Our losses were *six dead and nine wounded;* those of the enemy were more than 3,000 dead and as many more wounded." The defense was made by the brave American general with *volunteers from Tennessee and national militia from Kentucky with a few others from New Orleans* and a very small number of regular troops.

The great merit of General Jackson in these critical circumstances, in addition to his valor which no one disputes, was in having been able to inspire confidence in the inhabitants of New Orleans by the forcefulness of his character. The legislature of Louisiana had been hesitant, the people of the city came to the point of showing signs of wishing to enter into negotiations with the English. From the moment that he arrived in the city he put an end to all uncertainty. In a message addressed to the governor he said: "He that is not with us is against us. Those who have been drawn by lot must be obliged with severe penalties to join the line. We should fear more the hidden enemy than those whom we can see. The fatherland must be defended, and it will be."

In these trying circumstances the general had no troops, and it is easy to imagine the difficulties in which he must have found himself, with the terror that a numerous and well-disciplined army at the gates of the city inspired in the mothers, wives and daughters of those who were called to a combat against what appeared to be such great odds.

When he left the city for the battlefield with a few hundred men, he wrote to Mr. Edward Livingston, author of the law codes of Louisiana, and today minister plenipotentiary to France, saying to him: "Assure the inhabitants that the enemy will not get as far as the city and try to calm them." But in the difficult situation in which he found himself he took on the powers of a dictator and declared martial law. He punished several deserters with death; he interned to the interior at a distance of 120 miles many Frenchmen who refused to take up arms; he arrested the French consul who tried to resist the carrying out of martial law; he banished a judge who provided an act of *habeas corpus* to free the French consul; in short he acted in accordance with what the unusual circumstances demanded of a man capable of such an undertaking. The people of New Orleans, convinced that the forcefulness of his character and the opportuneness of his provisions had saved the city, received him after the victory in triumph and as the liberator of the whole country.

I must not end this chapter without some mention of the regular troops of the United States and citing the testimony of respectable travelers in that area. The army of the American Union is composed of only six thousand men, but the order, the discipline, the spit and polish, the good manners are as though born in those soldiers. There is no officer who is not aware of his duties as a military man and as a citizen. His education is worthy of respect, and on this point I wish to cite the respectable testimony of the Duke of Saxony-Weimar who writes about some officers that he met in Washington in these terms:

> Most of the men with whom I have dealt are officers in the army. It would be difficult to find in Europe a corps of officers of better condition than that of this small American army. No one can

25

be an officer if he has not had an outstanding education. Almost all are taken from the military academy at West Point; there are not those hasty promotions as in Europe. When you meet an American officer, you can be sure that he has all the qualities that will bring him esteem in the most select society.

The prince who writes this is the brother-in-law of the present King of England.

The Prince of Wurtemberg, who traveled in the United States in the year 1828, wrote on the same subject: "There is no country in the world," he said,

where the soldiers are put to work more usefully. In Europe the soldier puts in the whole day in exercises, parades, cleaning his clothes and his arms, or in idleness. The American soldier is constantly occupied in some work. The rigorous discipline to which he is subjected keeps him up to a level of preparedness that is maintained in other countries with considerable effort. *No soldier in the world is better fed, better clothed and better paid than those of the United States.* The government of this country has grafted its military institution on to the civil administration, and the result has been not only the improvement of the army, but a masterpiece of military order.

The manner of enlisting recruits is shown by the following advertisement that is seen in public newspapers: "Needed for the service of the country of the United States so many hundred men between the ages of eighteen and thirty-five years, healthy, and five feet six inches tall. A bonus of $5.00, plenty of food and clothing, with $5.00 salary per month. Those who wish may apply at such and such a place."

The lottery system, or draft, which up to the time of my departure was in force in our republic, is especially odious, and when I was governor of the State of Mexico, I confess that many times I winked at the fact that it was not carried out, in view of the repeated and painful petitions from laborers and workers. Only in the direst circumstances, such as those in which General Jackson found himself as we have seen, is everyone obliged to serve in the armed forces. The method of conscription in France alienated many people from the cause of Napoleon.

As he goes from the Mexican Republic to the states which permit slavery in our sister republic, the philosopher cannot fail to feel the contrast that is noted between the two countries, nor fail to experience a pleasant memory for those who have abolished this degrading traffic and caused to disappear among us the vestiges of so humiliating a condition of the human race. General Guerrero issued the decree December 16, 1829, by virtue of extraordinary powers, through the generous inspiration of Don José María Tornel. When I passed through New Orleans, there were more than one thousand slaves up for sale. These poor people are treated with great severity in Louisiana. They serve in homes and in inns and generally sleep on the ground.

When a master wishes to punish a slave, male or female, he will send that person to the jail with a note that contains the order for the number of lashes that the jailer is to administer. The poor man or woman returns home with the note that shows that the indicated punishment has been carried out. When the master deems it fitting, he orders that they tie the slave's hands, throw him face down upon the floor, and administer the beating in this manner. Often as one passes by the jail in the morning the cries and laments of those unfortunate people can be heard.

I am going to describe an event related by the Duke of Weimar, concerning whom I have already spoken, and who stopped at the same house where I was in New Orleans, with the difference that he traveled in 1826. "I cannot pass over in silence," says the prince,

a scene that I witnessed on March 22—one which excited my profound indignation. There was at the inn a young female slave from Virginia employed as chambermaid whose cleanliness and care in the service made everyone love her. A Frenchman who was staying at the inn asked for water early in the morning. The girl could not serve him with the speed that he wished since she was busy with other duties. He went downstairs, and when he found her in the patio busy with other chores, he struck her fiercely until he made her mouth and nose bleed. The poor creature, trying to defend herself, put her hand up to the attacker's throat, and he began to yell loudly. He escaped from the hands of the girl, went to his room, got together his clothing and trunks, and was getting ready to leave when the landlady, Madame Herries, trying to satisfy the cruel guest, ordered that they give the slave twenty-five lashes with a leather whip, and to double the pain of the victim this punishment was inflicted by her lover, who was a slave in the same house.

The Frenchman, not satisfied with this penalty, went to the police where when the unfortunate slave girl was brought in by two constables she was beaten again in the presence of the accuser. I am very sorry [adds the famous traveler] that I did not take the name of this evil Christian in order to publish it and denounce him to public scorn.

A few months before my arrival on March 7, 1830, the Louisiana legislature had passed two laws that contained extremely antiliberal provisions; they are as follows:

I.   Whoever writes, publishes or distributes any writing that *has a tendency* to create discontent among the free colored population in this state or to introduce rebellion among the slaves, shall suffer, according to the gravity of the deed in the judgment of the court of justice, capital punishment, life imprisonment, or public works for life.

II.   Whoever in public speeches, on the platform, in open meetings, in the pulpit, or anywhere else, whether it be in private conversations or by signs or actions, shall do or say anything that *may have a tendency to produce discontent* among the free colored people of the population of this State, or to incite rebellion among its slaves, or any one who shall knowingly have brought into it papers, pamphlets or books that may have the same tendency, shall suffer, according to the court's judgment the penalty of public works for not less than three years, nor more than twenty, or death.

III.   Any person who shall teach, or shall cause to be taught any slave to read or write, shall suffer the penalty of from one to twelve months in prison.

The other law is as follows:

I.   It sets forth a law for the expulsion of all free colored people who may have entered the state since the year 1807, and prohibits the entry of any person of this class into the state.

II.   It establishes the penalty of public works for life for all free colored persons who having returned to the state do not leave it.

III.   It establishes that any white person who may be convicted of being the author, printer, or editor of any writing in the state, or even of using language, that has the purpose of disturbing the peace of the same with relation to the slaves or people of this state, or even to diminish the respect that the colored people should have for the whites, shall be fined the sum of $300 to $1,000 and condemned to prison for not less than six months and not more than three years. But if the persons who commit these offenses should be *colored* they shall suffer a fine of not more than $1,000 and be condemned to public works for from three to five years, and banishment forever after that time.

IV.   It establishes that in these cases it shall be the obligation of the public prosecutor or the general attorney, and of the private attorneys of the districts, under the pain of loss of job, to prosecute the colored persons who may have violated this law, or *as often as they may be required to prosecute the said colored persons by any citizen of the state.*

These laws were signed by Mr. Roman, president of the House of Representatives, Mr. Smith, president of the Senate, and Mr. Dupré, governor of the state at that time. Today Mr. Roman is governor.

Sad indeed is the situation of a state where its legislators consider necessary such offensive measures of repression against the rights of man. Those who know the spirit of liberty that prevails in all the deliberations of those who guide the United States can only think, in view of these acts of notorious injustice towards a group of individuals of the human race, that very strong motives, that an inevitable necessity, *dura necessitas,* obliges these people to sanction such laws. There are those among these legislators who go from the halls of their sessions to pay homage and adoration to the beautiful quadroons, with whom they would bind themselves in the sacred bonds of matrimony if an invincible prejudice did not interpose itself to prevent such unions. I have known respectable persons who lived condemned to an involuntary celibacy because they could not unite with the women who because of their charms, beauty and affectionate solicitude had made captive their wills. There are several examples of these clandestine concessions in the state of Louisiana.

This type of exceptional laws has an extraordinary influence on the moral progress and the civilization of the states that permit slaves, such as Georgia, South Carolina and Louisiana. It is sufficient to cast a glance over the present state of publishing in those parts, compared to that of other states free of slaves, and one will notice immediately the advantages of the latter. Let us pick out three free states and three where slavery is permitted. In 1810 there were published in the state of New York sixty-six newspapers; in 1830 there were two hundred twelve. In 1810 there were published in Pennsylvania sixty-one; in 1830, eighty-five. In 1810 there were fourteen published in Ohio; in 1830, sixty-six. Let us see now the slave states. In 1810 in South Carolina ten newspapers were published; in 1830, sixteen. In Georgia in 1810, thirteen; in 1830, an equal number. In Louisiana *ten* were published; today the number has gone down to *nine.* It is to be noted that while the population of this last state has increased from the 20,854 that it had at that time to the 115,262 that it had reached in 1830, the newspapers have decreased in number, following a course that is contrary to the progress of civilization and trade.

The sugar cane plantations, the lemon and orange and other aromatic trees of our hot lands that are to be found on the plantations reminded me of the beautiful holdings of Cuautla and Cuernavaca in the state of Mexico. But here agriculture is more advanced, and the ease of export and locomotion, with the advantage that the planters have in cultivating with slaves, makes it possible for them to sell their sugar at very low prices. The quality of the sugar is never as fine as that which we have in the states of Veracruz, Puebla and Mexico. There is always a greater amount of dirt in the sugars from Louisiana and Havana. The same thing happens with our sweets from Yucatan, which bring even less than those of Havana.

The heat was excessive at the time when I arrived in New Orleans; there were some days when the thermometer went up to 98° and even 100° Fahrenheit. All the well-to-do people traveled up the river in search of a better climate.

I was very glad to find in New Orleans some old friends with whom I had traveled in Europe previously, or whom I had met in this city. Among these were Mr. Charles Black, city treasurer, and Mr. Fleytas, a rich planter, the ex-count of Montezuma, the family of Mr. Duncan and other important people of the country. Mr. Curson, a man of much education who had traveled a great deal in America and Europe, favored me with his advice and reflections. He gave me letters of recommendation for several people, among them the English minister to Washington, Mr. Vaughn. In Mexico Mr. A. Butler, the business attaché of the United States, gave me letters that were very useful to me.

On June 15, General Mejía and I took passage on the steamer *Louisiana*. This is one of the better steamboats of the line that offers all the comforts compatible with a floating home. Most of these boats are of four to five hundred tons, and they are constructed with the triple purpose of carrying poor people and a cargo of sugar, coffee and rum when they go up; cotton, flour, meat, hides, etc., when they come down. On the upper deck they are like our bullrings, or like the baths that are found in Paris on the Seine. They have their balconies which serve for the travelers to amuse themselves, and their inside cabins where there are a bed, washstand and mirror for sleeping and dressing. There are staterooms for different classes. The passage from New Orleans to Louisville costs forty dollars. The distance is close to 1,200 miles.

The 16th we went aboard at 12:00 noon, and a little before the departure of the boat the sheriff presented himself asking for Mr. Zavala. The sheriff was accompanied by a man whom I did not know. The officer told me that that individual's name was Browerman and that he had presented himself at the city court asking that I pay ninety-four dollars that he said that I owed him for repairing a coach when I was governor of the State of Mexico. Note the evil workings of this man who waited until the moment of the departure of the steamer, which made it necessary for me either to be delayed, which would put me terribly behind schedule, or to pay him, although I was certain that I did not owe that amount, for I had paid him in Mexico when it was due. But I had not kept the receipt, and

I cannot imagine how there can be any right for such a demand in a foreign country, far from the place where the debt is supposed to have been contracted. The only recourse that I had was to get Mr. Breadlove, Mexican vice-consul, who fortunately was on the boat, to stand good for me. Thus I got out of this small and unpleasant embarrassment.

After two years of travel in which this matter was forgotten I had to pay in Mexico on October 4, 1833, the sum of $105.50, which included court costs, with judgment without my consent, which receipt I still have, as well as those of all the artists, innkeepers, and others that I have paid, in order to avoid another similar happening. I have with me a trunk full of receipts.

ON THE MISSISSIPPI
Loading Cotton

Currier & Ives, 1870

CHAPTER III.

The day was beautiful, the sun was shining with all its splendor, and its rays, reflected by the waters of the river, multiplied its effect and increased the fire that seemed to burn the earth. The wind blew hot, and the only comfort was found in the sight of the clumps of trees along the banks and the hope of a more temperate atmosphere at the end of the day. There were six ladies, and among them one from Guatemala, who was following her husband Don Mariano de Aycinena, exiled from his country for political matters, like so many others.

Also on board was a man from Yucatan, Don Joaquin Gutierrez, a young man with refined manners, pleasant ways, and that easy and friendly lack of shyness that is found among educated people who have traveled and lived in good society. Count Cornaro, a person distinguished because of his birth and elegant manner, who was coming from Mexico, was also on the boat. There were a number of other people, all capable of making a truly interesting company.

In the navigation of the Mississippi there are not the risks of storms, hurricanes and coral reefs that cause so much and such terrible damage to the ships that sail the ocean. But the frequent encounters with the enormous tree trunks that come down the river are apt to cause trouble for the steamers. There is another greater risk, but it has lessened a great deal because of the precautions that have been taken. I speak of the explosions of the receptacles or boilers for the steam that is confined to move the machinery. When this happens, and frequent cases have been seen on the Mississippi steamboats, many people perish, either directly from the scalding water, or because with the shipwreck the passengers are exposed to the turbulent river, or finally, from the force with which the exploding machinery strikes people in its path. The boats also are apt to run aground on banks of sand or mud, but they are easily pulled free by other steamboats that pass frequently.

One hundred miles from New Orleans is a small place called Baton Rouge, where they manufacture sugar, syrups and rum. In this town there are a military garrison and a fortress. We passed by there on June 18. The climate is very little different from that of the capital. The 19th we passed by Natchez, famous for M. de Chateaubriand's interesting novel which bears that title.

Mrs. Trollope, who has written of her trip to the United States with the spirit of satire and sarcasm that often leads to excess, speaks of the steamboats on this run and of the associations to be found on them:

> I advise those who wish to get a favorable impression of the manners and customs of the Americans that they not begin a trip on the Mississippi because I declare in all sincerity that I would give my preference to a well cared for pigsty with a herd of pigs to the cabins on these boats. I know of scarcely anything so repugnant for an Englishman as the incessant spitting of the Americans.

Elsewhere, when she speaks of the passengers, of whom she says that most of them use the title of colonel, general or major:

Their absolute lack of table manners, the voracious speed with which they grab their plates to devour their food, the strange and unusual expressions that they use, the frequent spitting, from which it was hard to keep our clothes free, the horrible habit of eating by putting their knives into their mouths up to the handle, and the most horrible habit yet of picking their teeth with their penknives after eating, led us to believe immediately that we were not surrounded by generals, colonels and majors of the Old World, and that meal time was not a time for pleasure.

Those who have traveled on steamboats from the Thames to Calais, to Ostend, Boulogne, etc., after having done so in the United States, cannot help being surprised that Mrs. Trollope should use this language, when evidently those in the United States are much more comfortable, more respectable, cleaner, and in every respect better. What shall we say of those of the Seine, the Gironde and other rivers of France? It is impossible to conceive how these countries so civilized and advanced in every type of social comfort can maintain boats that are so filthy and disgusting.

As for the habit of the North Americans to spit frequently, we should not hide the fact that it is a disgusting fault in good society and is due to a habit that they have generally of chewing tobacco, as we Americans of the South have the habit of smoking it. What would Mrs. Trollope say if she were to see our charming Mexican women continually blowing smoke through their mouths and noses, staining their small and well-shaped hands with the oil from the cigarette paper, contaminating their clothing with tobacco smoke and giving their breath a disagreeable odor? On the boats smoking is not allowed except in a place designated for it, in order to avoid the discomfort that the ladies have from the smoke, as well as many delicate people who neither smoke nor chew tobacco.

Although for miles and miles the banks of the Mississippi offer only a constant and uniform view without the interruption of towns, or mountains or hills, there is always a surprising spectacle presented by the pleasant sight of the continual passing of palmettos, palm trees, the great oak trees, firs, sycamores and other gigantic productions of the vegetable kingdom all intertwined with the vines that serve as the nests and perches for a varied multitude of birds that raise their songs in those eternal and solitary rural settings.

How the spirit is transported as it contemplates the inner being of these infinite places of solitude where no human footstep has ever fallen. Those trees, like our great mountains, seem like contemporaries of creation itself! Looking at all this one is able to get an idea of how still life could be brought alive under the romantic brush of Chateaubriand and could lift up his ardent heart to the degree of enthusiasm that made it possible for him to bring his readers to have a part in his brilliant pages. The Mississippi, like the Nile, the Marañon and the Orinoco and other great rivers of America and Asia, cannot fail to produce strong impressions and ideas of the grandeur and majesty of the Creator as one contemplates them. Nature in her primitive state with all her rough spots, her air of abandon, to put it thusly, her silence, her languor, but at the same time with all her fertility, her riches, her magnificence, her hopes, is always for the eyes of the sensitive man an object worthy of profound reflections.

The Mississippi is joined and augmented by the Red River, the White River, the Arkansas, Ohio, Missouri and many other rivers of lesser importance. The Mississippi varies in depth and width according to the places through which it passes, and naturally becomes smaller as one approaches its headwaters. In New Orleans it is about 120 feet deep; in Natchez, 80; this is 300 miles upstream. From the Balize to Pittsburgh, to which one travels by steamboat along the Ohio, there is a distance of 2,012 miles, which amounts to more than 700 leagues in Mexico. The impetus to growth in commerce and civilization as a result of the introduction of steamboats is tremendous.

Formerly it took three or four months to make this trip from New Orleans. Today one arrives in Louisville in ten days, 1,100 miles; another day to Cincinnati, 120 miles; in four to Wheeling, 380 miles, and in a day and a half to Pittsburgh, about 280 miles. It is not uncommon to see families go to visit one or another of these places, 100, 200, or 300 leagues, to return home in two or three days. It is as though one were going from Mexico City to Zacatecas or to Durango. The trip from New Orleans to Pittsburgh is a greater distance than from Veracruz to Sinaloa.

Every twenty-four hours our boat would stop to take on wood to keep the fire going that was necessary to run the machinery. The daily consumption of firewood according to my calculations amounted to twenty-eight or thirty dollars. On the swampy banks there are wretched settlements of small wooden houses, standing on stilts that sustain them and preserve them from the dampness and the lizards, and these miserable huts are the homes of the men who provide the wood for the three hundred boats that traverse the mighty river. The Americans call them *squatters*, no doubt because their houses are so small that they cannot stand up. Mrs. Trollope paints a very melancholy picture of these people:

From time to time [says this traveler], there come into view a few cabins of the woodcutters who provide the steamboats with the necessary fuel, and they live in this traffic at the risk, or rather I will say, with the certainty of a premature death in exchange for dollars and whiskey. These dismal houses are for the most part flooded during the winter, and the best of them are on stilts that keep the inhabitants from drowning when the waters of the river rise. These unfortunate beings are the victims of high fevers that they face without fear, helped along by the stimulus of spirituous liquors of which they make use. The sallow appearance of their wretched children and women is a cause for horror, and although this sight was repeated frequently, it never ceased to make the same impression upon me. Their color is a bluish pallor, and they all look dropsical. A cow with two or three pigs, with water almost up to their knees, distinguish those that are better off among these hapless people, and one thing I can tell you is that never did I see human nature reduced to such a state of degradation as appears among the woodcutters of the unhealthful banks of the Mississippi.

Indeed Mrs. Trollope's description is exact. But I have seen several of these small settlements increase in size in places where the height of the land along the banks permitted it and form villages in which they are beginning to build houses of some comfort. Our own Indians along Lake Chalco and the swamps of the Valley of Toluca find themselves in the same situation as these squatters. But there is a difference in that our Indians can improve the lands a great deal, build their houses on solid ground, raise animals and harvest crops; while these cannot leave the small circles in which they have set up their courtyards of lumber and firewood because the flooding of the river will not permit it. In a small town three leagues from Toluca called San Pedro de los Petates the Indians live in the waters that come down from the river at flood time. They die very young, and the last cholera epidemic that caused so many deaths in the capital of the state almost put an end to that small village.

In the navigation of this river one encounters a great number of rafts that bring goods down to New Orleans—especially lumber for homes and buildings. These rafts are often five or six hundred feet in length and twelve to fifteen feet wide, made of wooden planks nailed and joined, upon which they put others and then the animals, seeds and other goods. In the middle there is a room where they sleep and prepare their meals. They come down with the current, which runs at four or five miles an hour after the Missouri and the Ohio have joined the river. In New Orleans they break these rafts up and sell the lumber. A few years ago to make a round trip to Louisville took eight months. Today they do it in two weeks. Could there be anything more fitting than to erect in each town a bronze statue to the immortal Fulton who

"WOODING UP" ON THE MISSISSIPPI

Currier & Ives, 1863

BOUND DOWN THE RIVER

Currier & Ives, 1870

applied steam to navigation? Such is the greatness of a man of genius who brings about a revolution beneficial to humankind! Gioya, John Guttemberg, Columbus and Fulton will live eternally.

One of the great rivers that flows into the Mississippi is the Arkansas; its course is known for more than nineteen hundred miles, and it is navigable for more than six hundred. The banks of this river have so much limestone that some people say that the stock die when they eat the soil. In the rainy season small steamboats can even get close to the mountains. On this side is the White River, which is navigable for more than four hundred miles in the Arkansas Territory which borders the lands of New Mexico and California. The inhabitants of this part of the United States are generally not very civilized, and there are many who are much like our Indians, although they are always more proud. They always carry knives shaped like a cutlass, which they use against wolves, bears and other wild beasts.

In our most remote small towns, one can feel the effects of the slavery under which we lived under the old regime. Civilization is nothing more than the effects of terror impressed upon the minds of the inhabitants, which causes them not to show themselves hostile to travelers, nor to live together in a state of open war with continual reprisals.

In the places of which I am speaking where there is neither civilization, nor fear, nor religion, men only respect each other for their individual strength and power. It would not be out of line to relate in this work a few anecdotes that often give a better idea of the character of a people than do exact descriptions. ''April 10, 1830,'' says Mr. Stuart in his trip to the United States,

> in one of the places where the boat stopped to take on wood, the captain urged me to get off in order to hear from the mouth of the mayor himself an event that he did not think that I would believe if he told me himself. The justice of the peace was a respectable American of good manners; he lived in a house that was neat and comfortable, and he invited me to enjoy a rye whiskey, which in his opinion was the best of that kind in the United States. He told me that some small boats which were coming down the river loaded with different goods of the country had stopped nearby during the night, and that on one of these boats a murder had been committed, and that the murderer had been surprised in the act. This caused great excitement among the passengers, among whom were friends of the murdered man. Since the punishment would be delayed for many days if the guilty man were sent to Arkansas to be judged by the court, and there would be no witnesses to the deed there, they decided to hold the trial right on the boat. Having tried him, they sentenced him

to be hanged, which was done a few hours after the crime was committed. The mayor could not have prevented it even if he had tried.

There is another curious affair which gives an idea also of the civil situation of those remote lands, and which I wish to relate because I think it would not be strange to find it repeated in some parts of Mexico such as Texas, California, and New Mexico.

A little above the town of Memphis there is a place that is called Little Prairie in the state of Missouri. At that point we found a cultivated field cleared by a colonist named Brown. This fellow had bought those lands from the government, paying $2.50 or $3.00 an acre for them. He had not yet received the title when a certain man named Eastwood had taken possession of some adjacent lands that also belonged to Brown. Eastwood was busy plowing them when Brown, accompanied by two daughters that he had, decided to oust that intruder. He sent his older daughter to bring a rifle or American musket. He was held back, however, from carrying out such a desperate decision by the fear that his daughter would be held equally guilty as an accomplice if he fired on Eastwood. The action of this man was not, however, as absurd as might be imagined by a reader from a civilized place. It is very common in the western states and territories of the United States, and in Texas, California and New Mexico of our republic, that those who get there first take possession of lands without any title, cultivate them and live on them until a legal owner may come to occupy them. In such a case the one who cultivated the land is reimbursed for his work according to some agreement. There is no law for such a claim, but it has become the custom in many places.

A few miles beyond the confluence of the Ohio and the Mississippi there are a considerable number of islands that are being settled and must be wonderfully fertile. Among them is one called Wolf Island, about one mile square, that belongs to Mr. James Hunter. In a book which contains directions for travelers on the Mississippi, printed in Pittsburg, is the following curious statement: "Mr. James Hunter, the only man that I have known that has the pleasure of being called a professional gambler, is the only one who lives on Wolf Island." He carries on a lucrative trade in hogs, cows, chickens, milk, etc., which he sells to the boats that ply the river.

The small town of Memphis, in the state of Tennessee, is on the left bank of the river on one of the few hills along the swampy banks. There are not many places on the Mississippi so lovely and majestic. At that spot the river looks like a beautiful lake, and an island that divides its abundant waters gives a picturesque aspect because of the trees which cover it. The town is on an elevated point about three hundred feet above the Wolf, which is one of the innumerable tributaries of the Mississippi. Memphis is a modern town that is growing rapidly and carries on trade in lumber, dried beef, cheeses, and other foodstuffs with the boats, as well as with the nearby state of Louisiana.

The constitution of Tennessee was written in Knoxville in 1796. The legislative power resides in a general assembly composed of a senate and a house of representatives. The members of these bodies are elected biennially the first Thursday and Friday of the month of August.

The number of representatives is sixty, which are apportioned according to the number of taxpayers of each county. The number of senators cannot be more than half nor less than a third of the number of representatives.

The executive power is given to the governor, who is elected at the same time as the senators and representatives by the people; his term runs for two years, and he cannot be reelected more than three times.

The sessions are convened in Nashville the third Monday of the following September, each two years. But the assembly can be called into session by the governor on suitable occasions. The right of suffrage is given to all free men twenty-one years of age who have any property in the county in which they vote, or to anyone other than a slave who has lived in the county for six months prior to the election. The judicial power is the same as that in other states.

Before leaving the state of Tennessee, I must speak of a religious ceremony that is observed in all the states, but the broad lands of Tennessee offer a vaster field for carrying it out. I wish to speak of the *Camp Meetings*, which have been described differently by English travelers, among them the celebrated Mrs. Trollope, whose work has been so popular in England. I shall relate what I have seen and what I have been told by impartial and educated people so that the reader may form a precise opinion. This is one of the most imposing religious practices that have a remarkable influence on the manners and customs of the country, as will be noted from the faithful account that I am going to give of it.

Unless one has seen it, he cannot have any idea of the excitement and enthusiasm in a district of more than fifty miles radius with the approach of these religious gatherings, and unless one has been a witness, he cannot imagine how thoroughly the preachers have understood the effects that they have, and how well they have been able to take advantage of it. Let us suppose the spot and setting where for the past two years these have been held most frequently, and that by its silence offers truly interesting scenes—one of the most beautiful and fertile valleys in the mountains of Tennessee. The news circulates two or three months in advance. On the day indicated coaches, carts, chairs, people on horseback, countless on foot, wagons with provisions of bedding, camp tents and utensils, necessary for a week's stay begin to arrive. Those who have seen our fairs of San Juan de los Lagos, Chalma and Guadalupe in our Mexican republic can have some sort of hazy idea of these numerous assemblies. In order to provide themselves with the necessary water, the people scatter out among the somber forests and dark woods of Tennessee, on the banks of one of those streams that wind among the trees.

"Attending this religious assembly are the rich, the ambitious," Mr. Flint goes on,

because public opinion, all powerful in that country, dictates it. They also go there to extend their influence, or so that their failure to attend may not reduce it. Aspirants for public office attend also to gain followers and popularity. Many are there out of curiosity, and there are also those who go for the fun of it. Youth and beauty are also mysterious motives which it is wise not to examine too closely. Then there are children, whose curious eyes take in with remarkable speed everything that surrounds them, middle-aged men, fathers and mothers of families, whose way of life is already settled, waiting in holy expectation to hear the divine word, and finally the old people of both sexes with their white hair, with the thought of the eternity that they are approaching. These types of persons make up these congregations that count their numbers in the thousands.

A swarm of preachers, who under diverse denominations explain the gospel, hasten to show off their eloquence, their learning and their piety to the congregation. Young preachers who in the vigor of their age, aided by sonorous and powerful voices, struggled to shine. Others who have proclaimed the gospel as pilgrims of the cross from the most remote areas of the north to the shores of the Gulf of Mexico, ready to offer words that express profound feelings, the fruits of their experience garnered in their long and painful journeys, exercising for fifty years their ministry, whose trembling accents and appearance produce a greater impression than their words, announce that for the last time they are directing their terrible exhortations to mortals. Such are the ministers who occupy the attention of the immense audience.

A line of campaign tents is set up on the banks of the streams, and the religious city is raised in a few hours among the trees. A multitude of lamps and torches hung in the branches cause a magic effect amidst that somber rural setting. The state of the most brilliant theater of Europe is a feeble painting beside this wondrous spectacle.

In this setting those attending, among the sweetest transports of social feeling, added to the general enthusiasm of the expectation, go from one tent to another to exchange greetings and embraces of apostolic congratulations and to speak of the solemn occasion that brings them together. They have tea and supper, and by this time the peaceful rays of the moon are beginning to cut through the branches of the trees.

It should be noted that the time is always calculated for when there will be a moon to enhance the majesty of these solemn occasions. A clear sky permits one to see a few stars that shine feebly. All this together produces a natural atmosphere that is worthy of the grandeur of the Creator.

A venerable old man, dressed with elegant simplicity, mounts to the pulpit, cleans his dust-covered spectacles, and in a voice that expresses the emotion of his soul intones the hymn so that the entire congregation can repeat it, and so that all voices are joined with his. We would consider sad indeed the heart that did not beat violently as it comes to this song similar to the "sound of many waters" whose echo is sent back by the nearby mountains and forests. Such are the scenes, the associations, and such the influence of things eternal upon a nature that is so impressionable and so constituted as is ours that a small effort is sufficient in a matter such as religion to fill the heart and the eyes.

The honored speaker talks of God, of Eternity, of the final judgment, and of everything that can cause a strong impression. He speaks of his experiences, his works, his travels, his persecutions and good receptions, and of all that he has seen in hope, in peace, in triumph, in the fruit of his predecessors. When he talks of the short space that is left to him of life, he says that he regrets it only "because he will not in the silence of death be able to proclaim the benefits and goodness of his crucified Redeemer."

One does not have to be an accomplished orator to produce in those surroundings profound religious feelings. Nor should it be a cause for wonder that when the preacher pauses a few times to dry his eyes his whole audience dissolves into tears and breaks into demonstrations of penitence. Nor should it cause surprise that many whose pride persuades them of their superiority to the common mass of society and of a noble lack of sensitivity to such objects, should be dragged in spite of themselves towards that general feeling, that they should become women and children in their turn, and that although they have come to be amused, they should acknowledge repentance.

In spite of all that has been said to expose to laughter and public ridicule these spectacles that are so common in our parts, it cannot be denied that when everything is considered their influence is salutary, and the general result of their practice upon social interests is good. It will be a long time, if the day ever comes, when the ministry will be supported by the community. Instead of this, nothing is more fitting to make up for the lack of influence that results from the constant duties of the established ministers than recourse to this sort of simultaneous explosion of religious feelings that shake the moral world and purify its atmosphere until the accumulated seeds of moral sickness demand a new purification.

Whatever may be the cause, it is evident that these religious spectacles have brought about a noticeable improvement in the customs, manners, ways and habits of the people in the states of Tennessee, Mississippi, Missouri, Kentucky, Ohio, Indiana, and Illinois. In many places taverns and gambling halls have decreased in number or disappeared, and those who formerly frequented these places go to religious assemblies. The Methodists have also brought great and incalculable benefits to the way of life.

The picture which I have just presented, taken from a work by Mr. Flint, one of the best educated of Americans and one worthy of esteem because of his brilliant qualities, gives an exact idea of what goes on in these gatherings. Those of the Methodists in the eastern states are almost the same, and perhaps I shall have occasion to speak of them.

Compare this religious festival with those that we have in the republic, which are more or less like those of Spain and all of Italy, an hour or two in the temple, where the people take very little part in the religious feelings that should occupy them in those circumstances. The pomp of our Catholic worship, so imposing and from which one could take so much good in the improvement of moral character, loses all its effect because of the absolute lack of communication between the priesthood and the people. The mass is said in Latin in a low voice, hurriedly and according to formula; the preaching generally speaking is a weaving of words without coherence, without conscience and without divine comfort. The rest of the day, after the ceremonies, the lower classes eat and drink; those of the upper class play and dance. Look at our religious festivals. And what shall we say of the Indians in Chalma, in Guadalupe and in other shrines. Ah! The pen falls from the hand in order not to expose to the civilized world a horde of idolaters who come to deliver into the hands of lazy friars the fruits of their year's work to enrich them, while they, their women and children have no clothing, not even a bed. And the Spaniards, our fathers, have dared call this religion!!!

On June 27 we arrived at Shippingport, a small town a mile from Louisville. At this point we took coaches which were ready, and they took us to Louisville. During the course of our sailing we had lived in an agreeable society. Some ladies played the harpsichord, others the guitar, and they sang very charmingly and without having to be begged.

There was tea or coffee early in the morning, a good breakfast at nine o'clock, lunch at noon, dinner at four, and tea or supper in the evening. In this way there was a very short interval from one meal to the next, in addition to the serving of beer, champagne, cider, etc. On these trips, according to the observation of M. Farel, one meets on the same boat gentlemen, merchants, workers, congressmen and legislators, captains, generals and judges, all seated around one table in a truly republican simplicity. One does not note uncouthness in the conduct of the most humble person of those at the table, and in truth the refinement of their manners is remarkable—that is when compared with people of the same class in France or England.

What is true is that when a worker finds himself in this country with a certain importance in the social scale, he makes an effort to show himself worthy of being in the same society and at the same table with rich people and those of first rank. It is true that the upper classes lose something of their refinement by their continued contact with less polished people, but the latter gain a great deal at the same time. All are well dressed, and in the United States there are no ragged people.

Louisville is located on the left bank of the Ohio, in the state of Kentucky. The opposite bank belongs to Indiana. The city has probably twelve thousand inhabitants and is growing considerably, although not to the same extent as Cincinnati and New Orleans. Its principal north-south street must be about one mile long, and it has only four streets in this direction. It is the depot for many foreign goods that are imported to the interior through that city; it also serves as a port for exporting flour from wheat, barley and other grains as well as corn meal.

From Louisville I wrote to Mr. McClure asking him about a young Indian boy that I had entrusted to his care when he was in Mexico and I was governor of the state in 1828. Mr. McClure was in charge of the educational establishment that Mr. Owen founded in New Harmony, Indiana, about thirty leagues from Louisville. I shall speak of Mr. McClure and of the reason that I had for delivering to him the boy to whom I gave the name of Toribio Zavala.

Mr. Owen, so well known in literary circles for his vast knowledge, his eloquence and the singularity of his doctrines, formed the project of starting in the United States his system of instruction under Mr. McClure. It was a practical school of crafts, trades,

46

reading and writing, the object of which was to be to occupy the boys in work that would give them enough to support themselves. Mr. Poinsett, United States minister to Mexico, introduced me to Mr. Owen and Mr. McClure when I was governor of the state of Mexico, and I confess that I was much taken by the project of those two philosophers. Later we shall see how their establishment was dissolved.

In the same year they presented to me an Indian boy from the town of Zempoala in Mexico about eight years old, more or less, who, as I was told by the schoolmaster who brought him to my house, was an orphan that he had taken in and whose prodigious memory he had developed. I examined him in the presence of a few people asking him several questions on geography, astronomy, spelling, versification and grammar, religion and morals, to all of which the boy answered with ease and without embarrassment. He had given him the name of Toribio Pauper because of his poverty, and I substituted my own family name. Thinking that the young fellow could have a better career in Mr. McClure's establishment, I turned the boy over to him, paying only for the expenses of the trip to New Harmony. I found out later that the establishment was dissolved and that my Zempoala lad had already found a way to make a living in the country.

In the state of Indiana the executive power resides in a governor who is elected by the people every three years and can be reelected one time. The lieutenant governor is elected at the same time; he presides over the senate, and exercises the duties of the governor in his absence.

There is a senate and a house of representatives. The members of the first are elected every three years; those of the second each year. The number of representatives cannot be less than thirty-six nor more than one hundred. This arrangement is based on the number of white males twenty-one years of age. The number of senators in the same proportion cannot be less than one third nor more than one half the number of representatives.

These and a third of the members of the senate are elected annually the first Monday in August. The governor and the lieutenant governor are elected every three years on the same day.

The legislature convenes in Indianapolis the first Monday in December.

The right of suffrage is granted to every citizen twenty-one years of age who has resided in the state for one year.

The judicial power is administered by a supreme court of justice and circuit courts. The supreme court consists of three judges, and the circuit courts of one presiding judge and two associates. All the

47

judges serve for a term of seven years. The governor names those of the supreme court with the consent of the senate. The presiding judges of the circuit courts are named by the house of representatives and the associates by the people.

In Louisville there is a small theater where, it is curious to note, they have separate entrances and seats for the women who are not received into society. When I passed through this city, the famous actress Mrs. Drake was playing; she is one of the best comediennes in the United States and can hold her own in the theaters of Europe.

Besides Louisville, there are two other important cities in the state of Kentucky; they are Lexington and Frankfort. The second one is the capital of the state. Both are beautiful towns according to what I have been told by several persons.

The state of Kentucky was the favorite land of several tribes of Indians that had set it aside for hunting. It is said that in the remote forests where they are at the present time on the other side of the Missouri they sigh for their ancient lands and the graves of their forefathers and have songs about their migration. Indeed, few states offer the appearance of abundant fertility as does Kentucky. Its beautiful forests covered with sturdy trees, oaks, sugar maples, sycamores, firs, chestnuts, etc., delight the eye of the traveler. Its products are wheat, tobacco, corn, barley and other valuable crops. Its people are notable for their height and large build, as well as for the beauty and regularity of their proportions.

In 1790 Kentucky separated from the state of Virginia, of which it was a part, and the constitution that was adopted then lasted until 1799, when it was replaced by the one now in force. Its legislative power consists of two houses, that of the representatives and the senate. The representatives are elected annually, and every four years they adjust the number according to the number of electors in each county. The present number is one hundred, which is the maximum, and it cannot go below fifty-eight. Senators are elected every year, one quarter at a time. The present number is thirty-eight, the maximum, and twenty-four is the minimum.

The executive power is in the hands of a governor elected for four years, who cannot be reelected within a period of seven years. A lieutenant governor is elected at the same time, and his duties are to preside over the senate and act in the absence of the governor.

The representatives and a fourth of the senators are elected annually by the people the first Monday in August. The governor and lieutenant governor are elected likewise by the people on the same day every four years and take office on the fourth Tuesday of the same month. Voting is open for three days, and it is done by voice vote and not by written ballot. The sessions are convened annually in Frankfort on the first Monday in December.

The constitution grants the right of suffrage to all male citizens (with the exception of colored people) who have reached the age of twenty-one and have resided in the state for two years.

The judicial power is administered by a supreme court of justice called the appellate court, and other lesser tribunals or courts that the assembly establishes. The judges and justices of the peace serve as long as they are on good behavior.

To the southwest are the states of Indiana and Illinois and the territory of Missouri.* The Mississippi River which runs along these states has on its banks cities that carry on trade with our territory of New Mexico, and from St. Louis numerous caravans leave for as far away as Santa Fe and California. Before many years those vast lands will be populated by strangers in search of a better climate and vacant lands to set up new establishments, and then one will see descending the Rio Grande travelers who will have come by the St. Lawrence, through New York or along the Mississippi and have made across the country a journey of six thousand or eight thousand miles. While the states to the south in the Mexican republic are occupied with civil wars and domestic quarrels, those of the north, dedicated to trade, agriculture and navigation, will give examples of morality and useful work to their quarrelsome brothers who will be fighting for power and supremacy.

On June 27 we continued our journey to Cincinnati on a smaller steamboat the *B. Franklin* that was very comfortable. We paid five dollars per person and sailed for thirty hours. We arrived in Cincinnati as the people were celebrating the arrival of General Jackson, president of the United States. It is easy to imagine that there were no battalions in line, nor artillery, nor armed people, nor priests, bishops or canons who were coming ceremonially to receive the chief of the government of the Union. There was none of that. But what one did see was a numerous crowd of people running along the banks of the river to receive and to see their first citizen, the honorable old man who had liberated New Orleans and given Florida to the United States and who today was guiding the destinies of the country with prudence, care and purity of intentions. There was music with banners, flags, shouts and cries of joy. Everything was natural and spontaneous. It was more like the fiestas in our towns when people are celebrating some saint than those ceremonies

*Translator's note: Zavala has his geography confused as Indiana and Illinois are more to the *northwest* than to the *southwest* of Kentucky. Neither does Indiana border the Mississippi River. Evidently, Zavala did not note accurately when he passed from the Mississippi onto the Ohio River.

set up on days of homage in which one does not see in people's faces any vestige of true interest or a feeling of sympathy. Jackson was received with enthusiasm, especially by the workers, laborers and craftsmen.

The next day General Mejía and I went to visit the patriarch president. I had for him a letter of recommendation from Mr. Butler, chargé of business affairs from the United States to our government, and Señor Mejía had known him since the time that he was in Washington as secretary to the Mexican legation. The honorable elderly man was staying in a modestly furnished house and was seated in an armchair and surrounded by twenty-five or thirty persons who by their dress seemed to be workmen and craftsmen, thus making for him the simplest court in the world. He appeared to be one of those ancient heroes of Homer, who after having performed great deeds in war had retired to live among their fellow citizens whom they governed as children. The general received us cordially and asked us about his friend General Guerrero. He regretted his fate and had no doubt that the people's cause which he was defending would have a complete triumph.

Cincinnati is a city of twenty-five thousand inhabitants situated on the banks of the Ohio River in the state of the same name. It is not threatened by the waters of the river like New Orleans; its elevated position protects it even from those periodic overflows that cause so much disaster in towns that are not so elevated. Before the introduction of the steamboat twenty years ago Cincinnati had at the most six thousand inhabitants, and ten years before that ten or twelve houses. Its rapid growth has been due to the ease of communication, the fertility of the soil and the numbers of immigrants that come from Europe and even from the eastern states. Many colonists who came and established themselves in Massachusetts, Vermont, Maine and New England generally, after having cleared and cultivated the land, built new homes and set up valuable establishments, put their real and personal property up for sale, weary, as they say, of hearing for so many years the barking of the neighbor's dog and the village bell. With their families and no belongings they came to establish new homes in the western states. Some come to Arkansas, others to Missouri, Ohio, Indiana, Illinois, and finally today many are going to Texas, New Mexico, and even Chihuahua. The places that they are leaving are filled by new immigrants from Europe. In this manner North America and following that the Mexican republic are enriched by the crafts, industry and elements of European civilization, while that part of the Old World is relieved of a part of its population that cannot maintain its land because the aristocracy needs gardens, woods, meadows and huge terrain from which to reap large rentals. In other places such as Switzerland and Wurtemberg it is because there is not sufficient land for the population.

Cincinnati is surrounded by beautiful hills covered with trees that in the summer offer the most picturesque scenes. The view of the city from the river, and that of the river and nearby banks from the elevated hill where the city is, are likewise pleasing and varied. There are eighteen churches, of which two are Episcopal, one a Roman Catholic cathedral, one a synagogue, another Unitarian, another Universalist, another Lutheran, Reformed Quaker, and the others are Presbyterian, Methodist, and Anabaptist. Many houses are beautiful with the first story of granite and white marble and the rest of brick. Generally they are small compared to our houses in Mexico, but they have all possible conveniences. The streets are not as clean as should be expected in a city founded on the slope of a hill on the banks of a great river. The lack of underground pipes and sewers causes the accumulation of filthy materials and the formation of mudholes, which are made even worse by the hogs. Food is very cheap as can be seen from the list made up by Mr. Bullock whom we knew in Mexico. Forty-five cents for a turkey, fifty cents for a roast pig, ten cents a pound for beef and three cents for a pound of pork. Other articles cost proportionately.

In Cincinnati there are cotton and woolen factories, as there are installations for the manufacture of articles of lead which is brought in in great quantities from the state of Illinois. But the prime elements of its amazing social progress and growth in population are to be found in the fertility, the ease of communication with the other states, and the form of government which makes it easy for a man to develop all his intellectual and material faculties. What would Cincinnati be without the constitutional provision which permits the free exercise of all forms of worship?

Mrs. Trollope, when she speaks of this prodigious multiplication and increase of inhabitants, wealth and prosperity of Cincinnati, says that it cannot be otherwise in a country where idleness is not welcome, and where one who does not work does not eat. "During my stay in this city," says this lady,

> or in its environs, which was close to two years, I never saw a beggar, nor even a man who although he had considerable wealth did not work actively to increase it. Like bees they are ever eagerly in search of that Hybla honey called money. Neither fine arts, nor the sciences, nor the attractions of pleasures can separate them from their labors. This singleness of purpose, favored by the spirit of enterprise, together

with sharpness and lack of ethics when it is a matter of self-interest, can obtain the object under consideration with advantage.

I have read much [she continues] about *the few and simple necessities of man*, and until now I had given a certain indulgent acquiescence to those who feel that each new necessity is a new enemy. Those who give themselves over to reasoning of this nature in their comfortable boudoirs of London or Paris know little about the subject. If it were food that nourishes a man, all that he would need, the faculties of a pig would be sufficient for him. But if we analyze the hour of pleasure, we will find that it is produced by pleasant sensations, occasioned by a thousand delicate impressions on as many nerves. When these nerves are inactive because they have never been touched, exterior objects are less important because they are perceived less. But when the whole machine of the human body is fully active, when each sense gives to the brain testimony of its impressions of pleasure or of pain, then each object that is presented to our senses comes to be a cause of wretchedness or of happiness. Let people who are made like that carefully avoid traveling in the United States; or if they do, let them not remain longer than is necessary to deposit in the memory those images that by force of contrast can appear pleasant to them in the future.

Look and pass by and then we shall reason concerning them.

The traveler continues, as she gives a very unflattering description of the manners and civility of the people of the western states, with such acrimony that she seems to have set out to hold up to ridicule the industrious colonists and their beautiful daughters, and to paint a melancholy picture of the whole country, with the purpose of discouraging her fellow countrymen and other Europeans from emigrating to those parts. But, is it fair to compare London with Cincinnati, Liverpool with New Orleans, Birmingham with Pittsburgh, in brief England with the United States? The strangest thing is that in order to measure the civilization of Cincinnati one should speak of the society of London and Paris. It is not surprising thus to find the Catholic cathedral small and insignificant when compared with Notre Dame of Paris, and the same with the Protestant church when compared with St. Paul's of London.

There is no doubt that generally speaking the people of the United States are self-centered, uncommunicative and distrustful. In addition they have a certain harshness in their dealings that makes their society unpleasant when one has not established relations in the country. It has often happened with me that I have traveled in the same coach, on the same boat with Americans without speaking a single word during the trip. Business people who have dedicated their whole lives to improving their lot with work, accustomed to seeing in all dealings of human life nothing more than the exchange of one product for another or for money, may be said not to make a single move or to come to any decision that does not have as its object pecuniary advancement. They make no move to get into conversation with a man whom they do not know, and they even avoid it unless their penetrating eye perceives that they can gain some advantage from knowing him, or at least that it will not be to their disadvantage.

On the other hand, one may be sure that there are no more moral people than those of the United States of the North. Constant application to work makes men virtuous or independent, but at the same time proud and distrustful. A shoemaker, a tailor, a blacksmith who sets himself up in one of those new towns with a capital of twenty-five dollars, rents a wooden room and buys the raw materials of his trade at the end of ten years of work and rigorous economy has a house, a garden, and his well-equipped workshop. Such a man (and there are tens of thousands of these in the United States) fears that a loafer will come along and swindle him out of the fruits of his labor, or that a man without a conscience will seduce his daughter or his wife, and as a consequence he holds back from close communication with any person that is not very well known to him.

One can imagine that this excessive precaution leads naturally to extreme incivility, and indeed, the traveler who arrives in that country without connections lives in isolation in the midst of human kind. What a difference between these people and those of Mexico! We are essentially outgoing; it seems that we are impelled to become involved with all those about us, of whatever class and condition they may be. Our forefathers the Spaniards did not hand down to us that harsh and haughty character that they made us feel so strongly under their domination. I do not know whether or not in our extreme amiability there is a touch of servility or of the habit of passive obedience. I am inclined to suspect there is because we are not always sincere in our flattery or in our compliments, and we have a saying that "one kisses hands that he would like to see burned."

"I visited one house," says Mrs. Trollope,

that attracted my attention because of its solitary and rustic location, and interested me because of the dependence of the family upon their own resources. It was a cultivated spot in the midst of the forest. The house was built upon an elevated hill so steep that they needed a long set of steps to get to the frontier style front door, while the back opened out upon a large patio on the same level.

At the foot of this steep rise was a waterfall of clear water that ran into a pond formed in front of the dwelling. At one side there was a plot planted in corn, and on the other a corral for hogs, chickens, cows, etc. There was also near the house a small garden planted with potatoes, a few apple and peach trees. The house was made of logs and consisted of two rooms besides a small kitchen. The two rooms were well furnished with good beds, chairs, wardrobes, etc. The farmer's wife and a young girl who seemed to be her sister were spinning, and three boys were playing about outside. The woman told me that they spun and wove all that they needed in the home made of cotton and wool, and they knit their stockings. The husband, although he was not a shoemaker by profession, made the shoes. In the home they made soap, candles, and even sugar, taken from a sugar tree that they called the maple tree, which is found in those forests. "The only thing that we need money for," she said, *"is for tea, coffee and whiskey, and we provide that easily by sending each week to the market a bar of butter and some chickens."* They did not use wheat, and from the corn which they harvested from their planting they made their bread and several kinds of pastries; they used it also for the animals in the winter. The women did not seem healthy, and they said that they had had intermittent fevers, but that they were better. The mother seemed satisfied and proud of her independent state, although she said in a somber tone: "It is very rare that we see people, and my greatest pleasure is the hope of seeing the sun rise and set a hundred times without seeing any other human being besides those of the family."

I believe that this minute description deserves the attention of the readers because there are a great many like this family in the woods and forests of Indiana, Tennessee, Ohio, Illinois, Missouri, and other states. They are to be found also in our Mexican republic, although they are generally poor Indians who have no other dwelling than a straw hut, for a bed the ground and a *petate* or straw mat, a tortilla, salt and chili for food, and for clothing a piece of old rag around the body. What a difference!

I am of the same opinion as Mrs. Trollope that this manner of living is a little savage and not natural. That solitude—that isolation from the rest of mankind, that eternal silence of the forests in which they live—does not seem to befit the noble attributes of man. They never hear the sound of a bell that unites mortals in places set aside for prayer, where men find the goodwill of their brothers; there is no consecrated cemetery to receive their remains when they die; no canticles of religion come to breathe their sweet breath in a last farewell over their tomb; the husband, the father or the son opens with his hands the grave that will cover them forever beside a tree near the house; they themselves bury the body, and the sound of the wind as it moves in the branches of the trees is their only requiem.

Upon our arrival in Cincinnati there was much talk in the public papers and in society of the famous philosopher Miss Wright, whose vehement eloquence and seductive doctrines in a person of her sex, set forth in assemblies where were gathered all who could get into the halls and theaters in which she gave her lectures, attracted the attention of the Americans. This lady received an outstanding education in England and let her talents shine in many notable gatherings.

She had the farfetched idea of becoming the head of a sect; since there was no revelation in her system, she did not follow the direction of Saints Teresa and Agreda, but she did plunge into the philosophical doctrines of Rousseau and of Owen. She preached the absolute equality of classes and conditions, religious scepticism, voluntary divorce and other similar things. If there were anyone who doubted our spirit of tolerance in the United States of the North, Mr. Owen's establishments and Miss Wright's lectures would be enough to convince the least disposed to believe it. This apostle of philosophism was listened to by all classes of society in all the cities in which she saw fit to present herself to the public. She left the United States in 1829 without having made any converts.

Among the notable things in the domestic society of the United States, especially in the interior, should be listed the false modesty that degenerates into hypocrisy in conversation. A person who at the table might ask for a *chicken leg* would offend the *chaste and virtuous* ears of the ladies, and anyone who was so imprudent as to put forth the profane words of lady's chemise, shift, underskirt, petticoat, or corset would be held in very low esteem in society. These scruples remind me of those of our nuns who find themselves embarrassed to pronounce certain words. It is impossible, for example, to persuade an American woman to go out on the street when she is pregnant, unless it be at night.

The reader will not be averse to hearing the story of the memorable literary-philosophical-religious challenge given by Mr. Owen in Cincinnati the year before my arrival in that city. The object was to provoke a debate with all who might wish, setting forth as a conclusion that *there was no true religion,* and that all of them were based on imposture and deceit. Mr. Owen had circulated his challenge everywhere for more than a year. The preacher Alexander Campbell, a Presbyterian, had publicly accepted it with the same solemnity. The appointed day was the second Monday of May in 1829, and indeed a

Methodist church was readied for the noisy discussion. The building was filled with people of both sexes, seated on opposite sides.

Both debaters spoke with eloquence, decorum and mutual and fitting respect. After the discussion, Mr. Campbell asked the audience to be seated. Then he addressed them and said: "Those who profess the Christian religion, of whatever denomination they may be, stand up."

Nine out of ten stood up, and with that he declared the triumph of his cause. Mr. Owen protested saying that many people did not make known their opinion because they feared that credulous people would not buy their goods and would cut off trade with them. Thus ended the famous debate, which is another proof of the philosophical tolerance of the United States in one of the least civilized places of that republic.

This is the same Mr. Owen who founded the school of *mental independence* of New Harmony. He bought the establishment and lands from some fellow members who under the supervision of Mr. Rapp had constructed buildings and cultivated more than ten thousand acres of land on the banks of the Wabash River, one of the tributaries of the Ohio. Mr. Robert Owen put more than two hundred thousand dollars into this enterprise.

At the beginning of his establishment in 1824 he aroused great interest in the United States. Many distinguished people of all classes of society wrote to him asking for information concerning the rules, method, principles and objectives of the founder, indicating a desire to join his society. A year later Mr. Owen left for Europe, leaving his two sons and Mr. McClure in charge of the college.

In 1826 the society had about a thousand members who lived under a regimen of perfect equality and had to eat at one table. A respectable traveler says that Mr. Owen showed him the complete establishment and relates things worthy of knowing. At night a concert was given in a large hall in which all the members of the establishment were gathered. The music was perfectly executed. In the intermissions some piece of William Shakespeare or some other poet was recited, and then there were dances. In the daytime some exercised themselvese at fencing, others were engaged in making shoes and chairs, others in blacksmithing, tailoring and other mechanical trades. Most of the young women were busy making straw hats.

On Sunday morning all the members met together, and Mr. Owen, pastor of this philosophical church, delivered a discourse on the advantages of the society. In the visits that he had with the ladies he found one that was playing the piano with great perfection. After a little while a man came in and told her that it was her turn to milk the cows for the community.

56

The doctrines of the society were: that it is absurd to promise conjugal love for a lifetime; that children should not be an impediment to separation, and that they should belong to the community after the age of two years; that the society endorsed no religion, leaving each member to maintain his own belief; that all were equal, etc. Mr. Owen was so infatuated with his system that he seriously thought that he could establish it throughout the world. I remember having read the proposal that he made to Mr. Poinsett, calling him to be the reviver of the New World on those principles, while he (Mr. Owen) returned to Europe to busy himself in converting the Old World, in order to cut off *at the root all crime, abolish all punishment, equalize needs and desires, and avoid all dissension.* He was so thoroughly convinced concerning his system that it never occurred to him that anyone could doubt it.

Already by 1827 discontent had appeared in the community. Many people, especially the women, did not adjust to absolute equality and avoided contact with the tatterdemalions or ragged ones. The major charge brought against Mr. Owen was that he had from the beginning taken into the society without any distinction people of all classes, without examining their character, their mode of life, their previous education, qualities, etc., consequently producing a mixture *so heterogenous that assimilation was impossible.* I am going to extract a few paragraphs from the famous declaration of political independence, or as he called it *mental independence,* proclaimed by Mr. Owen on June 4, 1826.

My friends, we have before us a noble objective that should be won by one party or another in this or in some other country. It is a matter of nothing less than the destruction of the triple cause which deprives man of his mental liberty, compels him to commit crime and to suffer all the woes that that crime brings with it. Permit me now to ask you whether you are inclined to imitate the example of your forefathers and wish to run the risks to which they were exposed. Are you disposed to carry out a mental revolution as superior in its benefits and results to the first revolution in this country as the mental powers of man exceed his physical powers?

If you are so disposed, with the greatest satisfaction I will join you in this arduous undertaking, the latest and boldest which mortals in the irrational state in which they found themselves have dared to carry out.

But, my friends, knowing as I do the immeasurable magnitude of the benefits that this mental revolution must bring and secure permanently for the human race of future ages, I judge the continued stay here for a little longer of a few individuals as a thing worthy of little consideration in comparison with the goal that we propose. Therefore, since I cannot know the present disposition of your souls, and since on the other hand the prolongation of my life at the age which I now have is very uncertain, I have calmly and deliberately determined on this portentous and happy occasion to break completely what remains of the mental chain which for so many years has unfortunately afflicted our nature, and for this time human understanding shall stand in complete liberty.

As the fruits of forty years of experience, due to a very peculiar set of widely varying, extensive and unusual circumstances that are perhaps not to be found in any other man, during which period my understanding has been continually occupied with investigating the cause of every human suffering, whose knowledge has come to me from its true origin, I declare you and to the whole world that man has until this moment been in all parts of the globe a slave to the most monstrous trinity that has ever been put together to cause ill to the physical and mental faculties of the human race.

I denounce to you as such: 1. Individual or private property. 2. The absurd and irrational religious systems. 3. Marriage as an individual property combined with one of these irrational systems of religion.

It is very difficult to say which of these great sources of all crime should be placed first or last because they are so intimately connected and consecrated together by time that they cannot be separated without being destroyed. Each one of them supports the other two.

This formidable trinity composed of ignorance, superstition and hypocrisy is the only demon or devil that has ever existed and is the eternal torment of the human race. It is calculated in all its consequences to produce the most frightful wretchedness to which nature is susceptible in the soul and in the body. The division of property among individuals has prepared the seeds, cultivated the increase and led to the maturity of all the evils of poverty and wealth that exist in a people at one and the same time. The industrious fellow undergoes privation, and the idler finds himself loaded with wealth that he does not deserve.

Religion or superstition, which is the same thing, for all religions are superstitious, have as their objective the destruction of reason and the rationalization of all the mental faculties of man and to make him the most abject slave by means of imaginary entities created solely by disordered imaginations. Superstition obliges him to believe and to say that he believes that there exists a Supreme Being who possesses all power, infinite goodness and infinite wisdom; that he has been able to make and has made all things; that evil and sufferings abound everywhere; that this Being who makes and produces all things is not the direct or indirect author of evil and suffering. Such is the foundation upon which all the mysteries of superstition are erected in the whole world. Its inconsistency and inconceivable madness have been such that they have occasioned continual wars and massacres throughout the world, have caused private divisions and have led to all imaginable evils. It is possible that superstitions have caused more than a third of the crimes and misfortunes of the human race.

The forms and rituals of matrimony, in the manner that up until now they have been celebrated and later maintained, point out that they were invented and introduced among people during the same period that property was divided among a few chiefs with superstition coming to their support, since this was the only device that they could put forth in order to authorize retaining their division of the public spoils and creating among themselves an aristocracy of wealth, power and doctrine.

As the fruit of the experience of a lifetime consecrated to the investigation of these important objectives, I declare to you without any fear because of a conviction as deep and as intimate as can exist in the human mind that this composite of ignorance and fraud is the only and the real cause of crime and of all the miseries that emanate from it and that are spread about in human society.

For forty years I have dedicated my heart and my soul, day after day without ceasing, to preparing the means and combining the circumstances that have enabled me to give the kiss of death to tyranny and despotism that for years without number have held human understanding bound with chains and fetters of mysterious forms from which no mortal has dared to undertake to liberate the unfortunate prisoners. The time had not yet come for the fulfillment of this great event until this very hour. Such has been the extraordinary course of events that the declaration of political independence in 1776 has produced this result, to wit: the declaration of mental independence of 1826, half a century after the first one. Rejoice with me, my friends, because your mental independence is now as well assured as your political independence.

With the circumstances in which this mental revolution has been realized no human power can destroy or bring to naught what has already been done. This truth has passed from me beyond the possibility of any revocation, and has been received in your hearts; within a short time it will be heard throughout America, and from there it will pass to the north and to the south, to the east and to the west as far as the word of man is heard. And with the same swiftness with which it circulates human nature will give it acceptance and universal approval. Rejoice then once more with me, my friends, because this light is now placed upon the mountain; from there it will become ever greater day by day until it is seen, felt and understood throughout all the nations of the earth.

For the fulfillment of this great objective we are preparing the means by educating our children in useful and industrious habits, with natural and consequently rational ideas and points of view, with sincerity in all that they do, and lastly inspiring in them tender and affectionate feelings one for another—charity in all the meaning of this word for all their fellow beings.

By these means, uniting your separate interests, abandoning the use of money in your business transactions, adopting the exchange of the articles of your industry on the basis of work for equal work, providing that the surplus of your wealth be distributed among those who do not have the wherewithal to put them in a position to improve their lot and to acquire the same advantages, and finally by the abstention from spirituous liquors you will promote in a special manner the objective of all wise governments and of all men who are truly enlightened.

This prayer and its publication in some newspapers were sufficient to complete the dissolution of the society. The same thing happened in France with the St. Simonians who preached the same doctrines, although accompanied by more religious apparatus.

CHAPTER IV.

For a Mexican who has never left his country, or who has not done so in a long time, the first impression as he arrives at any point in the United States or England is that of seeing all classes of people dressed. They say that when the Emperor Alexander visited London in 1814, he said to those about him that he found no common people in that capital. What a pleasant spectacle to the eye of the beholder is that of a society that announces by its appearance of decorum and decency the industry, the comforts and even the morality of a people! On the contrary, how unpleasant is the aspect of nudity and lack of cleanliness and what a sad idea a nation gives of the state of its civilization and of its morality when it is inhabited by such people! In a work on Spain that he published in Paris a certain M. Faure four years ago put on the title page of the book an engraving of a student wearing a torn cloak and other rags, with a staff in his hand, *begging alms for the love of God*. This alone gave an idea of the object which most attracted the attention of the French traveler in the Pyrenean Peninsula.

If I were trying to produce a work that was a luxury item with engravings, I would have prepared immediately beautiful plates on which would be pictured steamboats, workmen leveling the land and laying planks of wood and iron to form roads, meadows bathed by streams, cities divided by navigable rivers, cities being born of the earth and dedicating themselves to improving it immediately, rooms filled with children of both sexes learning to read and to write, workers and craftsmen with plow or instrument in one hand and the newspaper in the other, six thousand temples of diverse cults in which man raises his vows to the Creator in accordance with the dictates of his heart, in short tranquility and abundance bringing happiness to fifteen million people. Such is the idea that I have of the United States of the North and the impressions that I received from New Orleans to Cincinnati.

The constitution of the state of Ohio was drawn up in the town of Chillicothe in 1802. There are two chambers as in the others. The representatives are elected annually the second Tuesday in October, and the number is proportional to the white population of males above the age of twenty-one years, but should never exceed seventy-two members, nor fall below thirty-two. The senators are elected every two years in the same manner, with the number proportioned to half that of the other chamber.

There is a governor who exercises the executive power, elected by the people every two years, the second Tuesday in October. He begins his term the first Monday of the following December.

The capital is Columbus, where the general assembly of the state convenes the first Monday of December.

The right of suffrage is universal within the white class.

The judicial power rests in the supreme court of justice, in the Courts of Common Pleas of each county, and others that the legislative power may establish from time to time for the expediting of justice. The judges are elected by secret vote every seven years in a joint session of both houses. There are juries as in the other states.

On June 29, I embarked upon the steamer *Magnolia* that was leaving for Wheeling. On board the boat, the day of July 3 was designated for celebrating the anniversary of the independence of the United States because the fourth, which is the legal day, fell on Sunday, and it could not be celebrated then since that day was consecrated by religion for worshiping the creator, each man according to his sect. There were fifteen or twenty persons on board, certainly not a sufficient number to give an idea of what a great nation, infused on that solemn day with the noble feeling of its liberty, does in such august circumstances. I shall not speak then on this occasion of what happens on this day of general enthusiasm in the United States; I have only recalled this circumstance in order to indicate that even in the most isolated and remote places, the North Americans celebrate with religious and patriotic rejoicing the anniversary of the declaration of their independence, and I shall mention the toast that I gave on that day, which was as follows:

Mexican citizens express their good wishes for liberty wherever they may be. On this solemn day dedicated to celebrating that of the United States of North America, I dare to join my own to those of free men who are celebrating the anniversary of their independence. Hear then my wishes: That providence maintain this people in its present institutions for many centuries, and that Mexico may imitate it successfully.

Señor Mejía spoke in the same vein, and the Americans joined their good wishes to ours.

On the afternoon of that day we arrived in Wheeling, a manufacturing city where they make fine and everyday crystal, in the state of Virginia, where passengers disembark to go to the states of Virginia, Pennsylvania, Maryland, New York, etc. Here I separated from Señor Mejía, who was to continue his journey to Washington across the Alleghenies. These mountains, which play a great role in the climatology of the United States, deserve special mention in this work.

From Wheeling there is a road that leads to the states of the East and the North, as I have said, passing through Little Washington, Laurel Hill, Brownsville, Hagerstown and Baltimore. From this latter city they had begun to build a railroad, which in 1830 was only thirteen miles long, and today in 1834 is about one hundred miles in length.

The Allegheny Mountains, which in some parts they call the Appalachians, are entirely separated from the general system of the Andes. At no point do they rise to more than 6,112 feet above sea level. Their principal ranges extend from the northeast to the southwest, from the St. Lawrence to the Alabama and the Yarou Rivers. The eastern chain is known as the Blue Ridge Mountains. These extend from the state of Georgia to the northeast as far as the state of New York. A little farther north, to the west of the Hudson River, there is a small group of mountains known as the Catskills, which the North Americans point out to the travelers from Albany from the steamboats as a marvel for altitude. Farther on are the Green Mountains. The western chain is the Alleghenies, and they are known in the vicinity of Wheeling by the name of the Cumberland Mountains; they cross Tennessee, Virginia and a part of Pennsylvania. Beyond the Susquehanna River this range of mountains takes a more easterly direction and joins the chain of those in the state of Vermont.

There are several small rivers on the way to Wheeling, and a rather deep creek on the first day crosses the road thirty times, making necessary as many bridges among which there are some of great taste and elegance. The views of the mountains are enchanting for the variety of the trees, the fragrance of the flowers and aromatic herbs, broken rocks, valleys, landscapes, cultivated areas, country homes, cattle, plains, etc.

While Señor Mejía was taking this road, I continued my journey to Pittsburg, the manufacturing city of the states of the west. Pittsburg is located at the confluence of the Monongahela and Allegheny Rivers that form the Ohio. The coal smoke that covers the city night and day makes it a little sad. The great number of factories of porcelain and glass of all kinds, as well as every sort of instrument of iron, steel, lead and other metals in common use, place this city among the most progressive in the United States. Its location at the head of the Ohio River and at a point that puts it in a position to be in touch by water with any place in the world after a two-thousand-mile trip down the river offers a unique advantage of this sort. In Pittsburg ocean-going vessels are built, and it seems as something out of a fairy tale to see such things being done at such a distance. Perhaps the day will come when our own Rio Grande of the North will see steamships coming down to carry the products of Chihuahua to London or Bordeaux.

When I passed through Pittsburg workmen were digging a canal to connect the Ohio River with Lake Erie, thus making it possible to go to New York by water, and to leave by the same means for the Mississippi, traveling along the Hudson, the Clinton Canal, Lake Erie, the Ohio Canal and the rivers as far as the Balize. This work was finished in 1833.

Another undertaking of greater importance, and one which General Bernardo figured would be worth twenty-five million dollars, was a proposed canal that would cross from the Chesapeake Bay at the lighthouse of Baltimore, following the Potomac that flows by Washington, and Pittsburg, crossing the Allegheny Mountains to the Ohio River. This canal would be 341 miles long, 60 feet wide and 6 feet deep. The general preference for the railroad has caused this great enterprise to be suspended for the present.

The city of Pittsburg is in the state of Pennsylvania; it has about thirty to thirty-five thousand inhabitants. There are Germans, English, French, Irish, Scots, in short all that wish to live by the fruits of their industry. If in these states they were to adopt a law like the one lately proposed by Señor Tornel in Mexico to prohibit foreigners from engaging in retail trade, never would one see such progress, such prosperity. What did Señor Tornel learn on his trip and his long stay in Baltimore and Philadelphia?

I left Pittsburg by stagecoach taking the Erie Road through the towns of Butler, Mercer, Meadville, all new, but all of them witnessing the spirit of life that animates their inhabitants. Always to be found are schools, newspapers, and three or four churches or chapels where they gather on Sunday to pay tribute to the Supreme Being with their worship. In Meadville there is also a college where they teach moral philosophy, physics, Greek and Latin grammar and the elements of mathematics. I arrived in Erie on July 8, and in that port we embarked on a steamer on the beautiful lake of the same

64

name that receives its waters from several rivers and from Lakes Superior, Huron and Michigan.

The next day I arrived in Buffalo which is situated on the right bank of the famous Niagara River as it leaves Lake Erie to flow into Lake Ontario. I stopped at an inn called The Eagle, one of the most cheerful buildings that I have ever seen in my life, all of wood and capable of lodging two hundred persons with comfort. Buffalo is one of the prodigies of the United States, one of those cities that were born in this century and are already competing with the older ones because of their beauty and their trade. In 1814 it was completely reduced to ashes by the English, and today it has ten thousand inhabitants, five churches and more than two thousand houses, although almost all of them are of wood. According to general information that I have received and continue to receive 120,000 persons pass through Buffalo annually, and there is not a day on which there are not at least 1,000 travelers in the city. It is one of the principal trade centers of this small Mediterranean Sea called Erie, surrounded by new towns, and the vehicle of communication between Canada, the states of the east, Europe, and the states and territories of the west which are called to play a great role within the next century.

I will copy what I wrote in my travel diary on Saturday, July 10, 1830:

We left Buffalo at nine thirty in the morning, and we arrived, after an hour's travel at Black Rock, which is a town located on the right bank of the Niagara River. This river flows from Lake Erie to empty into Lake Ontario after having run thirty-five miles and having formed the most amazing falls that bears its name. Black Rock is opposite Waterloo, the English town that is on the other bank of the river. One leaves the coach in Black Rock and crosses the river on what they call a horse ferry because one or two horses move the oars by means of a machine. In Black Rock begins the famous canal of the state of New York which connects with the river of the north or the Hudson at the city of Albany.

We continued our trip in stagecoaches which were waiting for us, traveling along the banks of the river through the beautiful plains of English Canada. Near Chippewa, which is a town two miles from Niagara Falls, is the field where the Americans and the English did battle in 1814. I went over these places with the book which gives a description of all these beautiful spots in my hand, and I felt an indescribable respect at the sight of the monuments erected to the memory of those who died in battle. The same thing happened to me in Mexico when I passed by the crosses and the Calderon bridge. In this small village near the Falls, a woman who had a shop in her tavern took out to show us two skulls of persons who had died in action there and which she kept very carefully.

We arrived at the great cataract of Niagara at noon. One cannot conceive the surprise that this spectacle causes, a mighty river that dashes down from a height of 170 feet into an unknown depth. The force of the waters causes clouds to be formed from the vapor into which these waters are converted. A thick column rises up over the cataract; the noise is deafening; the gaze remains fixed involuntarily for some time upon this phenomenon, this marvel of nature. The precipices which surround it; the movement of the waters that give vista and perspective and warn of the danger; the broken sides of the neighboring hills; the variety of trees such as chestnuts, cherries, acacias, firs, poplars, and the evergreen pines; in short the swift currents that before plunging into that abyss seem to stop on the rocks that they encounter, all produce sensations of wonder, pleasure, horror and melancholy. It seems that the soul feels itself oppressed by feelings that it cannot resist. The waters of the torrent smother all ideas in the imagination; it is a giant of a hundred arms that presses the mortal against its body with irresistible force. Such was the effect that the presence of Niagara had on me.

On the English side there is a good inn from which can be seen what is called Horseshoe Falls, and on the other side that they call the American side, is another inn; the falls are not as magnificent, nor is there as great a mass of water as on the English side. At this point the river is divided by an island called Goat Island, located right on the edge of the abyss of the cataract. Between this and the American side they have built a wooden bridge that trembles all over when walked upon. From this point the spectator sees the torrent that runs beneath his feet and plunges with indescribable swiftness into the unknown depths to continue its course then peacefully into Lake Ontario, which receives this mighty river, and afterwards it continues further down under the name of the St. Lawrence.

Many unfortunate things have happened at this cataract. Some persons have sought and found in its abyss a quick death; others have escaped. Well known is what happened to the famous Chateaubriand who was miraculously rescued when his horse, frightened by a snake, plunged toward the main cataract. Well known also is the beautiful description of Niagara at the end of his *Atala*.

All the banks of the Niagara River as far as Lake Ontario have been the theater of a deadly war in the years 1812, 1813, and 1814, between the Americans and the English. On the left bank of the river ten miles below the falls there is a column of granite one hundred feet

N. Currier, undated

The Harry T. Peters Collection, Museum of the City of New York

NIAGARA FALLS

high, erected on a hill in memory of the English General Brock, who died in an action against the American militia in October of 1812.

It is worthy of note that the English troops were all regulars commanded by war generals educated on the battlefields of Europe; such were General Freeddale who was mortally wounded in the battle of Chippewa, General Drummond wounded likewise in another action that took place two weeks later in Bridgewater, and General Riall who was taken prisoner. The American generals Brown, Scott and Ripley showed themselves to be worthy of such enemies although they had never been in any war action. General Scott, who gave brilliant proofs of bravery and intelligence in action at Chippewa and at Bridgewater, was not long before the campaign a famous lawyer in the state of Virginia. The first action in which he took part was at Queenston, where General Brock of whom I have spoken died.

The Niagara River and the lakes form a very weak barrier to prevent Canada from one day being a part of the United States of the North. Although that English colony has no reason to complain of its mother country in the matter of its political constitution, there are, nevertheless, some trade restrictions that are always an obstacle to progress. The capital of Upper Canada is York.

From Niagara I went to Queenston, an English town on the left bank of the river and on the shores of Lake Ontario. Opposite it is Lewiston on the American side, where there is an inn that is large and comfortable. I went up again to visit the falls on the side of Manchester. Although I may seem to repeat myself, I am going to copy what I wrote about the same places on Monday, July 12, 1830:

There is a very beautiful inn, and the view of the falls from this side reveals it in all its perfection. The Americans have built a bridge over to Goat Island, an island that became theirs after the last war. It is wonderful to see how they have been able to tame the terrible current that plunges down from the rocks. Genius and desire for gain have united to perform miracles of the art. On the island there is an inn where they have set up a sort of museum, and various curious objects can be seen, such as fossils, minerals, animals, etc. Among those there is a dead swan perfectly preserved that was caught in the cataract in 1828. Everything is surprising and magnificent; to walk over the suspension bridge high above the falls gives one a feeling of horror.

All these places were uninhabited when M. de Chateaubriand made his journey among the savages in 1792.

The sky is pure above my head, the waves are clear beneath my canoe which glides before a light breeze. To my left I see hills cut off sharply and flanked with rocks from which hang vines with blue and white flowers, festoons of wild roses, grasses of all kinds; to the right vast meadows. As the canoe advances, more and more new perspectives open up. Some times there are smiling and solitary valleys, at others hills bare and without vegetation. Here there is a forest of cypress trees that form shady porticos, farther on a grove of sugar maples where the sun penetrates as through a blond lace. Yes, primitive liberty, at last I have found you!

I travel like that bird that flies before me, that takes its course by chance and that is only worried about the selection of the tree in which it will build its dwelling. Here I am such as the Almighty has created me, sovereign over nature, carried in triumph upon the waters, while the inhabitants of the rivers accompany my course, the denizens of the air sing me their hymns, the beasts of the earth greet me, and the trees bow their heads as I pass by. Is it upon the forehead of the man of society or upon mine that is engraved the seal of our noble origin? Run, shut yourselves up in your cities; go subject yourselves to your strict laws; earn your bread by the sweat of your brow or devour the food of the poor. Kill because of an argument, to have one chief instead of another; doubt the existence of God or worship him under superstitious forms; for my part, I shall wander at will through these solitary places, in which my heart will beat freely, and my thoughts will run unshackled and unchained. I shall be as free as nature; I shall recognize no other sovereign than the one who gave light and existence to so many suns and who with one impulse of his arm caused so many worlds to rotate.

With an ineffable pleasure I read these pages when I was traveling through those same places then covered with towns, where civilization and the hand of man have not breathed the deadly breath of slavery or of superstition. I was leaving the anarchy of Mexico where I had seen myself so often exposed to being the victim of parties, and now wandered freely along the delightful banks of the Niagara, among the eternal forests of Canada, getting away as much as I could into those solitary places where as a man unknown in countries so remote, I gave myself over entirely to my meditations. Oh Niagara! With my eyes fixed upon your swift currents, they seemed to indicate that I was completely engrossed in the grandiose spectacle, I was seeing in you the most melancholy representation of our disastrous revolutions. I was reading in the succession of your waves the generations that hasten on to eternity, and in the cataracts that proceed to your abyss the strength of some men that impels others to succeed them in their places.

In Fort Niagara there is a detachment of American troops, and in Fort George English troops. Borders and fortresses are the only places where regular troops are seen in the United States. It goes without saying that they are well dressed and well fed. There are few desertions, while they are rather frequent among Canadian troops, or so I am told.

CHAPTER V.

In Queenston I took passage on a steamboat called the *Alciope,* which although comfortable was not comparable to those of the Ohio and the Mississippi. The passage cost me ten dollars to Montreal, one of the largest and richest cities of Canada. We traveled the day and the night of the thirteenth across Lake Ontario, and after having covered 150 miles we stopped in Kingston to take on firewood. From this town which is situated on the east bank of the lake they have begun the construction of a canal which they call the Rideau Canal, and which is to terminate in Montreal. The object is to facilitate the navigation of the St. Lawrence River below, which cannot be passed, at least not without considerable danger, because of the small cataracts that are encountered betewen this point and Montreal. The cost of this canal is reckoned at £500,000 ($2,500,000).

There is also another canal already begun in Upper Canada* between Lakes Erie and Ontario to overcome the roughness of the Niagara River and to make possible communication by water between the two sides. This is the Welland Canal where there is a cut that

_____

*Translator's note: Zavala uses the terms *Upper Canada* and *Lower Canada* to refer to the provinces of Ontario and Quebec, respectively. These terms were common in his day.

approximates our outlet at Huehuetoca, although it is not so immense nor so deep. The cut is twenty-seven feet across. This canal must be about forty-five miles long. Our canal at Huehuetoca is probably ten miles long at the most; but the cut of Nochistongo is considerably longer.* Here is the real beginning of the St. Lawrence River, which is famous for its width and its thousand islands.

Montreal, a city of 25,000 to 30,000 inhabitants, is located on the left bank of the St. Lawrence River, on a high bluff and surrounded by fertile hills that are well cultivated and that give a pretty view. There is a considerable going and coming of Indians, most of whom are savages that come to trade their beaver, nutria, buffalo, deer, panther and other skins and hides for foreign merchandise such as glass, crystal, clothing, brandy, powder, lead, etc. Most of the houses are built of brick and stones with square cut masonry and also granite. There are some monuments worthy of attention such as that erected to the memory of Admiral Nelson on which in bas relief the Nile is represented by a crocodile and the sea by well-designed boats.

Most of the people are Catholic, and there is a rather large cathedral in very bad taste, Gothic style, of limestone. The houses have their roofs covered with tin, which causes them to present a beautiful view from the hills when the sun or the moon shines upon them. The people are strangely dressed; they speak a mixed French which scarcely resembles the speech of Paris. Most of the merchants and large land-owners are English. The inn in which I stayed, that was called Good Enough, has very good service, although more expensive than the inns of the United States.

There are several convents in Montreal, founded during the time when it belonged to the French. There has been no change in their establishments since the Government considers them only as companies or associations. The nuns go out on the street when they wish, but they generally keep their vows and serve the sick.

As travelers who have written on the United States have never failed to draw a parallel between the St. Lawrence and the Mississippi Rivers because of the visible and remarkable contrasts that are to be found between them, I think that I should follow the same example so that the reader may get some idea of the diverse manifestations of nature. The St. Lawrence is quite varied in its banks and presents diverse scenes. The Mississippi is uniform, the same and monotonous; the former has a swift and tumultuous stream; the latter runs majestically and does not appear to be carrying the immense volume of water that it discharges into the ocean; the former has pure crystalline ripples; the latter is turbulent and muddy; the former has its source in

*Translator's note: Huehuetoca and Nochistongo are places in Mexico to which Zavala refers.

72

Lake Ontario, so great and majestic as it empties into the gulf of the same name; the latter is fed by mighty rivers that increase its volume; the former runs for three thousand miles; the latter does not exceed five hundred;* the St. Lawrence is neither increased nor decreased in volume; the Mississippi floods, rises and threatens with its overflow the towns, villages, and cities that are nourished by its waters. The St. Lawrence passes through many lakes; the Mississippi runs through the midst of forests; the first is great and beautiful; the second is somber and sublime; in short the St. Lawrence brings pleasant impressions to the imagination; the Mississippi oppresses it with its immensity.

In twenty-four hours of sailing on the St. Lawrence River in a steamboat we went from Montreal to Quebec, the capital of Lower Canada. We arrived at the hour when they were sounding retreat at the fort, and the military music produced a very pleasant feeling.

Quebec consists of the upper city and the lower city because it is erected on the hills that rise gradually in some places and suddenly in others, forming a wall on the river. The lower part is unhealthful, dirty, inhabited by poor people with wretched houses; the upper part does not have so many or such beautiful buildings as does Montreal, but it is not lacking in beauty and in houses that are comfortable and of good appearance. The cathedral is a formless mass, without architectural taste or form. The fortress, which is now being finished on Cape Diamond, is without doubt one of the most grandiose works of military art, both for its location and for its architecture. It must have cost the English government more than two million dollars. The Fields of Abraham is a plain that dominates the city, and it has been the theater of glorious actions, both in the war with France and in the war of independence. At different times the English General Wolfe and the American Colonel Montgomery died there, and their ashes were later transported to St. Paul's Church in New York. This whole plain is filled with the vestiges of war, and there are some monuments erected to the memory of the English leaders.

On my trip to Quebec I talked with Mr. Coveocy, a respectable elderly man of that city who was born in Boston. Few, very few, Americans hold Mr. Coveocy's opinions with regards to the future destiny of Canada. He thinks that within a period of time a part of the state of Vermont and even of Maine will unite with Canada in order, as he says, to complete their territory. I on the contrary indicated to him that I believed that all the English part of that area would be independent, or would form states in the American confederation in the course of time.

*Translator's note: Zavala must have gotten his numbers reversed here; that would make his figures more in line with present day calculations.

He spoke to me very enthusiastically of a M. Bailli, a reformer of the Catholic Church in Lower Canada in the years from 90 to 94 of the past century, who reduced the number of holidays by cutting them to six per year, not counting Sundays, which he accomplished with a great deal of difficulty and amid clamors of fanaticism. He brought to my attention that only the coasts were populated, as happens with new countries, where the colonists naturally seek the river banks and the shores of the sea.

As far as the addition of Upper Canada to the United States, I am going to transcribe here the reflections of an English traveler, who under the title of *Men and Manners in America,* has given a not very impartial description of the United States, although the force of truth often causes him to confess to its rapid progress and local advantages. "The legislative chambers were not meeting when I passed through Canada," says the traveler,

and consequently I know little of the questions under consideration. However, I have some information from a M. Papineau, who represents with much decorum the role of the O'Connell of the colonies. The field is not vast, but he does what he can, and he enjoys the dignity of being the perpetual thorn stuck in the side of the governors. M. Papineau and his party show themeslves always unhappy with English domination. But, what more do they want? They pay no taxes. John Bull (the English people) spends his money with great liberality among the Canadians, as they themselves can see in the magnificent fortifications of Cape Diamond and the Rideau Canal. This latter should bring immense benefits to both provinces— benefits that the Canadians would never have had if left to their own devices.

What would they have then? At least Lower Canada would not join the United States, and it is very poor and destitute of means to be able to subsist by itself. Take away English capital from this colony, and there would remain only poverty and solitude.

With respect to Upper Canada, we see rapidly approaching the time of its union with the United States. All things tend to the consummation of this matter. The canals that put that long pipeline of lakes in communication with the Ohio and Hudson Rivers will accelerate the accomplishment of this. The workers of Upper Canada have easier trade with the markets of New York and New Orleans than with that of Quebec. The masses of the people are republican in their political ideas and anarchist in their morals. Let's admit it then—the loss for England does not count for that much. The eagle's wing is not diminished because one of its feathers falls out.

74

When I was in Quebec (July of 1830), the heat was much greater than I had experienced in Yucatan or Veracruz. The thermometer stood at 102° F., and never in my life have I felt more miserable. The heat lasts two months, and already in September one begins to feel the cold which increases considerably until the end of January when the country is all covered with snow and ice. The summer passes so quickly that it does not permit corn to mature, and consequently this precious grain is not planted in Canada. They have wheat, barley, rye, buckwheat from which they make delicious pancakes, and oats. The fruits are not good, although they do have cherries, mulberries of various types, apples and peaches.

There are two noteworthy falls near Quebec. One of them is Montmorency Falls, which although it is higher than that of Niagara did not give me the pleasant impression that the other one did, even though its appearance is more rustic. The quantity of water that falls from 148 feet* is not a sixth of the other, but it makes more noise, no doubt because the vast receptacle does not have sufficient water to diminish the force of the falling mass. The other cascade is the *Chaudiére* or Cauldron, which has a hundred-foot perpendicular fall and produces the effect of causing the water to boil furiously and plunge into the St. Lawrence River.

The village of Loreto which is nearby offers, as in many of our very old towns, the melancholy sight of ruins. The last remains of a powerful tribe of Huron Indians live there. Brandy and gunpowder have done their work, and only two hundred persons are left of this people, noble and warlike in another day. They have adopted the religion and the language of their conquerors. There is a church in this town, and a priest who lives among his parishioners who love him. Christianity is the only benefit that the Indians have received from the whites. The latter have cheated, robbed, corrupted and ruined them in this world, and then they do them the favor of providing them with salvation in the next. The benefit is in truth sublime, but the poor Indians must mistrust a gift that comes from such people.

In the two provinces of Canada there are legislative chambers, and the laws receive their sanction from the governor who is named by the king of England. There are also certain laws of property and of special importance that require the approval of the government of His Britannic Majesty. Otherwise, there is freedom of the press, trial by jury, and the other same great social guarantees as in England. The French language is that of the public registers in Lower Canada, and the discussions are in this language.

*Translator's note: Zavala is mistaken as Montmorency Falls is about *275 feet* high, not *148 feet*.

75

I left Quebec and returned to Montreal, passing through the town of Sorel on the Richelieu River which has its source in Lake Champlain and empties into the St. Lawrence. This would be an excellent means of communication with the state of New York through Lake Champlain and Lake George, of which I shall speak later. I returned to Montreal and was there for only an hour.

In Montreal I crossed the river and set foot on land in a very beautiful place called La Prairie, where there is a convent of the Sisters of Charity, and I continued by stagecoach as far as St. Jean, a place located on the east bank of Lake Champlain. There I boarded the steamer *B. Franklin,* on which I again found the cleanliness and comforts of American vessels of this type. Since leaving Niagara I had been associated in making the trip to Canada with Mr. M. Evans, a merchant of New Orleans, and Laville de Beau, a landowner of Louisiana. In Fort Niagara we joined a friendly family from Pittsburg called Simpson and Dahra, and in this company we continued the pleasant crossing of Lake Champlain. After traveling thirty-four miles one comes to Black Island, beautiful, fertile and unhealthful, and three miles farther up again enters the territory of the United States, where a guard asks very courteously if one has any contraband material, and without further formality allows the travelers to proceed.

We passed through Plattsburgh, a town of considerable size in the state of New York which gave its name to a naval battle between the American and English fleets in 1814 when the Americans overcame the British, and ten thousand Englishmen had to retreat under the orders of General Provost, whose plan was nothing less than cutting the communications between New England and the rest of the United States.

After 142 miles of traveling on Lake Champlain, we landed in Whitehall, which is on the western side of the lake, from where Lake George is scarcely more than the distance of one mile. On this isthmus are the remains of the old fortress called Ticonderoga, the theater of bloody warfare, both when the French held Canada and later in the two wars between the English and the Americans. I visited these ruins where there is now nothing more than piles of stones and sand with some old walls.

Lake Champlain is in no place more than five miles wide. On the west* side it has to the south the mountains of Vermont that are called the Green Mountains, among the highest of this cordillera. Between the two lakes there is a small town called Alexandria with a cascade that tumbles gradually, something like fifty feet to form a brilliant

---

*Translator's note: Zavala is mistaken as Vermont is to the *east*, not the *west*, of Lake Champlain.

spectacle. We ate there and took the steamer on Lake George, which is even more narrow than the other lake, deep, with clear transparent waters, and closed in on both sides by high rocks so that it appears to be a channel. All these mountains and forests are sparsely populated; from time to time one sees a few houses high up that inspire the desire to occupy them in men weary of the world and of business, who seek in vain the illusions of the country and of solitude after having uselessly pursued a happiness that ever escapes from their hands.

Few places indeed have inspired in me so burning a desire to retire to the country life as those delightful and romantic shores of the Niagara River and Lake George. What solitude so well accompanied by the beauties of nature! Cliffs, streams, crystalline and navigable waters, exquisite fish, magnificent vistas, even the ruins of Crown Point and Ticonderoga, everything inspires sublime, simple and natural ideas.

The lake ends at Caldwell. One cannot pass these places without remembering two terribly tragic events that took place in the vicinity of these lakes. In the war between the French and the English in 1759, at the capture of Quebec for the second time, Mr. Schoonhoven and seven Americans were taken prisoners by a band of savages near Sandy Hill. Taken to a meadow they were made to sit down in a row upon a tree trunk, and then an Indian armed with an axe killed them one by one by breaking their heads. When they came to Mr. Schoonhoven, the chief ordered the bloody scene to stop, and addressing him he said:

> Do you remember one day when you were at a dance and several of us Indians presented ourselves at the affair, and when your companions were opposed to letting us in, you commanded that we be permitted to take part in the festivities? I believe I find in your face the same traces of affinity with the Indians; now you will see that we now how to appreciate these acts.

He then ordered that they free Mr. Schoonhoven and one of his companions who was still alive. *Sunt hic etiam praemia laudis* ("Such indeed are the rewards of a praiseworthy action").

During the War for Independence, in 1777, a young American named Jones, captain of the English troops, was engaged to a young lady named Miss McCrea. Her house was between the contending armies. Captain Jones, in order to get married, dispatched a party of Indians who were in the service of the English to escort his bride to the fort, which was the general headquarters. Not content with the first escort, he sent another also of Indians, offering a barrel of brandy as a reward to those who went. Both parties joined ranks and argued as to which ones would conduct the lady. The sad result was that the young lady was killed and fell victim to a fight begun to honor her.

77

In Caldwell we took the stagecoach to go to Saratoga. After a few miles we came upon Glens Falls, famous for its high cliffs, rock formations and great numbers of fossils. This cataract is on the famous Hudson River, which pours its great waters into New York Bay. We went on to Saratoga, which at that time was filled with travelers who come from all over the United States to take the celebrated mineral waters in the springs there, to dance, and to make acquaintances that may later decide the fate of the persons involved.

Saratoga is a town of the state of New York which has four excellent inns, each of which may lodge two hundred persons at least, not to mention a large number of smaller houses that they call boarding-houses. The principal inns are the Congress Hotel and the United States Hotel. More than one thousand persons go and come daily in this delightful place during the months of June, July, and August. As a center for mineral waters, the people there have tried to beautify it with groves, walks, gardens and everything that they can to make it pleasant for those who for pure pleasure or for their health go to drink the waters at the Congress.

There are fourteen springs of different combinations of salts, gases and minerals. Most of them contain sodium chloride, sodium carbonate, calcium carbonate, magnesium carbonate and iron carbonate in varying proportions. In the one which they call ''Congress Water'' there is a large quantity of carbonation, and the travelers drink two or three glasses every morning before breakfast to cleanse their stomachs gently. It is not distasteful like the water of the springs in our village of Guadalupe or the city of Hidalgo, which contain sulphur, petroleum, and much carbonation. When I passed through Saratoga, I was presented to the Count of Survilliers, José Bonaparte, ex-king of Spain, of whom I shall speak on another occasion.

In the vicinity there are still to be seen relics of campaigns of the War for Independence. The English General Burgoyne, after having taken Fort Ticonderoga, made his way with ten thousand regular soldiers and many thousands of savage Indians whom he had as auxiliaries towards Saratoga and Albany, in the center of the state of New York. In a proclamation which he published in June of 1777, he said that what he would be doing was more of a military passage than a campaign. Such was the pride that the easy taking of Fort Ticonderoga had inspired in him. He had conceived the idea of taking Albany, which seemed easy enough to him because of the terror that had been created by his sudden appearance on the left bank of the Hudson, the object of his desires as a barrier between the states of the west and New England. But the victory at Bennington, accomplished by the American Colonel Stark against the British troops commanded by Colonel Baun who was killed in battle, opened the eyes of the English general to the fact that he had to fight with a formidable enemy.

Worthy of attention is the discourse of Colonel Stark to his troops before the battle: "Today we must rout the enemy," he said to them, "otherwise, Mary Stark (his wife) will be a widow before the sun goes down."

After this action General Burgoyne fought two very bloody battles and was forced to surrender October 17 of the same year, leaving the field to the Americans. This campaign was directed by General Gates, who was born in England but was a faithful and noble defender of the American cause.

Subsequent to the expedition of the English General Burgoyne many incidents took place that are worthy of relating because of their unusual nature. This leader had received no communications from General Henry Clinton, who was to come to his aid by coming up the Hudson River. The courier named Taylor, who was carrying information on this important news to General Burgoyne, was taken prisoner by the advanced forces of the American General George Clinton. Poor Taylor swallowed something that he took from the bag, but he was observed. They gave him a strong dose of tartar emetic, whereupon he threw up a small hollow silver ball, and in it was found the letter from Clinton to Burgoyne. Taylor was tried and executed.

In the first attack of September 27 it was noted that a greater number of officers died than was in proportion to the number of troops. The American sharpshooters had stationed themselves in the branches of the trees, from where they aimed at the officers by choice. In the action of October 7 the principal leaders of the English army died. General Fraser, Colonel Breytman and Mr. Clarke, aid to General Burgoyne, fell victims to the American riflemen.

General Fraser was an active officer, a man of bravery and ability. General Morgan was the one charged to make first contact with a body of American *chasseurs*. In the fiercest part of the action the American general chose six of his best riflemen and said to them: "You see that man? I admire him for his valor and his energy, but he must die; do what you must and carry out your duty."

This was the sentence of death for the brave English general; within a quarter of an hour he was dead. The account of this event and the tragic action is taken from the description written by a German lady who found herself on the same battlefield or in the vicinity where her husband Baron de Reidesdel served under the command of the British general:

> Harsh and severe tests awaited us the seventh day of October when our misfortunes began. I was having breakfast with my husband, and I

N. Currier, 1852

SURRENDER OF GENERAL BURGOYNE AT SARATOGA N.Y.

80

realized that some serious business was at hand. I was expecting to dine with Generals Burgoyne, Tillips and Fraser. I saw much movement among the troops. My husband said that it was only a review, which told me nothing. I met many armed Indians, who to my questions only answered *guerre, guerre,* giving me to understand no doubt that they were going into battle. This made me hasten my retreat to the house where I had scarcely arrived when I began to hear cannon shots and gunfire that became louder and louder. At four o'clock in the afternoon, instead of the guests whom I was expecting to come to eat, I saw a litter enter bearing General Fraser mortally wounded. I had his bed placed in the same room that was to have been used for dining with him and the others. I sat down sadly in one corner waiting from one moment to the next for news of my husband.

General Fraser said to the surgeon: "Tell me if my wound is mortal; I don't wish you to be easy with me." The surgeon told him that the bullet had pierced the stomach and had cut the principal tendons of that organ. The general was buried the next day in the midst of the bullets and the fire of the two opposing armies. Colonel Wilkinson, whom we met in Mexico where he died, and with whom I had a special friendship, took part in this action. He says in his history that he was following a party of the enemy when he discovered near a fence a man stretched out who said to him: "Protect me, my colonel, from the bullets of this boy." He turned his head and saw a lad of fourteen or fifteen years pointing his rifle at the poor Major Ackland, who, gravely wounded, had been carried to that point by a corps officer who was with him, and Colonel Wilkinson delivered both of them from the deadly shots of the small American.

Most interesting is the story that Baroness de Reidesdel tells of the efforts of the wife of Major Ackland, who accompanied her husband in all his perils and was with him in the enemy camp itself. We also have the same sort of examples of conjugal love and feminine heroism in our Mexican war.

A NIGHT ON THE HUDSON
"Through at Daylight"

Currier & Ives, 1864

82

CHAPTER VI.

On July 24 I left Saratoga for Ballston which is on the way to Albany. This is also a town of mineral waters, of about two thousand inhabitants and with good inns. I did not stop there except for the time that it took to visit its springs, and journeyed on to the capital of the state of New York, the city of Albany on the right bank of the Hudson River. Six miles before you get to Albany is Troy, a pleasant village pleasantly located on the opposite bank of the river which has about four hundred inhabitants. On another occasion I shall turn my attention to Albany when I speak of my travels to New England in this same work.

July 25, 1830, I boarded the steamer *United States,* on which were traveling at least three hundred passengers, both men and women, all well dressed, especially the women, whose neatness and elegance were a real pleasure. In spite of the large number of people, all of them were very much at ease; some wished to stroll upon the deck, some to go below to the salons. For everyone there was a place at the tables set up for eating and dining. At dinner the food was plentiful, well seasoned, with good service, in short, with all the enticing comforts. We went down the picturesque Hudson River at a rapid pace, and at West Point we had the pleasure of meeting Señor Mejía and his family who were on their way down to New York, from where they had come to see the famous military establishment of this place. We arrived in New York at seven o'clock in the evening, having sailed 148 miles from Albany in twelve hours.

I stayed at Mrs. Street's Boarding House, No. 36, Broadway. This is one of the numerous stopping places that are neither public nor private, and in which a certain number of persons lodge under stipulated conditions. Those established on the street called Broadway in New York are the best, and one lives there in great comfort, in a select social group, and without the noise and confusion and going and coming of the large places.

Three times I have gone into New York by the bay, four by the Raritan, once from the east coming from Boston, and three or four by the Hudson River from the north. As I shall speak of the latter ones on another occasion, I shall begin now with the entrance of the magnificent bay of this great trade center.

As one approaches the coasts of New York there come into sight the heights of the state of New Jersey on the left side, and those of Long Island to the right. On Sandy Hook, which is a small sand hill on the southwest coast, there is a magnificent lighthouse, besides others that may be seen along the coast. The entrance becomes more narrow in about fifteen miles at Staten Island, which extends from the Raritan River as far as the straits which are called the Narrows, at the end of which a fortress has been built and is under the command of General Bernard.

The view is at once picturesque, magnificent and imposing; beautiful country homes on both sides surrounded by trees planted symmetrically on land that rises gradually and displays a prodigious fertility; the sight of the two rivers that descend leaving the city in the middle; a multitude of ships of all types and sizes that come and go taking different directions with full sail; steamships that cross each other's paths, and like great whales make their way lifting with their prows mountains of foaming water and leaving behind thick black smoke from their stacks; five hundred boats anchored on both sides of the angle formed by the rivers between which is located the city. This apex is covered with groves of trees, and the whole makes a pleasant ensemble that inspires the imagination and lifts up the spirit. New York is no doubt one of the most beautiful and most convenient ports in the world, and is also after London and Liverpool the city with the greatest maritime trade.

The city is located on the island of Manhattan formed by the North River, the Passaic and the East River, which is rather an arm of the sea. Long Island is a tongue of land separated on the south and is an island one hundred miles long and five or six miles wide. On this portion of land there are some rather large towns, among them Brooklyn, which is opposite the city, Jamaica, Flushing and other small towns and villages that are increasing in population and wealth in an extraordinary manner that is noted throughout the United States.

The state of New York has a population of two million inhabitants. In the city there are more than one hundred churches or chapels of different denominations; among these are eighteen Episcopal churches, twenty-five Presbyterian, twenty Methodist, nineteen Anabaptist, five Catholic, and the rest are Quakers, Unitarians and other sects. New York has approximately 220,000 inhabitants.

The city is irregular in form, and the streets are generally crooked. There are some, however, that can compare with the best of London or Paris. Such are Broadway, which divides the city and runs from the northwest to the southeast for about four miles, more than eighty feet wide, with stone sidewalks about six feet wide, made beautiful by quite handsome buildings, stores, shops, and all the brilliant things that there are in New York; Chatham, likewise made up of many very good buildings; Canal, Bowery, Blekery, Bonn, Greenwich, and others. Broadway is the place where all the best-dressed people promenade—ladies, young sports, strangers; it is at one and the same time a park, a street, and a promenade. More crowded than Regent Street in London, cleaner and more beautiful than the Boulevards of Paris, straighter and longer than Alcalá Street in Madrid. In New York there are no public promenades, with the exception of the small park at the Battery. There are no public fountains, and the drinking water is rather bad.

The advantageous location of New York, and more than anything else the system of liberty without petty passport restrictions, under the protection of just and wise laws, with absolute freedom of worship, have led this city to such a degree of prosperity and greatness in forty years that it is today the metropolis of the New World. In 1778 New York had only 22,000 inhabitants; in 1795 it had grown to 33,000; in 1800 it had 60,000; in 1820 it had increased to 123,000; in 1825 it had 166,000; and today, as I have said, it has 220,000. What city in the world has had such rapid growth?

The value of the merchandise that is imported and exported through this city is calculated to amount to $100,000,000; the income from the mails gives the treasury annually $120,000. What movement is necessary to produce such vast and extensive exchange!

There are more than seventy steamboats that leave the wharves to cross the bay. Some serve for crossing the Hudson and East Rivers to carry people that are going and coming from Brooklyn, Hoboken, Staten Island, and they are running all day long until twelve o'clock at night. Others leave for Flushing, New Haven, Hartford, Albany, Raritan, etc. During the summer up into the fall that bay appears to be one perpetual fair.

One of the most beautiful buildings of New York is the one called the City Hall, which is where the courts are held also. This is located in the midst of a tree-covered plaza called the Park, in the center of the city. It is 216 feet long and 105 feet wide. The facade is of beautiful white marble, and this building would be very elegant if it were better proportioned. But it is lower than it should be for its size. There are two other famous plazas in this city—one, Hudson Square, where there is a park surrounded by a high iron fencing with lots of scrolls; the other, Washington Square, which is outside the city, and which within a few years will be surrounded by buildings, shops, stores and houses.

In New York there are three theaters, and these are the Park, the Bowery and the Opera. Generally speaking North Americans are not very fond of this sort of entertainment which presupposes a degree of urbanity that cannot be said to be most noticeable among those people. Where taste for society and amusements has increased in the cities, such as Boston, Philadelphia, New York and a few others, one notices always that the people are not very enthusiastic about attending these functions. What a difference from the eagerness with which people rush to the doors of the theaters, balls and concerts in the cities of Europe, especially in France! The fifteen theaters of the city of Paris are filled nightly, and the managers make a living with good profits. In New York one theater of Italian opera cannot support itself at the same time as the other two in which they present separate bits of song and drama. I have noted a much greater inclination to the theater in the people of the Mexican republic than in the states of the North. The reason for this difference must be sought in the diverse circumstances under which these two peoples have developed. The North Americans are made up for the most part of agricultural immigrants who, because they were obliged in the beginning to work in the fields, have not had the time or the stimulation to dedicate their hours of rest to any exciting pastime. On the other hand, the spirit of sectarianism, which at first tended to a rigorous asceticism among the Presbyterians who migrated to those parts, left in its wake an insurmountable aversion to such presentations since they were prohibited by religion.

In the Spanish colonies there was an absolute separation between the conquerors and the conquered. The former had the wealth, privileges and the pleasures that provide both the inclination and the tastes that they engender. The descendants of the conquerors inherited from their parents the Spaniards the taste for music and entertainment, which were in accord with the Catholic religion, whose head in Rome gave encouragement to all sorts of

N. Currier, c. 1847

CHATHAM SQUARE, NEW YORK

spectacles. Instead of dedicating themselves to working the land or to other arduous occupations, they gave themselves over to noisy festivals to which on the other hand their warm or temperate climates invited them. Furthermore, there was not the dire necessity of accumulating for the winter provisions, firewood and clothing. The prime mover for work is necessity, then come pleasures. Thus then one sees a Mexican spend a peso which he had obtained without much difficulty in the theater, on the bullfight, or at a dance; while a North American would be afraid to take one dollar out of a hundred for such an investment.

In New York there are more than five hundred coaches for hire, not as comfortable as those of Mexico and Paris, but fast and elegant. There is scarcely room for four persons in a coach, and it costs one dollar per hour. A host of foreigners from every country keep these carriages continually occupied.

The principal hotels or public inns in this city are the City Hotel, Congress Hall, the National Hotel, the American Hotel, the Washington Hotel, the Franklin Hotel, all on Broadway. The rate is twelve dollars per week for room and meals, which consist of breakfast, dinner, tea and supper. The Washington Hotel is in a building that is quite large with a beautiful facade. Nearby are the Arcade Baths which are the best in the city, established by a Spaniard named Quesada. There are also many others that are second-rate, in addition to the boardinghouses of which I have spoken, which number more than eight hundred.

In no country in the world is there as great a number of newspapers in proportion to the population as in the United States of the North. In New York in 1831 there were twenty-eight newspapers, most of them rather large. In every town that has as many as two thousand inhabitants, the first thing that the people do is to build a small church, construct one or two buildings for schools and set up a print shop. When I read some days past of a project presented to the senate of Mexico by Señor Pacheco Leal on March 21 of this year, according to which there was to be set up a credit of $100,000 for the publication of a newspaper, I remembered the distance that exists between liberty that strives for thought and the publication of opinions and ideas in the country that we have taken as a model and our poor republic in which those who try to direct public affairs, far from moving openly towards the emancipation of our past servitude, try to maintain a monopoly on thought and put obstacles in the way of the intellectual progress of their fellow citizens. I cannot understand how men who profess popular republican principles can, even for a moment, adopt such projects that are in direct conflict with popular sovereignty.

I have said that in New York there were one hundred churches, but I have not spoken of the manner in which the clergy is supported, and this deserves a special explanation.

The American people are most religious, even to the extent of being fanatic in some places and congregations; but worship is entirely in the hands of the people. Neither the general government nor that of the states intervenes in any manner in religious matters. The need for having a church or chapel to meet in on the Sabbath, as they say, according to the precepts of Genesis, brings together these assemblies of the same denomination, who are in agreement as to how their worship is to be carried out. They name their ministers, support them, and exercise over them the authority that a company would have that pays its workers. To facilitate the exercise of their liturgical and economic government they elect a certain number of persons who have the powers of administration delegated by the congregation. Among the Protestants, Lutherans, Presbyterians, Episcopalians, etc., the people elect their ministers, and they dismiss them for bad conduct. Among Catholics the same thing occurs, but they go through the form of asking the bishop, and he never refuses them. Catholic bishops are appointed by the Pope, and the people receive these or not as they please. The Episcopalians, when they have a vacancy, meet to name their prelates. All of this is in accordance with the first centuries of Christianity, and *compatible* with the system of popular equality. *Any other method in which the government has a part in the affairs of worship is destructive to liberty.*

I cannot resist the desire to insert here a document that gives a clear and perceptive idea of the whole political system of the United States of the North as it concerns religious matters. The one who is speaking is an Episcopal bishop, Mr. Hobart, who died in a town in New York while carrying out his holy ministry during the time that I was in that state. Upon the death of Governor DeWitt Clinton, one of the most beneficent and honored men of the United States, the mayor of the city of New York sent a note to Bishop Hobart asking him to please make known in a solemn manner in the churches of his denomination the regrettable death of the governor of the state. Here is what the bishop replied on February 16, 1828:

> Sir, I have received today from the secretary of the city corporation a copy of the resolution of the city council, in which the request is made of the reverend clergy of the city that they publish tomorrow in corresponding and solemn form in their churches the very regrettable misfortune suffered by our common fatherland in the death of our first magistrate and fellow citizen DeWitt Clinton.

Since I find it necessary to refuse to comply with this demand in Trinity Church and in St. John's and St. Paul's chapels, I hope that you permit me to set forth the reasons that I have for this in order to avoid a bad interpretation in this particular.

The prostitution of religion to secular political use has worked great harm, and I conceive that the careful separation of the Church from the intervention of the State, which characterizes our republican constitution, has been for the purpose of preventing and avoiding that religion and its ministers should become instruments that some might use for political gain. All right, if the municipal authority wishes the clergy to communicate "in a solemn and proper manner" the death of the first magistrate of the state, this same petition can be extended successively to all distinguished citizens in public office, and in this manner the intervention of the clergy can be made to increase the influence of political men and of their political measures. The regrettable results of this danger have been seen in the ancient world, and against it we should strive to free ourselves in our fortunate country.

Whatever may be the character of the individual, he can never be worthy of this sacred religious distinction. In the circumstances of great political excitement an individual can be hated by some and the idol of others, and in this case the clergy, whose province is to administer to all in its spiritual functions, would be obliged to take sides between the parties and to experience dire conflicts. In almost all cases the ministers of religion, in their capacity as *eulogists,* find themselves embarrassed among the diverse opinions of their listeners, among which there are persons who wish for extraordinary eulogies, while there are others to whom moderate praise will seem excessive. Therefore, there is no point of view, as I see it, from which serious objections will not be met with in fulfilling the demands of the municipality.

As far as my own feelings are concerned, it would afford me great satisfaction to give public testimonial to the eminent talents, civic services and private virtues of the first magistrate whom we mourn. Very worthy of consideration also are the petitions of the municipal dignitaries of the city in which I carry out my ministry. But superior considerations of duty prevent me from complying with a demand which in the principle involved and the precedents that it establishes, seem to me a dangerous tendency with respect to the spirit of our free constitution, to the spirit of religion and to the character and influence of its ministers. I have the honor, etc.

J. J. HOBART.

Among ministers respectable for their learning and their virtues that I have known in the United States special mention is due Father José María Varela, a native of the island of Cuba, who emigrated from his country because of his liberal principles during the period of the persecutions of Ferdinand VII. Another is Doctor Power; both of them are Catholics, both well educated and examples of Christian virtues. The Catholic religion is making considerable progress in the United States, especially in the states of Maryland, Louisiana, and Mississippi. The most extensive are the Presbyterians, Methodists, Episcopalians and Anabaptists. The people on the whole are religious and moral.

In New York, as in the other cities of the United States, the people come together when they think it necessary to discuss political questions of general interest. There are not only assemblies to inform public opinion concerning elections; we have seen them also deliberate concerning difficult banking theories, tariffs and duties, and other issues that have been debated recently in the United States.

In New York they meet regularly in Tammany Hall, the Masonic Hall, the City Hall and in the Stock Exchange, which are the largest and most convenient buildings for the purpose. It is surprising to see the order with which they convene and dismiss these assemblies, which always begin by naming a president, two vice-presidents and secretaries to direct the discussions. Very seldom does one see excesses or hear boisterous voices and much less disorders of any other sort. When the discussion begins the president proposes the questions that are to be dealt with and grants the floor to whoever asks to be recognized. Usually they have already written the resolutions that the individuals that are directing them consider to be the consensus of those present. As each party has its determined location, it is already known more or less what the resolutions will be. Thus we have seen that the backers of General Jackson always meet in Tammany Hall, just as those on the other side meet in the Masonic Hall. Consequently, the resolutions of the first group have always been against the Bank of the United States, against the election of Mr. Clay, etc.

On the following day they publish the resolutions in the newspapers and on posters that are put up in public places. Thus they are made known throughout the other states, in which assemblies are formed in the same manner, and at the end of a couple of months it can be stated mathematically how many citizens think one way, and how many the other. When the majority has spoken, the question is considered settled, and no one thinks of appealing the decision by force of arms to undo what has been done. In some complicated questions as that of the Bank, in which great interests are opposed, what usually happens is to delay the resolution because the people cannot understand it in the first discussions, and the complication makes it difficult to know what is best.

In one of these meetings held in the month of January of this year on the question of the Bank of the United States, the following resolutions were passed:

1) The opinion of this assembly is that the prejudices suffered by all classes are due to the unconstitutional intervention of the president of the United States to arrange for the circulation of securities.

2) The manner in which the executive power has taken upon itself the disposition of the government's funds indicates a tendency to arbitrary action and proves that it intends to govern without any consideration for the constitution or the laws of this country.

3) Thirty persons shall be named to form a commission of public welfare whose duty shall be to come to an agreement with the commission of the Union; engage in correspondence with the other commissions organized to apply opportune remedies to the ills that afflict the country, and finally to take suitable measures to the end that the public administration shall operate in conformity with the constitution.

4) The unworthy and brutal manner in which General Jackson has conducted himself with the commission of workers and craftsmen of this city debases the high rank that he occupies in his capacity as the president of the United States, and offends the entire body of the signatories, of whom the commissioners were the representatives. Concerning Martin Van Buren, the highly improper reception that he gave the commissioners themselves is an indication of the low esteem in which he holds the working and industrious class of this city.

This fiery accord, the product of the assembly held in the Stock Exchange, was contradicted three days later by another of a more numerous gathering held in Tammany Hall, in which they approved the resolutions of the president. Thus the most troublesome questions were aired, but they never arrived at a plan of action.

The state of New York has eighty banks, whose total capital amounts to $27,800,000. There are $43,712,958 in circulation in discounts issued by these banks, for the most part in paper, and this produces an unbelievable activity in all branches of industry. Among these banks there exist some small ones whose funds are in the range of $100,000 and they circulate $200,000 or $300,000; as soon as a city of any size is organized, people begin to think about starting a bank. In the state legislature there were petitions for granting a charter to fifty new banks, or to renew those of existing ones. These banks have a solid basis for existence in that the lenders take the funds to invest in productive uses such as raising crops, purchasing cattle, building houses, boats, and other always useful enterprises that produce profits greater than the interest paid. This is the reason why one has seen these speculations prosper when they create imaginary values and put into circulation capital that does not exist.

From New York packet boats depart regularly three or four times per month for Liverpool, London, Le Havre, New Orleans, Charleston; and others not so regularly and frequently for Veracruz, Jamaica, Havana and the Spanish Main. Among the first there are boats that are outstanding for the comfort, cleanliness and even elegance of their cabins. The service is generally good, the food plentiful and the wines according to one's own choice. Always in greater numbers are the passengers on the return trip from Europe, especially of poor people who are emigrating. There is no packet boat that does not carry forty or fifty emigrants bound for America to seek lands, work, and liberty.

The greater part of the inhabitants of New York City and the state are descendants of the Dutch. They preserve their ways, customs, and in many places their language. To this is due the fact that most of the houses are painted in bright colors, which gives to the city and smaller towns an air of happiness that is pleasing to the traveler.

NEW YORK FERRY BOAT

N. Currier, undated

94

CHAPTER VII.

Colonization of Texas.—Formation of the company.—Type of inhabitants in that area.—Its future destiny.—Meeting my son in New York.—Persons that I dealt with.—The fair sex.—Museums.—Public education.—Participation of the people in public affairs.—Courts.

One of the first things that I did when I arrived in New York was to bring about the formation of a company to carry out the conditions of an agreement entered into by me with the government of the State of Coahuila and Texas relative to colonizing lands that lie between the Sabine River, Galveston Bay, the town of Nacogdoches and the sea. I could not carry out such an undertaking alone because it required considerable funds, and as a consequence I solicited persons that might wish to have a part in the enterprise. Don José Vilhein, from Mexico, who has a grant adjoining mine, gave me complete authority to establish a colony for both of us, and Mr. David Burnet, who has another grant in the interior where ours end, also joined with us, with the result that the three colonies provide a great extension of land that can be colonized where we should in a given time establish close to two thousand families.

This undertaking was carried out among more than fifty persons from various states, and we had named as trustees of this vast enterprise Messrs. Dey, Curtis, and Summer, who were in charge of the funds and all that was necessary to fulfill the colonization laws of the State of Coahuila and Texas concerning the grants made by the government of the State to the citizens Lorenzo de Zavala, José Vilhein and David G. Burnet.

My enemies in Mexico had many disagreeable remarks to make concerning this action, not only innocent but beneficial to the country; they said that I had sold a part of Texas to the United States, and that I had made myself rich by that sale. Time and my own poverty have caused all this slander to disappear. The government of the State has made a fair disposition of my patriotic efforts and has granted me an extension of time in consideration of the obstacles that the administration of General Bustamante placed in the way of the enterprise, and the persecution that General Teran directed against my young colony by not permitting the colonists sent by the company to disembark, or by taking them to other points. All of this is public knowledge in those parts, and the supreme government of the State itself lodged a complaint against Teran.

In my *Historical Essay* on the revolutions of Mexico I have set forth my opinions concerning that beautiful and rich portion of land known formerly as the province of Texas and today as an integral part of the State of Coahuila and Texas. Once the way was opened to colonization, as it should have been, under a system of free government, it was necessary that a new generation should appear within a few years and populate a part of the Mexican republic, and consequently that this new population should be entirely heterogenous with respect to the other provinces or states of the country. Fifteen or twenty thousand foreigners distributed over the vast areas of Mexico, Oaxaca, Veracruz, etc., scattered among the former inhabitants cannot cause any sudden change in their ways, manners and customs. Rather they adopt the tendencies, manners, language, religion, politics and even the vices of the multitude that surrounds them. An Englishman will be a Mexican in Mexico City, and a Mexican an Englishman in London.

The same thing will not happen with colonies. Completely empty woods and lands, uninhabited a dozen years ago, converted into villages and towns suddenly by Germans, Irish, and North Americans, must of necessity form an entirely different nation, and it would be absurd to try to get them to renounce their religion, their customs and their deepest convictions. What will be the result?

I have stated it many times. They will not be able to subject themselves to a military regime and an ecclesiastical government such as unfortunately have continued in Mexican territory in spite of the republican-democratic constitutions. They will point out the institutions that should govern the country, and they will want it not to be a deceit, an illusion, but a reality. When a military leader tries to intervene in civil transactions, they will resist, and they will triumph. They will organize popular assemblies to deal with political matters as is done in the United States and in England. They will build chapels for different faiths to worship the Creator according to

96

their beliefs. Religious practices are a social necessity, one of the great consolations for the ills of humanity. Will the government of Mexico send a legion of soldiers to Texas to enforce Article 3 of the Mexican constitution which prohibits the exercise of any other faith than the Catholic? Within a few years this fortunate conquest of civilization will continue its course through other states towards the south, and those of Tamaulipas, Nuevo Leon, San Luis, Chihuahua, Durango, Jalisco and Zacatecas will be the freest ones in the Mexican confederation. Meanwhile, those of Mexico, Puebla, Veracruz, Oaxaca, Michoacan and Chiapas will have to experience for some time the military and ecclesiastical influence.

When I arrived in New York I had the pleasure of embracing my son Lorenzo at the literary establishment of Mr. and Mrs. Peugne, where I had sent him five years before. Nothing can compare to the pleasant and gentle impression that one gets when after a long absence he meets the object of his affection and love. But these feelings become even more pleasing when a man sees in them the heir of his name, his name image and his representatives, to put it thusly, in posterity. The seeds of virtue and instruction that the worthy directors of that school planted in the soul of my son had taken hold and sent out deep roots. All this was sufficient reward for my past sufferings. A little while later I sent him to another school in Round Hill in the state of Massachusetts, under the direction of Mr. Cogswell, a man who was very respected for his learning and excellent character.

In New York I came to know the famous Albert Gallatin, one of the best educated and most respectable men in the United States, although born in Switzerland. He has been secretary of the treasury, and one of the companions of the first founders of the constitution and of the institutions. I also became friends with Don Tomás Gener, a Spanish immigrant, who had been a member of the Chamber of Deputies in 1823, and was held in high esteem in New York for his learing, his honesty and respectable manners. There was General Laight, with whose friendly family my son found the comfort and favors of a generous hospitality; Mr. James Prentiss; Mr. Webb, editor of the morning *Courier and Enquirer;* Mr. Fisher, editor of the *Advertiser and Advocate;* Mr. Dwight, editor of the *Daily Advertiser.*

Later on I shall mention other persons that I had the satisfaction of coming in contact with and that are important in that country. In the same boardinghouse or *pensión* where I stayed there was a Dane named Sigmund Leidesdorf, who had lived for many years in Santa Fé de Bogotá as an agent of one of the loan companies of London. This individual with whom I have since been a close friend is a person who knows of many things, has a very pleasant disposition, correct manners and is well informed in the matter of credits, banks and even of finance. General Bolívar had ordered him to leave the country because of his friendly relations with General Santander, with our chargé d'affaires Don Anastasio Torrens, and the British consul Mr. Henderson, all of whom Bolívar ordered to be relieved of their passports. Mr. Leidesdorf's opinion concerning the Liberator of Colombia was not very favorable.

Among the causes for surprise to a Mexican who travels for the first time in the United States, one is the beauty of the women. All travelers speak of this great advantage of those parts, and a Mexican has much more reason to do so. Indeed, among us the fair sex possesses charm, regular proportions, is endowed generally with much spirit and an irrepressible friendliness. But there is not that multitude of beauties that one encounters at every step in the states of the North. Even in the Mexican republic it is noted that the women of the north are more beautiful than those of the south; those of Sonora and New Mexico are famous for their beauty throughout the country. North American women have very good color, large bright eyes, well-shaped hands and feet; but they are very far from the elegance and voluptuous manner of walking of our Mexican women, of whom it may be said *incessu patent deae* (by their walk they reveal themselves to be goddesses).

In New York there are two museums that, as others in the United States and England, are privately owned. The one belonging to Mr. Peels is the oldest, although there are in the other one a larger number of very well-preserved animals. Mr. Peels' museum has rather the usual pictures, portraits of the principal persons of North America and a self-portrait of the founder of the museum. There is also a lyceum to which foreigners are admitted when presented by one of its members, and here they can read newspapers from this and foreign countries. The lyceum which they call American Lyceum, and of which I am a member, is for the purpose of promoting primary education.

This field is one of those receiving the most attention in that city. New York has more than three hundred schools, most of them free, in which are enrolled more than forty thousand children of both sexes. I have never seen a man who does not know how to read, and there are very few who do not know how to write among those in the cities of the United States. This accounts for the fact that they read newspapers, take part in the discussions of great interest and make up a mass of powerful public opinion. There is not nor has there been any country where the citizens have or have had so decisive and direct an influence on the decisions of its government. In Athens and in Rome a public directed by ambitious or salaried orators apparently made their decisions after the examination of matters that were subjected to their deliberation. Everything was the work of party enthusiasm or spirit, from which resulted those acts of injustice which posterity has condemned, and which led those republics to their ruin. Pericles in Athens and Cicero in Rome were not the only ones who dominated and directed the multitude by their eloquence. Aristophanes began the misfortune of Socrates, and Anytus aroused the feelings of the people against that wisest of men. Claudius began the troubles of the great Roman orator Cicero, and Anthony bore him to his death.

In the United States of the North although the people govern, and the chambers are their faithful interpreters, the decisions come from long and deep discussions. The meetings or popular assemblies in which political questions are debated do not settle anything definitely. They only set forth the opinion of a small fraction of the country, which finds or does not find sympathy and cooperation from other gatherings in the Union. Meanwhile the same questions are discussed in the newspapers, and the North American under a tree if he be a farmer or a shepherd, or in his office if a lawyer, or behind his counter if a merchant, or in his shop if a craftsman, reads and clarifies his ideas calmly and maturely. Such a government is the Utopia sought by political writers.

The administration of justice in the United States is not entirely free of judicial chicanery. Nevertheless, everywhere one observes the admirable simplicity of their government. "It is difficult to conceive," says an English traveler,

> less ceremony in the administration of justice than in the United States. Judges and lawyers without wigs or robes, dressed as they wish or as they go out on the street. There are no maces nor any symbol of authority, with the exception of various staffs which I observed that some constables or bailiffs of the court had in their hands. The witnesses gave their declarations with the appearance of the greatest ease or indifference as they do in England. No one seemed to think that he was in the presence of the court or should therefore maintain a certain decorum.
>
> The judges were probably about fifty years of age and went through no special ritual in the performance of their duties. The lawyers, although younger insofar as I could tell, did their part with zeal and ability in defense of their clients. The only disagreeable thing about the whole procedure—in which I was happy to see justice done with purity and good faith—was the continual spitting on the part of everyone present.

When I had satisfied my curiosity in this court, [the traveler continues] I went to another which I found to be the supreme court of the state. At the moment it was occupied with a case concerning bank bills. The dryness of the subject matter caused me to leave, but before I did I noticed the jurors were called in to give their verdict. I must admit that I was surprised to see three fourths of them busy eating bread and cheese, and that their foreman announced the sentence with his mouth full, getting the syllables out in between his chewing. To tell the truth, an American seems to see a judge just as any other craftsman, such as a carpenter, a tailor or a shoemaker, and it does not occur to him that one who administers justice is worthy of any more respect than one who manufactures hair dressing or candles. The judge and the candlemaker are both paid for their work, and *Jonathan* firmly believes that as long as he has money in his pocket there is no reason to fear that he won't have laws or skillets.

I cannot, however, persuade myself concerning this matter that legislation is founded upon solid and brilliant principles. A very learned lawyer asked me the other night if the visits that I had made to the courts had not cured me of my fondness for the formulas of *John Bull* (the English) and the togas, wigs, maces and other inconsequential apparatus and ridiculous insignia that they use there and that could only be imposed upon weak minds. I answered no, and that on the contrary, since my arrival in New York I had been even more convinced of the propriety of that apparatus. There followed a long discussion on the subject during which each one maintained his own opinion, and it must be said with due regard to fairness that my opponent used arguments based upon liberty that were expressed with force and energy. I refrain from giving this discussion in detail because a protocol signed by one of the parties is evidently only a partial document, and when a casuist enjoys the privilege of bringing forth the arguments of both parties, he must be endowed with a superhuman detachment in order not to present those against him as weak, putting himself on the side of the gods while he leaves his adversary that of Cato.

It is usual in these countries to ask, and generally with a certain air of triumph, if it is believed in England that wisdom consists of a wig, and if a few ounces of horsehair placed upon the heads of judges plastered with pomades and starch can be imagined to increase the knowledge of the individuals done up in so bothersome a manner. The answer is no—no Englishman believes that the head in its natural state or decorated with these things can be more or less disposed to judgment and legal criteria, and still I do not hesitate to admit that in some parts a judge in shirt sleeves seated upon a simple wooden bench can be as effective and useful an administrator of right as one who is bewigged and covered with a toga of ermine and scarlet.

But this does not necessarily indicate that Americans do not consider these apparatuses useful. If a man were a being of pure reason, forms would not be necessary; but whoever passes laws under such a concept would prove that he does not know human nature. Man is a being of feelings and imagination, and even in religious matters the constant experience of the world has shown the necessity of certain external rites and solemn observances in order to stimulate devotion and to accustom one to finding his faculties for worship of a mysterious and incomprehensible being ''whose kingdom is where there is no time or space.'' It is difficult to conceive upon what principle those who approve of the stole on the priest and the chevrons on the general can condemn as irrational the insignia of judges. Let the Americans be consistent by adorning their judges with titles of honor; they should protect them from the rusticity and common familiarity of their people.

Thus this traveler explains himself, and he does not seem to be very logical since he wishes to make a precedent out of the fact that judges should be dressed in court with trappings that were used four hundred years ago, upon the principle, with which I agree, that certain symbols of dignity are necessary to impose respect. Indeed, these symbolic vestments used by the judges in England and by the presiding officers of their chambers can contribute nothing to the majesty of the laws or to the inviolability of the oracles of justice. The English parliament is respected and obeyed intrinsically because of the justice of its agreements and the wisdom of its deliberations, and considered extrinsically for the profound policy of its decisions. Thus, like magistrates of that same nation, it is worthy of the praises given it by all the writers that speak of it because of the integrity, learning, and purity of its members. If the judges of England were to present themselves in their courts with the ordinary dress of society, they would not be therefore less respected. It is done that way in most of the courts of France and in those of the United States where the judges justly enjoy the most distinguished consideration.

If I could but transport my fellow citizens to these free lands to witness the simple and natural manner by which they reach their judgments, I should certainly succeed in seeing established in my country trial by juries, without which there can be no true liberty nor judicial independence. In some states of the Mexican republic some attempts were made, and their legislators stopped short at the beginning of their philosophical considerations because they found no oracles of Areopagus in the first deliberations of inexperienced men little accustomed to this type of judgments. In all countries the same thing happened at the beginning, and only the constancy and the conviction that this system was the only method of judging according to the principles of liberty caused the legislators to maintain this holy institution [of trial by jury].

"The penalties against robbery were severe," says Mr. Hallan in his *Constitutional History of England,* but they were nevertheless effective in deterring those acts of violence that arise naturally out of the gross and licentious customs of that period and from the imperfect dispositions that had been taken to insure the public peace. These acts were committed or advised often by persons whose fortune and power placed them beyond the laws."

Here then is the situation in which we find ourselves at the present time in Mexico, and the time most apropos for establishing the jury. I shall never tire of saying it. Under whatever form of government the Mexican republic may be, in the end, it will be a grave charge against its directors not to establish trial by jury.

CHAPTER VIII.

Washington Irving.—His writings.—New York's hospitality.—Anniversary of Mexico's independence.—Object of conversations with the Americans.—Inclination to the English.—Mr. Adams' account of recognition by Great Britain.—His speech to the king.—The reply of George III.—Celebrations in New York on the occasion of the revolution in France.—Master Burke.—Colored population.—England's conduct with reference to the slaves.—Reflections.—Anecdote.—Fires.—Aristocracy in the United States.—Mr. Livingston.

While I was in New York, Washington Irving arrived in the city on his way back from Europe. He was received by his fellow citizens with the enthusiasm inspired naturally by the presence of a compatriot whose works have merited approval in literary circles and deserved to be placed beside the classical authors. Washington Irving has written a considerable number of novels and other works that have elevated him to the rank of Goldsmith, Addison, and Robertson. It has been said of him that his *Braceridge Hall* was comparable to the *Vicar of Wakefield* by Goldsmith, his *Sketch Book* to the *Spectator* by Addison, and his history of Columbus to the histories of Robertson. His style is that of the Burkes and the Gibbons. He is, moreover, a true painter of customs such as Walter Scott. Cooper, another American writer, should not be passed over in silence. His novels are written with elegance, naturalness, and verisimilitude. The interest that they inspire is a real one that is not dissipated and does not disappear when the book leaves the hand, as happens generally. It leaves great and deep reflections.

In New York I received the most cordial hospitality from all the people to whom I was introduced. Many did me the honor of inviting me to their dinners and their tea parties. In the United States, as in England, the ladies retire after the dessert, and the men remain at the table for some time longer.

The tea parties are in fact social gatherings where generally there is singing and sometimes dancing. They serve fruits, tea, wines, sweets, cookies, pastries, or other similar things. Businessmen are not overlooked on these occasions. In September of 1830 we celebrated in New York at a banquet the anniversary of the independence of Mexico. Those present included Generals Negrete, Echavarry y Mejía, Count Cornaro, Don José Amaro Ruiz, the consul of Colombia Medina, several well-known North Americans and myself.

In no country in the world do they deal more constantly with mercantile business and how to make money. Very few people speak of abstract questions or matters without including some material interest. An American will ask a Mexican whether there are steamboats, whether there are factories, whether there are mines, whether money is to be found easily in such and such a state. A Mexican will ask what kind of government, what religion, what customs and what theaters, if any, he can expect to find in this or the other place. The North Americans are essentially grasping and hardworking. In England during the meal people talk about the quality of the wines, how the food is seasoned, the elegance of the table and other things having to do with what they are engaged in. In the United States the conversation will likely be about the price of cotton, of lumber, etc.

Although it is generally thought that the North Americans have, with respect to the English, the same averse feelings that have developed in the former Spanish colonies against the Spanish, this is not entirely true. The North Americans do detest royal authority, and everything that has any connection with monarchial institutions, and they do perhaps carry to the extreme their aversion to certain formulas and items of etiquette of the British; but as far as people are concerned, I am certain that the English find among North Americans the best of good feelings in treatment and hospitality, as well as in language and popular customs.

The pride of primogeniture and the advantages that the English have because of their antiquity sometimes brings about disagreeable differences between those on one side and the other; differences where the Americans always make a great show, with much justice, of their admirable progress and of their unquestionable liberty. But it must be agreed that the open and philosophical policy of the British government with respect to its former colonies has played a large part in keeping down these national hatreds, to which purpose the admonitions and good offices of Washington and his successors contributed constantly.

TABLA

DE LOS CAPITULOS

QUE CONTIENE ESTE TOMO.

First page of the contents from Zavala's *Viage a los Estados-Unidos del Norte America*. (Courtesy Texas State Archives.)

Although after the peace between Great Britain and the United States in 1783 the government of the former sent no minister nor agent to the new republic, the respectful and attentive manner with which George III received the minister John Adams, first American envoy to His Britannic Majesty, gave occasion to continue in the most perfect harmony in those thorny beginnings. Mr. Adams, who had been in Europe on other occasions with missions of an important nature, received in 1785 the delicate and prickly one of being representative at the Court of St. James in London as the first minister from the liberated colonies. I shall copy the account that this distinguished American dispatched to the secretary of state of his government because I think the reading of it will be interesting in the circumstances in which the Mexican republic finds itself at the moment of establishing the same sort of relations with its former mother country. "During my interview with the Marquis of Carmarthen," says Mr. Adams,

he informed me that it was the custom for all the ministers on their first presentation to His Majesty to pay him a courtesy in keeping with his credentials, and when Sir Clement Dormer, master of ceremonies, came to inform me that the secretary of state of the court would accompany me, he added that new ministers should also pay their respects to the queen. On Tuesday night Baron de Lynden, ambassador from Holland, came to see me and told me that he had come from the home of the ambassador from Sweden, Baron de Nolkin, and that they had spoken of the singular situation in which I found myself, and they both agreed on the need for my pronouncing a complimentary discourse to the king. All of this agreed with what Count de Vergennes had recently said to Mr. Jefferson. Since that was the way things were, and since I saw that it was the established custom in these two great courts, and that the Court of St. James and the ministers of the other nations were of the same opinion, I thought that I could not get out of it, although my first intention had been to deliver my credentials without saying anything and then withdraw at once.

Finally on Wednesday, June 1, the master of ceremonies came to my house for me, and we went together to the ministry of foreign affairs, where the Marquis de Carmarthen received me and introduced me to Mr. Frazier, the subsecretary. After a short conversation concerning the fact that they would take my luggage from France and Holland without duty, Lord Carmarthen invited me to get into his coach to go to the court. When we arrived at the antechamber, the master of ceremonies came out to receive me and stayed with me while the secretary of state went in to receive his orders from the king. While I was in this room, where all the ministers wait on such occasions, and which was full this time, you may imagine that I was the center of attention, and that all looks were turned in my direction.

Fortunately the ministers of Sweden and Holland lessened the embarrassment in which I found myself as they stayed close to me and kept up a pleasant conversation. Other gentlemen whom I had met previously likewise favored me with their conversation until the return of the minister, who advised me that His Majesty awaited us. I went with his lordship into the king's chamber. The door was closed, and I was left alone with His Majesty and the secretary of state. I made three bows, one at the door, another half way there, and another before His Majesty, according to the protocol of the courts of Northern Europe, and then as I addressed the king, I said to him:

"Sir, the United States has named me as its minister plenipotentiary to Your Majesty, and I have the honor of delivering the credentials that declare this. In obedience to its express commands, I have the satisfaction of assuring Your Majesty of the unanimous disposition on the part of the citizens of those States to cultivate the most friendly and open relations with Your Majesty, and of their most sincere wishes for the health of Your Majesty and of his royal family.

"The naming of a minister from the United States to the court of Your Majesty will mark an epoch in the history of England and America. I consider myself the most fortunate of my fellow citizens for having had first the distinguished honor of presenting myself to Your Majesty in a diplomatic role, and I shall hold myself to be the happiest of men if I can be a useful instrument for recommending repeatedly to my country the royal benevolence of Your Majesty, and continuing to restore complete confidence, esteem, and affection, or in other words, the former good feelings, and the former good humor between peoples who, although separated by an ocean and with different governments, have the same language, the same religion, and blood ties. I beg Your Majesty to permit me to add that although I have received the confidence of my country on numerous occasions, at no time has it been so pleasing and flattering as now."

The king listened to my whole discourse with dignity, but with a certain emotion. I do not know whether that was the effect of the nature of such an interview or perhaps of the visible agitation with which I delivered my discourse; what is certain is that he was very much moved and answered me with greater spirit than I had used as he said to me:

"Sir, the circumstances of this audience are very unusual, the language that you have used is so adequate, and the feelings that you have expressed are so opportune on this occasion that I must say that not only do I receive with pleasure the assurances of the friendly disposition of the people of the United States, but also it is a great satisfaction to me that the mission to represent them has fallen to you. I desire, sir, that you be persuaded and that the American people understand that anything that I have done in the recent conflict has been done only as my conscience has persuaded me was for the good of my people. I must speak to you frankly; I have been the last to come to terms with the separation, but now that it has been accomplished I have always said, and I repeat now that I will be the first to seek the friendship of the United States as an independent power. The moment that I see that the feelings that you have expressed are those of that people, in that moment I shall be able to say that the great sympathies that are born of one same religion, one same tongue, and one same blood will have their full effect.''

It must not be forgotten that the declaration of independence was made in July of 1776, and that in 1783 the United States was recognized as a sovereign nation by the mother country. Our republics of America, formerly Spanish, declared their independence more than twenty years ago, and for more than twelve years have been completely independent, without any obstacle or opposition on the part of Spain, nor even the capacity on her part to do anything. They are recognized as independent nations with duly constituted governments by the civilized nations, and the Spanish cabinet and its new Cortes are still considering whether they will *do us the favor of recognizing us.* Such a policy is mean and little in accord with the liberal principles that they have claimed to profess.

I was in New York when the news came about the famous revolution and the three days in July in Paris and its happy results. It is hard to believe the enthusiasm displayed by the people of the United States for an event that it would seem should not affect a commercial and agricultural nation dedicated to its profits and material improvement. But the feeling for liberty is deeply rooted in those independent souls who can never forsake their sympathies for the progress that other countries make to come closer to their social position. Mr. Monroe, who had been president of the United States, was the one who presided over the assembly or meeting of the workers, craftsmen, businessmen, and other classes gathered in Tammany Hall to take the necessary steps to put on a function worthy of the thing that was being celebrated. The procession was one of the most brilliant gatherings that I have ever seen. To understand the number of those who took part in it, suffice it to say that although they proceeded at a normal pace, the spectator could be in one place for three hours watching them go by.

It started off with a squadron of cavalry, then came the general in chief, Mr. Swartswout, with his aides-de-camp and a detachment of French, residents of New York, with uniforms of the national guard of

France. There followed an open coach in which rode ex-President Monroe, Mr. Gallatin and the speaker. After that came the commissions of the different trades and occupations with their corresponding emblems, banners, instruments, and then the musicians, singers, comedians.

There were printers carrying the type from their printshops, tailors, shoemakers, silversmiths, ironworkers, blacksmiths, businessmen, sailors, lawyers, doctors, students, every class beneath its own banner. Finally came the legislators, mayors, consuls, all of the most brilliant and respectable people. The procession began at Canal Street at nine o'clock in the morning and ended at Washington Square at six o'clock in the evening. There were more than one hundred thousand persons in the procession. The order, good behavior, decorum and general good manners that were evident from the beginning to the end corresponded to the wealth of the people, to the great occasion which they were celebrating, and to the majesty of the American nation.

During those days performing at the Park Theater was the prodigious Master Burke, an Irish lad of eleven years who played, sang, gave readings and did pantomime with the grace, finesse, strength and naturalness of the leading masters of the art. I was spellbound, as were the others in the audience, as I watched a boy three feet tall, with his feminine voice and delicate features, present himself upon the stage and show forth his prodigious abilities.

In the city of New York there are a considerable number of blacks and colored people, although as in the other states to the north of Maryland slavery is not permitted. But in spite of this emancipation of the African class and its descendants, it is excluded from all political rights, and even from the common trade with the others, living to a certain degree as though excommunicated. This situation is not very natural in a country where they profess the principles of the widest liberty. Nothing, however, can overcome the concern that exists with respect to this particular subject.

The colored people have their separate homes, hotels, and churches; they are the Jews of North America. This rejection by society degrades them and takes from them the incentive to work; they resign themselves to idleness and do not try to improve a hopeless situation, circumscribed within limits so narrow that there is scarcely room to calculate self-interest. Hence the vices and laziness which with very few exceptions holds this whole class down to the lowest ranks of society. This is the great argument against the emancipation of the slaves, an argument that discourages its most ardent supporters and that would make their efforts useless if the abolition of slavery were not demanded by a necessity that within a short time will admit no further delay.

England, in the midst of economic difficulties, contrary to its mercantile way of doing things, has just paid, with the high price of $100,000,000, a debt to humanity and national honor that for forty years has been maintained by the futile efforts of a powerless philanthropy. While isolated acts of violence—although one of these irrational happenings has no consequence—raises protests in an American city in favor of slavery, an assembly in London *composed of all parties,* where O'Connell sat on the side of the minister of colonies, where proud aristocracy fraternized with colored men, celebrated the anniversary of freeing of the slaves. Lord Murgrave, recently arrived from Jamaica where he presided over the first sessions of the emancipation, has declared that two more years of slavery would have caused the same disasters as in Santo Domingo. The whole noble example that was carried out peacefully with the best of order in the islands of British America cannot fail to have a good effect on the United States of the North.

All men who are aware of the fact that worry about the future must take into account the questions of the present are easily persuaded that society must give consideration to slavery before slavery produces its bloody eruptions in society. Abolition already has many supporters in the state legislatures. But how does one remedy that embarrassing situation of free colored people in the center of American society? Will the day come when they will be incorporated into the state and form an integral part of the community? We must hope so. The New York legislature took the first step when in 1829 it extended the right of suffrage to colored people who owned real property valued at $250, free of all debt.

I shall end this discussion with a story told by a traveler. The son of a general of Haiti, a very good friend of President Boyer, decided to make a trip to New York for the purpose of having a good time while he was learning something. This young man, although a mulatto, had very good manners and a neat and pleasant appearance and had a better education than is generally found in his country. Accustomed in his homeland to receiving the respect due his station, he expected to find in New York the consideration that money and fortune give, together with the pleasures that a rich and civilized city provides.

When he got off the ship, he ordered that his luggage be taken to the best hotel. But he found that they would not admit him because of his color. He went to another and another; but everywhere he met with the same result, until he found it necessary to take a room in the home of a black woman. The pride of the young Haitian was humiliated, all the more since he was dressed with elegance and adorned with gold chains, rings and diamond buttons, etc. Unfortunately he continued to experience the same insults everywhere he went; in the theater he was not admitted to the seats of the white people, nor in the churches, nor in any society. At the first opportunity he went back to his country vowing never to visit the United States again. If this young man had gone to Europe, he would certainly have found all the comforts and entertainment that he would have desired and that he could buy, sitting in the theater, in the hotel and in church next to the whitest and blondest English, French, or German lady.

"One cannot be in New York for twenty-four hours without hearing alarming shouts of *fire,*" says one traveler.

Indeed, a fire in that city is so common an occurrence that it never causes that anxiety and upset that it does in other parts less accustomed to this calamity. The *firemen* of New York are famous for their quick action and forcefulness, and since it is interesting to witness the exercise of these qualities, I decided to go to all the fires that might occur while I was in the city. The first four were of little consequence since three of them were already extinguished when I got there, and I only got to see the smoke of the fourth one. On the fifth I had better luck. Since I had gotten into the scene of the action farther than was proper, thinking that it was the same as the others, I finally had the satisfaction of witnessing the appearance of a respectable volume of flames coming out of the windows, chimneys and doors of the four stories of the house, accompanied by smoke, alarms, noise and confusion captable of fulfilling my reasonable desires.

Then a fire truck arrived, and the shouts and the grinding of the wheels of the machines announced the approach of help. Some time was spent in getting water, on which matter it is to be desired that the city improve the situation. Nevertheless, in a few minutes it was coming out in torrents, and the two elements began their battle. Those who perform this service are young citizens who because they dedicate themselves to this, and it is very severe, are exempt from serving in the militia. Their activity and daring are truly surprising. At once ladders were put in place, they climbed up to the chimneys, began to take out furniture which they threw into the street without much consideration for those who were there, at the risk of breaking their heads.

The traveler continues giving an animated description of the progress of the fire, the brilliant spectacle that it presented at night, of the confusion and alarm in neighboring houses, and he makes the observation that in these cases they should do as in London, where in order to avoid the crowds of idle people that hinder the operations and increase the difficulties, they are supposed to close the entrances and have them guarded by the police.

N. Currier, c. 1854

THE FIRE: "Now then with a will. Shake her up boys."

112

THE LIFE OF A FIREMAN

N. Currier, 1854

"When I suggested this idea for improvement to an American friend," he continues,

> he replied that it would be desirable, but that such means were not calculated for the American scene where exclusion of any sort is always contrary to popular sentiment. In this matter I cannot persuade myself that the exclusion of a group of idlers from the scene of a fire because they increase the difficulty of saving the property and the lives of some, can be considered as an attack upon liberty.

I have heard many people say that in the United States there is a true *aristocracy,* and others say that it is the country of liberty and of absolute *equality.* No law, no custom, no historical record exists in that country whose tendency would be to form an *aristocratic* class. Civil law calls all citizens before the same courts; political law clothes them with the same rights. But there is a law superior to human institutions, a law of inequality that nature has established, and that no legislator can do away with; a law that has more sway in free peoples than with despotic governments, but that always exercises a powerful influence. This law is that of mental capacity, the superiority of talent. What disposition, what rule can indeed cause a man of talent, of instruction and capacity to remain at the same social level, at the same degree of consideration and of influence as another man who is not endowed with the same qualities? Consequently, the second one cannot choose the same employment nor be received in society with the same esteem, nor attract the same respect and attention as the first one. This is already an inequality, and this exists in the United States as it does everywhere. Webster, Clay, Calhoun, Van Buren, Jackson, Forsythe, Poinsett and others are personages who are very superior to the rest of their fellow citizens.

There is another superiority which, although it is not natural, is a necessary consequence of the state in which society finds itself constituted in general, and that various Utopian philosophers have tried to modify without success. It is that of wealth. A rich man must have more concessions, must offer more hopes, must spend more than another one who is poor. He has more means of influence and a greater capacity for doing good and evil than another in whom wealth and talent are not found together. Such a man considers himself lifted up above the rest, and to a certain degree it is true because many depend upon him, because he does not need to work to live, because he can satisfy his necessities and his pleasures.

Here are two classes of people that in the United States of the North maintain a kind of habitual hierarchy whose natural privileges depend in no way whatsoever upon legislation. I remember that as I was going from Europe to the United States in 1831 on the beautiful packetboat *Francis I* there was at the same time on the boat a family of Mr. Francois Depau, a millionaire merchant of New York and one of the partners of the packetboat company. There were many distinguished passengers, among them General Santander, Señor Acosta, at the present time chargé d'affaires from Nueva Granada to the United States, a noble Italian named Suzarelli, in short, all of them people of education and high principles. Notwithstanding this, Mr. Depau and his family ate by themselves in the ladies' section, thus perhaps having to associate less with us. I confess that that conduct was offensive to me in such circumstances. But whom did it offend, or what right could there be to say anything against their ridiculous isolation? I looked at him with scorn, the same as my companions. Many from the United States of the North do this also.

Compare this with the Mexican aristocracy, and you will note the difference. Among us the laws and the former concerns maintain a true *aristocracy,* an *aristocracy* of privilege, in short an *aristocracy* of *exceptional* laws and therefore a dying one in a popular republican society. How can people who recognize entire classes as superior to others because of legal privileges convince one of their sincere and true love of liberty? In the United States the statesmen can pass on their venerable names to their children and grandchildren if these maintain with their own intelligence, patriotism, and honor the luster of their forebears. But it is seen that this is not a prerogative of the law; it is that of personal merit.

In this city I had the satisfaction of being presented to Mr. Edward Livingston, an illustrious legal authority in the United States, the author of the codes of Louisiana and senator at that time, then secretary of state and today minister plenipotentiary to the king of the French. Mr. Livingston himself has told me that after twelve years of continuous work in getting the codes completed to his satisfaction he retired at twelve o'clock at night and said to his wife: ''Now I am going to sleep with the satisfaction of having concluded my work at the end of twelve years.''

At two o'clock he heard a noise and then warning cries of the servants who were shouting *fire.* The room in which Mr. Livingston had the papers and books was the scene of a roaring fire. The fire consumed everything, and Mr. Livingston began his task anew the following day with the same constancy, until once more he finished his work worthy of a profound jurisconsult.

Mr. Livingston has likewise played a very distinguished part in the development of the office of the secretary of state which he held during the delicate questions of the *nullificationists* of Carolina. The skill with which he was able to manage the negotiations led things to a happy ending. The proclamation of President Jackson in the month of December in 1832, the work of Mr. Livingston, is a document of major importance in the annals of republican governments. In this paper are developed the principles of the form of government of those states with an insight and mastery worthy of the majesty of a great people.

CHAPTER IX.

Trip to Philadelphia.—Iron road.—New Jersey.—Its constitution.—Borden-town.—Joseph Bonaparte.—Delaware River.—William Penn.—Philadel-phia.—Water reservoir.—Theaters.—Miss Wright.—Pennsylvania navy.—Sea trade.—Independence Hall.—Washington Square.—Quakers.—Sundays. —Banks.—Their history.—Penitentiary.—Public education.—Respectable sub-jects.—Mr. Girard.

In August I left for Philadelphia and took passage for four dollars on the steamboat *Swan*, which is one of those of the line. The trip is made by going to the southwest through Raritan Bay, then into the Raritan River and landing at a small town called Washington, in the state of New Jersey. This is crossed by coach, and again one boards a steamer at Bordentown or Trenton. Today the course has been changed since the railroad was laid from Amboy to Camden. The journey lasts three hours through Raritan Bay, three hours by land, and three on the Delaware River to Philadelphia. The distance is about thirty-five leagues.

The state of New Jersey, which one crosses, lies between the ocean, the river on the north called the Hudson, the Delaware, and the states of New York and Pennsylvania. The principal cities are Burlington, New Brunswick and Trenton. The latter is the capital of the state. The constitution of New Jersey was written in 1776 and has not been revised since that time, with the exception of a few changes made by the legislature. The executive power, as in the other states, is exercised by the governor. There is a legislative council and a general assembly. The members of each are selected annually the second Tuesday in October. These two bodies make up the *legislature*.

The number of members in the council is fourteen, with one selected from each county. The general assembly is composed of forty-three individuals. But a law passed in 1828 added seven more members, and today the council is composed of fifty members taken from the counties in the following order: three from Bergen, five from Essex, four from Morris, three from Sussex, three from Sommersett, four from Monmouth, five from Burlington, four from Gloucester, three from Salem, three from Cumberland, one from Cape May.* The legislature meets annually in Trenton the fourth Tuesday in October. The governor is named annually by the vote of the council and of the assembly. The governor is president of the council, which in its first session names a vice-president from its own body, who exercises the functions of the governor in his absence.

The governor and the council make up the court of appeals in all cases of law in the final instance and have the power of pardon.

The constitution gives the right of suffrage to all persons who have property in the value of two hundred dollars and have resided for one year in the place of the county where they vote. The legislature declared in 1829 that every citizen twenty-one years of age with a capital of two hundred dollars could vote provided he were of the white race. By another decree blacks and women are deprived of the right to vote. In Canada the latter do have that right. The judges are named by the legislature—those of the supreme court for seven years, those of the lower courts for five years.

In Bordentown, a small town on the Delaware, is the beautiful country home of Joseph Bonaparte, ex-king of Naples and of Spain, today the Count de Survilliers. This famous personage, whom Spanish papers painted in such ugly colors, is very well educated, has a very pleasant personality and elegant and natural manners, and is endowed with social qualities that have brought him respect in the United States of the North, where he retired after the catastrophe of the Emperor Napoleon his brother. A respectable amount of money, which he was able to salvage from the political shipwreck, has put him in a brilliant situation in that country of trade and business. His magnificent house, gardens and parks on the banks of the delightful Delaware would be enough to make him happy if other *pursuits* did not take him away from the modest and peaceful sphere to which he has been reduced by the misfortunes of the great personage who elevated his whole family to the rank of kings.

The Delaware is a broad and beautiful river, navigable for steamboats as far as Trenton. The views on both sides, especially in the vicinity of Philadelphia, are magnificent and picturesque: country homes with presumptions of Greek architcture of very good style and

*Translator's note: Obviously the numbers do not add up to fifty, but the text has been checked against the first edition, and the reading is the same.

placed in the midst of groves artistically planted and watered by many streams; new villages made up of buildings of beautiful appearance, stores and factories. The vegetation is earlier than in New York. On the left side of the river the railroad runs now; in March of 1834 it reached Camden, and will probably extend as far as across from the city of Philadelphia within two more years.

This great city founded by William Penn, inhabited in the beginning by a few Quaker families, today presents the appearance of one of the illustrious cities of Europe, with greater beauty and much greater hopes of prosperity. From four leagues away on the river are discovered its towers, its tall buildings, its observatories, and the smoke that rises in a colossal column toward the sky.

I stayed in the Mansion House, one of the better hotels in the United States. There I found Mr. Poinsett, my old friend, who was busy writing an article about English politics for the *Quarterly Review*.

The city of Philadelphia is cut perfectly in parallel lines that form streets in the figures of parallelograms. There are numbers 1 to 11 from East to West; and from North to South the streets have the names of plants or fruits—such as Mulberry, Chestnut, etc. But in addition to the street No. 11, the city has already been extended five or six streets more that are not yet numbered. The sidewalks are of brick and are two yards wide. The streets are from fifteen to twenty yards wide, most of them with a border of acacia, chestnut, or walnut trees, which give a beautiful view and a pleasant shade in the summer.

There are magnificent buildings in the city. The stock exchange is being completed and is much better than the one in New York. The Bank of the United States is of beautiful white marble, an imitation, although imperfect, of the Parthenon in Athens. The facade is beautiful, but it lacks the lateral columns. Another bank opposite the one of Mr. Girard (Bank of Pennsylvania) has six beautiful columns of Ionic order, likewise of marble.

The reservoir and machinery for the provision of waters for the city on the banks of the delightful Schuylkill River are works of considerable size. They are built on one side of the river where the scene is truly interesting, and the works, whose utility has corresponded to the enterprise, are solid and beautiful at the same time. No stranger should fail to visit them. The river is at that point about nine hundred feet wide and twenty-five feet deep. A dam has been placed across it, a dike that leads a great part of the waters into the reservoir, and more to the mills that move the wheels destined to raise the water by means of pumps to an open tank in a rock elevated 270 feet above the level of the city, at a distance of one league. Eleven million gallons of water are raised daily to the receptacle. Not only is the water taken to the public fountains, and utilized for irrigating and other common uses, but few houses in Philadelphia do not have the advantage of running water on the upper floor. The undertaking cost $1,600,000, and the company today receives an interest of at least twelve percent per year.

In Philadelphia there are two theaters, one on Walnut Street, and another on Chestnut Street. Both are small, but of regular dimensions, each capable of seating six hundred people. Next to the second one is the museum, surely the richest and most abundant in all types of curious objects of any to be found in America. Exhibited there is ancient clothing of the Indians of the country, very similar to that of the Egyptians, and also the complete skeleton of the biggest mammoth that I have seen up to this time. Each one of the tusks is eight feet in length. In the museum are the portraits of the principal American personages, of many ladies, and of some wise European generals.

In one of these theaters Miss Wright gave her lessons in philosophy a short time before my arrival. The theater was filled with persons of both sexes, and they were listening to the philosopher preaching with an attention uninterrupted by signs of approval or disapproval. The main purpose of her preachings was to persuade her hearers that instead of employing the first day of the week in religious exercises and spending twenty million dollars a year supporting preachers, in building churches, and in enriching idle people, they should use their time and employ their money in discovering the hidden secrets of nature.

"Take as masters," she said emphatically, "experimental philosophers; convert your temples into halls of science, and dedicate your feast days to the study of your own bodies and to the examination of the beautiful material world."

The doctrines of Miss Wright, as I have said another time, are founded in philosophical deism, and they cannot suit a society. But in a free people, truly free, and not free by *proclamations and theoretical constitutions*, all thinking beings have the right to express their opinions, their systems, and their ideas, without the authorities or the mob's opposing this exercise of mental faculties.

One of the things that attracts the attention in Philadelphia is the amazing ship *Pennsylvania*, which without a doubt is the largest boat built up to the present time. It has, or is supposed to have, 150 cannons and 1,400 men. Its main anchor weighs 10,171 pounds. The length of the ship is 220 feet, and it is 58 feet wide. It has thirty-four beams on each deck; the main beam is two feet in diameter. It has five bridges. This boat as well as others and the war frigates that are built in the United States are covered with superstructures of wood that are taken down when they are launched.

The United States Navy has given unequivocal proofs during the last war with England of its capability, bravery, and discipline. What nation has been able to compete with the proud Albion, exclusive mistress of the ocean, except her emancipated daughter, that enterprising nation which lifts itself up each year to a greater height, that some day shall surpass the other powerful nations? The North Americans count with pride among their naval men the names of Stephen Decatur, the American Nelson, Patterson, Bainbridge, and Porter.

In this city was written the famous Declaration of Independence on July 4, 1776, and the hall still stands where the illustrious Americans signed it. In this hall is the statue of General Washington with this inscription at its base:

FIRST IN WAR
FIRST IN PEACE
FIRST IN THE HEARTS OF
HIS COUNTRYMEN

At the back of this building is a small plaza, one corner of which adjoins the beautiful Washington Square, one of the best places to walk in Philadelphia, marked off by iron railings very well made.

As we speak of a city founded by Quakers, and in which the major part of the people are of that faith, we should not pass in silence over the manner in which they observe their worship.

This famous sect, founded by George Fox in the seventeenth century in England, had as its object to follow strictly the doctrines of the gospel. Thus it is that the counsel to present the other cheek when one is struck, that of St. James to say *yea, yea, nay, nay* and never go beyond that, that of humility, and others similar formed the body of their doctrine, so that they did not admit war, nor oaths, nor any manner of luxury, etc.

Such people who on the other hand reproved other religious sects as profanations suffered cruel persecution from the beginnings of their church. Their opposition to taking oaths before courts, to taking up arms in defense of their country, and their hatred for the dominant sects were plausible pretexts for presenting them as enemies of religion and the community. The fantastic differences in their dress, in their language, and in their manners seemed to be the symbol of their sharp and perpetual separation from human society. Proscribed by law and by prejudice, they gladly accepted the mercy of King Charles II of England. They were the most consistent adherents of passive obedience which the gospel prescribes, because they resisted no affront, nor disarmed their enemies otherwise than by kindness and by their submission to the injustice of tyrants.

121

William Penn, one of the illustrious converts of this religious doctrine, after having employed all his talents without results for systematizing religious liberty under Charles II, saw himself obliged to come to America to seek asylum for his persecuted brothers, and he founded the city of Philadelphia and other towns of the state of Pennsylvania, a name derived from that of its founder. The admirable Locke, his friend, gave him the first laws for his colony. Charles II granted him all those lands for the debts of the crown to the admiral his father, and then he entered into treaties with the other provinces. Treaties made without oaths, says Voltaire, and the only ones that have not been broken. William Penn died in London in 1718 while negotiating for certain privileges for the trade of his colony.

The worship of the Quakers, like their dress, is extremely simple. There are no sacraments, there are no prayers, there are no saints. All of them keep their hats on, the women separated from the men. Any one who feels inspired goes up to the pulpit, or from his bench preaches, or counsels, or says some sentences. When a person begins to speak, he takes off his big hat, if a man, if a woman, she speaks with her hat on. It is a singular manner of worshiping God; but perhaps they say the same thing about our mass and our ceremonies. The important thing is that in general they are charitable, hardworking, and honorable. The women are modest and simple.

In Philadelphia Sunday is even sadder than in New York. All the women go to the churches of their respective sects, and they are there two hours in the morning and two more in the afternoon at least. Many men go also, but not all of them. On these days there is no music, nor games, nor any other type of entertainment. The streets where there are churches are closed with chains to prevent the passage of carriages whose noise would interrupt the worship service.

Philadelphia is the city of capital as New York is of commerce. In the former is the main branch of the Bank of the United States. This bank was created in 1816, with a charter for twenty years. It began its operation January 1 of that year with a nominal capital of thirty-five million dollars. The general government is a shareholder in this bank to the sum of seven million dollars, but in reality it has not delivered to the bank more than the two million dollars that it had deposited formerly, with the result that the shares that it has are the capital from a debt that has been opened for it on the books of the bank.

The other $28,000,000 in capital, divided into 280,000 shares at $100 each, were subscribed by individuals and were to be settled in three payments, to wit: $5 in money and $25 in specie or public paper at will at the time of the subscription, and the other $70 in two equal payments of $35 each, of which $10 would be paid in cash and $25 in public paper or in coin. The $5 per share of the first payment is the only payment that the bank has received in coin of gold and silver. The directors thought that it was not necessary to demand more.

"It is clear," one of them said, "that when the bank had begun its operations and put its paper into circulation, it could not oblige its shareholders to buy gold or silver coin to make the payment of $10 that was supposed to be made in cash when the second and third payments became due."

As a result a memorial was presented to Congress in 1819 that the bank had not really received more than $324,000 in cash, instead of the $2,800,000 that the shareholders were to have put in on the second payment, and that the third brought in an even smaller amount. The shareholders paid with paper and in part with bills of the bank itself that they had received, taking the legal discount and received guaranteed titles to the shares. Thus, instead of the bank's capital being, as required by the *charter* granted, $7,000,000 in cash and $28,000,000 in public funds, after making the three payments it was only $2,000,000 in silver or gold and $21,000,000 in public funds; the balance of $12,000,000 was satisfied with titles of shares of the first shareholders.

In a work that has as its principal purpose presenting to Mexicans the customs, manners, institutions, and establishments of the United States as a nominal model, to put it thus, for Mexican legislators, it should not appear as beyond its scope to give an extensive idea of the system of banks established in that country, which moreover can be rather useful for their financial system. Therefore, I am going to continue to indicate what has happened and what is happening among our neighbors to the north in this interesting area.

I have pointed out the manner in which the Bank of the United States was set up, and the reader will be surprised at the manner in which a State Bank called the Sulton Bank was founded in Boston in 1828. It can be affirmed that most of the banks of that country have been created on more or less the same basis. By a decree of the legislature of the State of Massachusetts, in March of 1828, the directors of the new Sulton Bank were authorized to establish it under the obligation that the capital would be $100,000 in gold or silver, divided into 1,000 shares at $100 each; that half of this sum would be paid before October 1 of that year, and the other half during the following six months; that the bank would not begin its discounts, loans or issuing of bills until there was in its hands the capital of $50,000.

To assure the execution of these clauses, it was added that the bank could not begin its operations until a commission of six members named by the governor of the State had verified the existence in the coffers of the bank of the sum expressed of $50,000 in hard money. The directors should declare under oath that that capital was the product of the payments made by the shareholders for the funds of the bank, and that it would remain as half of the total.

On September 26, 1828, the governor named the commission at the request of the directors. On the day that the visit was to be made the directors of the new bank asked the loan of the sum of $50,000 on bills from another bank called the City Bank, for just one day. This sum was counted and its existence verified by the commissioners as though coming from payments made by the shareholders, on the sworn statement of the directors, all according to the law that granted the charter.

When the formality was concluded, the money was returned to the lenders, and the bank had left only the small sum coming from the sharehohlders. This was the matter of an hour's time. The truth of this affair is set forth in a memorial directed to the senate of Massachusetts in January of 1830. In it is stated furthermore that the second payment was no more precisely made than the first; and in this manner the Sulton Bank, instead of a capital of $100,000, could scarcely count on a fourth of that amount.

Among the present stockholders of the State banks there are many who have paid in whole the total amount for the shares that they possess, especially those that have bought the original titles, with the result therefore that the first founders have made a great profit.

It is evident that the real capital of American banks differs greatly from the nominal capital, and since far from directing their operations regularly on this basis, they do not hesitate to issue bills of circulation or credit for sums that double or even triple the figures, the result is that the total of the obligations contracted by the banks with the public is always greater than the real assets that they have for fulfilling them. In ordinary times, as long as there is no sudden event, an unforeseen circumstance that produces in people's minds an uneasiness sufficiently great to cause the multitude to decide to go to the banks to demand payment in cash of the great mass of circulating bills in their hands, the directors of these establishments are always in a position to satisfy the ordinary demands. Having a knowledge of the daily flow of deposits and other payments, by very approximate calculations they are careful to keep in the cash reserves a sum in gold or silver equivalent to the amount of the bills that may be presented for cash.

But the moment that a grave circumstance such as a war or a commercial crisis is felt to be approaching, the confidence is weakened to the degree that it impels the holders to rush to the banks for money, and the latter find themselves with a sum three or four times greater than their cash reserves. With the impossibility of satisfying such demands the banks suspend payment and often take bankruptcy.

These crises, from which European banks established upon more solid bases and much more rational principles are not entirely exempt, are repeated frequently in the United States, and since 1828 have been the cause of 144 of the 544 banks in the country being declared in complete bankruptcy. Fifty suspended their payments and ceased their operations entirely. Even the Bank of the United States several times found itself embarrassed and compromised. The years 1814, 1819, 1825 and 1828 are the periods when these institutions found themselves in the hardest straits. The crisis of 1814, occasioned by a war that the Americans were then carrying on with the British, obliged all the banks of the Union, including the former Bank of the United States, whose time had not yet run out, to suspend redemption of their respective bills.

In 1816 and 1817 when the issuance of bills was considerable, there was so great an export of coin that the banks were not able to procure what was necessary to redeem their notes. The new Bank of the United States found itself obliged (as this year) to cause money to be brought from Europe to the United States, and in spite of all its efforts, at that time it could not get together in cash reserves more than three million dollars, a sum completely insufficient to maintain its operations and those of its eighteen branches in the states. It had to take recourse then in a partial suspension of payments in cash, fortunately coming out of this crisis in a short time. This did not happen with several private banks that closed their doors and dragged to ruin a considerable number of families.

Likewise the issuance of a large amount of notes was what brought about the difficulties in 1828. In this last period the directors of the Bank of the United States, in an effort to rid themselves of the competition of other banks, made every effort to extend the operations of their former branches in order to establish new offices. They issued a larger number of bills and authorized their different dependent banks, whose number had now reached twenty-four, to discount private bills. They had calculated that their bills and those of their branches would enjoy more consideration than those of the local banks, and it would be easy for them to substitute in circulation their own notes for those of the others by taking them. Then they could present all at once the notes for payment, or retain them on deposit, thus lessening their operations and drafts. They succeeded indeed in diminishing the operations of some banks, but they could not prevent others from increasing their discounts, which led to a new exportation of money from the country, and to its consequent scarcity, so that the banks could not find sufficient funds to meet their daily needs.

At the beginning of 1830 the total amount of gold and silver in circulation was valued at $10,000,000, $55,000,000 in bank notes, and in bank credits an equal amount. The existing sum in cash for assuring the payment of notes and bank credits, that is to say $110,000,000, consisted of only $22,000,000 in hard money.

The banking system, with the extension that it has been given in the United States, had in its beginning an extremely beneficial effect on the progress of industry in that country. However, as a consequence of the excessive issuance of bills, metal coinage has been exported, thus leaving in circulation the representative symbols in too large a proportion to maintain credit for very long. Indeed, the bills that the banks issued appeared to have the advantage of increasing the wealth of the country by raising the nominal value of all goods and property. But since the result of an abundant circulation is to raise the prices of merchandise in the country, it is clear that the time will come when they will not be able to export goods in exchange for foreign products because with the expense of transportation, duties and other things, they will not be able to meet the competition of foreign merchants. Then it will be necessary to resort to the export of hard cash to secure consumer goods in a nation where there are no mines, or where the products of the mines do not furnish a quarter of the cash necessities; it will bring about the scarcity that has caused the bankruptcies of which I have spoken.

These ideas on the banking system in the United States that I have taken from a book entitled *History of Paper Money and Banks in the United States* can give the readers an understanding of the great question that is being argued between the government of President Jackson and the supporters of the Bank of the United States. The president has believed that a renewal of the charter of the bank referred to would be a great disservice to the country, as much because it creates a sort of monetary aristocracy as because the system of banks is harmful to the nation.

There is an establishment in Philadelphia that it would be well to adopt in Mexico, if not on as extensive a scale, at least to a lesser degree. A league from the city is the penitentiary, which is a building with thick walls of gray granite thirty feet high. It incloses a space a mile in circumference, and in the center of it the prison is located. This consists of a rotunda from which there project seven radials that form as many corridors, each about eleven feet wide. Between one radial and another are distributed the small rooms where the prisoners are. Each one has a small courtyard where he goes out to get some fresh air three hours each day. Beneath the rooms runs a sewer with water for sanitary purposes. From the corridor which controls all the cells, through a small hole, can be seen what the prisoner is doing, and from the rotunda the only watchman they have, seated in the center, can look along all the corridors that converge upon the center. There are no guards or watchmen; there are only four helpers to take the meals to the prisoners, the number of which was 350 when I was there. Their food is plentiful and healthful, but if they resist working, the amount is cut down. There are connecting pipes that heat their rooms in the winter.

The sentenced prisoner is brought into the prison blindfolded. Then he is taken to a small room where they cut his hair, he goes into another to bathe, and here he gets his prison garb which consists of a jacket, a cap, a shirt and a pair of trousers. The old clothes are put away until he leaves. The director of the establishment who is an honored and respected Englishman, Scotch I *think*, told me that the work done produces all that is necessary to support the institution. Smoking is not permitted, nor can they drink anything besides water. They can only have the Bible or some book of devotion according to the sect of the prisoner. Many men who have been in this prison have gone out afterwards rehabilitated to continue a normal life.

Men that have been imprisoned three, four, or six years without communication with anyone, when they come out into the world, arrive with new clothes, with the reflective character that should be contracted in society, and without inclinations to vices, or at least with them very much lessened. The same thing does not happen with persons who have been in a prison with others, where unfortunately they do not acquire virtuous habits.

In the state of Pennsylvania there is a university where moral philosophy, history, Latin, Greek, Hebrew, metaphysics, ideology and mathematics are taught. The course is four years, a very short time to come out thoroughly educated in any branch. But generally speaking, in that republic they have preferred to promote primary education rather than to build establishments such as Oxford or Cambridge that contain the elements of advanced science, of those sciences that absorb the whole life in profound and elevated meditations. The prime necessity is to read and write. This the North Americans try to satisfy by giving to primary education all the general character that is compatible with the other social necessities. The basis of education in that country is to "extend the sphere of thought and to elevate the conscience by means of useful knowledge that makes man apt for dealing ably with the affairs of life and not to make himself ridiculous or the object of scorn because of a noticeable ignorance."

This does not mean that in the United States there are not men of great knowledge and scientific ability. Evidently there are, but not in the number corresponding to the population, as occurs in England, France and the other civilized nations of northern Europe. The translation that has just been published in Boston of the works of M. LaPlace is an unmistakable proof of the great advances of that city.

In Philadelphia I met Mr. Sergeant, a distinguished lawyer of the United States who was in Mexico as minister to the Congress of Tacubaya, where the ministers of the republics of America were supposed to be gathered, according to the agreement of the Congress of Panama in 1826. It is well known that this project was never carried out. Mr. Sergeant is an American very learned in his profession, and has a rather wide reputation, to the extent that it took him to the candidacy for the vice-presidency against Mr. Van Buren. I also spoke with Mr. Walsh, editor of the *National Gazette* and of the *Quarterly Review*, periodicals respected in both hemispheres for the ability with which they are written and the material that they contain, especially the second, with M. DuPonceau, a Frenchman of literature and patriarch of the literary societies of Philadelphia because of his age and vast education.

Mr. Girard, the richest banker that has lived since M. Rothschild, died this year (December of 1831); he was French, born in Bordeaux. Since in 1811 the former Bank of the United States ceased operations, Mr. Girard took advantage of the building and the credits with the lack of discounts that were no longer made, and extended his drafts and business. He left about eight million dollars, and the greater part of his fortune he distributed in the United States, especially in Pennsylvania and New York. In his will he placed an express clause that in none of the colleges that were to be established with his funds should any ecclesiastic of any religion be admitted. He detested any exclusive doctrine.

CHAPTER X.

In 1830 I visited the widow of Señor Don Agustín de Iturbide in Georgetown near Washington, where she was living and looking after the education of her children. In 1834 I had the pleasure of seeing this respectable Mexican family for a second time in Philadelphia, after the president of the Mexican republic, General Santa Anna, had lifted the banishment which condemned her to live outside her own country, although with a good pension. Señora Iturbide had achieved in good part the fruits of her endeavors; her older daughters, receiving an education according to the culture of the country, have followed the wishes of their teachers and have augmented the charms of their sex with the advantages of the mind and with the physical perfection of a material education.

The market in Philadelphia is one of the best that I have seen. It is on a street at least one hundred feet wide and one mile long, in the midst of which they have built a wooden shed open on both sides and covered with a roof overhead. A large crowd of people comes there in the mornings to buy necessary provisions from an abundant market, to which come contributions from the sea, the rivers, the land and the air. Indeed, one finds there fresh and salt water fish, wild animals, birds, vegetables, flowers, fruits, seeds, meats prepared with care and everything that the gourmet could wish to provide for his kitchen and to set a good table.

Four miles from Philadelphia is a small town called Frankfort, the home of Colonel Burnt, an old friend of Mr. Poinsett. The latter invited me to pay a visit to his friend, and I had the pleasure of a day in the home of Mr. Burnt. He commanded a body of calvary in the last war with England, and he had retired to live peacefully in a country home that he has in the town; it is very well cared for, well laid out, although small, but with all the comforts for a man alone. He had his principal holdings in Scotland, where after his death Mr. Poinsett, his executor, went to get them together. Mr. Burnt was a man of pleasant disposition, had a good education and was extremely modest. Some travelers in America have spoken of him in the same vein.

In Philadelphia I embarked on the steamboat *William Penn*, in company with Señor Mejía, who as I have said was secretary to the Mexican legation in the United States. After traveling down the river for three hours we disembarked upon an isthmus that is formed between the Delaware River, Chesapeake Bay and a canal that leads to the latter in the state of Delaware. This is one of the states that formed the first confederation which numbered thirteen. Its population will scarcely reach two hundred thousand inhabitants, but it prospers like the others because of the wisdom of its government, the industry of its inhabitants, its liberal institutions, economics and other circumstances that distinguish the fortunate states. The schools are established in Delaware upon the same basis as those of Boston, of which I shall speak later.

The constitution of this small state was written in 1792 and revised in 1831. The legislature is called the General Assembly, and is composed of a senate and house of representatives. It has nine senators, with three named from each of its counties, a third of them elected every four years.* There are twenty-one representatives, seven from each county, and all are elected every two years. The General Assembly meets in Dover, capital of the state, biennially, the first Tuesday in the month of January, unless the governor calls it into session before that time. The general election is held the second Tuesday in November of the preceding year.

The executive power is held by the governor elected by the people every four years, and he cannot be reelected for an immediately succeeding term. The judicial power resides in a Court of Errors and Appeals, a Supreme Court, another of Chancellery, another of orphans, another of hearing of last resort, another of general sessions of peace, liberty, prisoners, and one of registry, etc.

The right of suffrage is held by all male citizens who are white and twenty-one years of age, provided they have resided for one year in the

*Translator's note: Although Zavala seems to indicate that senators served twelve-year terms, in fact the Delaware constitution called for four-year terms.

state prior to the elections, and for one month in the county in which they are held, and in which they have paid taxes.

On the canal that leads from the Delaware River to Chesapeake Bay one travels fourteen miles and then walks twenty or thirty yards to take the steamer on the second. I boarded the *Charles Carroll*, of four hundred tons, with room for three hundred passengers and baggage. I arrived in Baltimore at five o'clock in the afternoon of the same day.

Baltimore, a city of one hundred thousand inhabitants, is located between the Patapsa, Potomac, and Susquehannah Rivers and almost in the life stream of the United States. It is the largest city in the state of Maryland, whose capital is Annapolis. Lord Baltimore, an English gentleman and a Catholic, was the founder of this colony, and the principles of tolerance and philosophy of that venerable colonizer were in contrast to the persecutions of the Puritans of New England.

I stayed at the City Hotel, which they call by another name, Barnum, because he is the owner of the hostel. It is the largest one in Baltimore, and its central location on the corner of the square where is located the monument to the memory of the victims of the war of 1814, together with the good service that is to be found there, make it one of the more popular ones. The service is usually by blacks and colored people and some Irish.

The monument of which I just spoke, called the Battle Monument, a sort of trophy erected in memory of the resistance to the attack which under the orders of General Ross the English made against the city, contains the names of the most notable persons who died in the action. The column rises to about fifty feet, represents the Roman fasces, the symbol of union, and at each corner there is a spigot. On top is located the statue of Victory. Nobler and simpler is the monument erected to the memory of the immortal Washington on a hill that overlooks the city. It consists of a white marble column 150 feet high, upon which is placed the statue of the hero.

The Catholic cathedral is considered as one of the best churches in the United States. It is a very small one compared with our cathedrals of Mexico City, Puebla, Merida and Jalisco and much more so when compared to those of the great and ancient cities of Europe. However, the interior aspect of this church is very pleasant for its cleanliness and for some of its images and pictures. It is in the form of a Greek cross with its cupola in the center. The type of architecture is irregular with leanings towards the Gothic. Another Catholic building attracts the attention of the traveler in Baltimore, and it is the chapel of St. Mary's College. Although located in the heart of the city, this building is as solitary and silent as though it were in the desert. It is surrounded by a small garden where there is a Mount of Calvary with a very tall cross. A narrow lane among the shrubs and cedars leads to a small chapel, comparable in its smallness and beauty to that of Santa Teresa in Mexico. A lamp, whose dim light filters through the glass that covers it, sheds upon the darkness a melancholy clarity, fitting for a soul that comes to lift its entreaties and prayers in a self-communion that should not be interrupted by any strong emotion. The light of day comes in through the windows that are covered with glass of crimson color which gives an aspect of sublimity and grandeur to that sacred place.

There is another well-known building in Baltimore, and it is the church of the Unitarians. This sect, more philosophical than religious, is making extraordinary progress in all parts of the United States, especially in New England. The Unitarians are as opposed to the trinity of the persons in the divinity, as the reformers to the mass. It is a modification of the doctrines of the Socianians, enlightened by the progress that philosophy has made in the nineteenth century.

The *infant school* of Mr. Ibberson is one of the most useful establishments, not only in Baltimore, but even in the United States. Children from the age of two years begin to receive by means of agreeable sensations and material lessons instruction which serves later as a basis for a more thorough knowledge of geography, natural history, botany and arithmetic. Instead of entertaining the children with dolls, tops, whistles and other childish toys, they are made familiar with the different kinds of animals painted in natural colors—birds, fishes, quadrupeds. A large map is placed on the wall with the rivers, seas, isthmuses, islands, continents; they make pictures which contain the letters of the alphabet. In short, they prepare the first elements of instruction in different pleasant ways, and when they get through, the children already know the letters and their combinations. They know the names of the animals, plants, flowers; they can pick out the continents, rivers, etc. Mr. Ibberson has about one hundred children of both sexes who will later spread the teaching abroad in their country.

The constitution of the state of Maryland was written in 1776. Since then it has been amended many times. The legislative power is exercised by the senate, which contains fifteen members, and by the House of Delegates composed of eighty members. Both together form the body called the General Assembly of Maryland. The members of the House of Delegates, four from each county, two from Baltimore and two from Annapolis, are elected annually by the people the first Monday in October. Those of the senate are elected every five years the third Monday in September, in the capital Annapolis by electors chosen by the people the first Monday of the same month of September. These electors, voting by written ballot, elect nine senators from the west shore and six from the east shore, and these serve for five years.

The executive power is in the hands of the governor, who is named by the two houses by a majority vote each year on the first Monday in January; he cannot be reelected more than twice so that one person cannot direct the destinies for more than three years; he is eligible to be elected for the same job after having been out of office for four years. The governor has a council of five delegates named by both houses.

The General Assembly meets in regular session the last Monday in December. The governor appoints the employees, and the council confirms them. According to the constitution the right of suffrage is held by all white men twenty-one years of age who have lived one year in the state and six months in the county, or in the cities of Annapolis or Baltimore. The chancellor and the judges are named by the governor with the approval of the council.

From Baltimore to Washington it is forty miles, which is covered by land. I took a private coach to make this journey more slowly and with greater comfort. I was accompanied by Don Anastasio Zercero, who met me in Baltimore, and who was at that time exiled by the Mexican republic for political matters.

Washington is a city erected upon the ashes to which it was reduced by the British troops and British navy in 1814 under General Ross and Admiral Cockburn. For many years Congress met in a provisional building until the Capitol was constructed, a magnificent work, which does no discredit to this venerable word. Built upon the highest point in the city, it dominates the whole place as does the Potomac River, which at that point is half a mile wide. It seems that from its superb cupola freedom and liberation of thought and ideas are announced to humanity, while in that original Capitol in Rome subjection, slavery and blind obedience were preached.

Who does not feel inspired with these noble feelings as he mounts the steps that lead to those chambers where discussions have as their purpose the true interests of the masses? There one finds no hereditary privileges, no lifetime incomes, no sacred persons. That assembly is judged also by the people who have the faculty of subjecting to examination in the press, in the clubs, in assemblies, the opinions and decisions of those mandated. I had come from Mexico when I visited the Capitol in Washington. What should I think of all that I saw, that I heard, that I felt, in the capital city of the Anglo-Saxon Union, in the very building where the legislators of the human race gather?

In this magnificent building the two chambers of the general congress meet, have their offices, and here are located the supreme court and the offices attached to it. The home of the president is on

133

the opposite side of the city, a mile from the Capitol. It is a beautiful building 175 feet long and 85 feet wide. It has only two stories, and although there are included in it all the comforts for a family, it is not a palace. On the same terrain, at some distance, there are four buildings that correspond to the four corners of the president's house, which are the offices of the state department.

Mr. Van Buren, who was secretary of state when I went to Washington the first time, did me the honor of inviting me to dinner. At the dinner were the foreign ministers and many of the more distinguished representatives and senators. Señor Tornel, the minister from Mexico to the United States at that time, had his residence in Baltimore.

Mr. Van Buren is a man about fifty years of age, small in stature, blond, with a very spiritual face and well educated. He is from the state of New York where he was governor when called to be secretary of state. After my departure from Washington he was sent to London as minister plenipotentiary while the chambers were in recess. The Senate did not approve his nomination, and the Democratic party, of which he was the head, to avenge him for this insult, named him vice-president in 1832.

Since I was near Mount Vernon, the residence of General Washington, I decided to cross the Potomac and make this little journey of fifteen miles in order to have the pleasure of walking in the same places where the venerable patriarch of liberty had lived and to meet his nephew, the heir to his home and virtues. I took a coach for hire, went over the very long bridge across the Potomac and arrived after five hours at Mount Vernon, a very pleasant place associated with such interesting memories. There I met Mr. Washington, one of the individuals of the Supreme Court of the United States, who with the greatest politeness showed me all of his uncle's rooms, which they have tried to keep just as he left them, out of a religious respect for his memory.* In the vestibule one can see hanging the keys to the Bastille which General Lafayette sent to his venerable friend.

General Washington was the oldest son of the second marriage of Augustine Washington of Virginia, grandson of John Washington, a gentleman of a respected family in the north of England, from where he migrated. Lawrence Washington, the oldest son of the father of George Washington by the first marriage, left the lands of

*Translator's note: Zavala seems to say that he talked with Bushrod Washington, a nephew of George Washington and a Supreme Court justice, who inherited Mount Vernon when Martha Washington died in 1802. However, Bushrod Washington died November 26, 1829, and Zavala did not visit Mount Vernon until the summer of 1830. Zavala probably talked with John Augustine Washington, who inherited Mount Vernon when his uncle Bushrod died.

Mount Vernon to George, who was born February 22, 1732, and after a glorious life died December 11, 1800.*

The state of Virginia, founded as an English colony under the direction of Mr. Smith, has become the second state after having been the first one of the Federation. The extraordinary character and amazing adventures of Smith will make an interesting episode on this journey.

Captain John Smith was born in 1579 in Willoughby, in the County of Lincoln. From a very tender age he astonished his companions and even his school master by the boldness of his pranks. He was thirteen years old when he got the desire to see the ocean. With this in mind he sold his books and toys, which brought him a small sum. He was getting ready to leave when his father died, and he fell under the tutelage of positive men to whom the romantic bent of the youth seemed a bitter madness, and although he was the object of a kindly watchfulness on their part, nevertheless, it was so narrow that it became unbearable to his independent spirit. As soon as he was fifteen years old, so that he might occupy his intellectual faculties he was placed in the store of a merchant who was not economical either in the lessons that he gave nor in the work that he had for him.

The merchant with whom Smith was learning was one of the principal ones of Lynn. He had much maritime business, and the young Smith hoped that his master would let him travel, and travel on the sea. However, since he heard nothing concerning his shipping out, and weary of that monotony, without taking leave he left the merchant and his business, and departed with only two or three dollars. His lucky star caused him to fall in with a young lord who was going with his numerous company on a trip to Europe. Smith settled down to his service, but this was not for long.

After some months he became displeased with his new master and went to enlist in the army in Holland. He spent three or four years there, and inspired by a Scottish gentleman who offered him excellent recommendations to the court of King James, he crossed the sea again and went to Scotland. When his hopes were dashed, he left the court and took the road again to his native country. There in horror at the fanatical patriotism of his fellow countrymen he went to live alone in the midst of the forest with some books on tactics and military history, a horse and a lance. Thus he divided his time between the study of war and the exercise of arms without seeing another person besides an Italian servant from the house of the Count of Lincoln.

*Translator's note: Zavala is mistaken as George Washington died December 14, 1799.

While engaged in these pastimes he came into possession of a part of his father's fortune. With the means to travel, he again had the desire to see the world. So here is Smith once more launched upon the ocean. He arrived in Flanders, and there he was robbed by four French swindlers; he followed them, found one of them, fought him, wounded him, made him confess his crime, and set out on the road again with some money that an old friend of the family had given him. He followed the coastline of France from Dunkirk to Marseilles, visiting the arsenals and fortifications. Then he set sail for Italy.

An Englishman and a heretic, he found himself to his misfortune in the midst of a crowd of pilgrims who were going to fulfill their promises to our Lady of Loreto and to Rome. The boat was overtaken by a storm; the pilgrims overpowered the heretic, and the new *Jonah* Smith was thrown into the sea. He had the good fortune to be able to swim to St. Mary's Island near Nice. He stopped there just long enough to take another boat that was leaving for Alexandria.

This ship, after completing its voyage, got into a dispute with another boat from Venice with a rich cargo, attacked it, captured it and stripped it. He had them let him off in Antibes with his part of the booty, went to Italy, crossed the Gulf of Venice, arrived in Styria and wound up by volunteering in the service of the emperor, who was at that time at war with the Turks.

Smith was not only brave and enterprising; he was also a resourceful man. He found the means to force the Turks to lift the siege of Olympach and thus earn the rank of captain in the regiment of the Count of Meldritch, a distinguished man from Transylvania. After many deeds, Smith found himself at the siege of Regal in Transylvania; the siege was long, and one day a herald presented himself in the Christian camp and announced that the lord *Turbashaw*, a famous Turk, challenged the bravest among them to single-handed combat, for the purpose, he said, of amusing the ladies and passing the time. By lot it was decided that from the Christian warriors Smith should be the one who must answer the Turk's challenge. The combat was solemnly held; the Turkish ladies adorned the parapets of Regal; the besiegers were stationed along their lines; the music sounded. Smith killed the Ottoman; another Turk undertook to avenge *Turbashaw*; Smith killed him also. A third one presented himself, the terrible Bonny-Mulgro of gigantic stature. At the first charge Smith was almost dismounted by a blow from the axe. The Turks burst into shouts of joy, and the Turkish women clapped; they even shouted and applauded when Bonny-Mulgro, run through by a sword thrust, lay stretched out on the ground and Smith cut off his head. A short time later the city was taken.

But the fortunes of war are changeable. Some time later the Christians were beaten; Smith was left for dead on the field of battle; the richness of his armor caused the Turks to take him for a distinguished personage; he was treated as a man worth a considerable ransom; cured quickly he was taken to the slave market of Axiopolis; there he was bought by a pasha, who sent him to the lady of his thoughts in Constantinople, saying (despicable show-off) that he was a Bohemian gentleman that he had taken in battle. This pretense turned out badly for the pasha; Charatza Tragabigzanda (this was the lady's name) knew Italian, and Smith spoke it also; he told her his adventures, his glory and his misfortunes; Tragabigzanda began to get angry at the boasting of the pasha; she was moved by Smith's misfortunes, and later she was inflamed by his noble actions and his perils like Desdemona, says one of the captain's biographers. Smith hoped for a little rest and happiness when the lady, either to circumvent the suspicions of her mother or to make Smith learn Turkish, sent him to her brother Timur-Pasha, whose residence was on the shores of the Sea of Azov.

The instructions from Tragabigzanda were very insistent; to her brother she confessed her feelings for the captive; but the pasha of the Sea of Azov was angry that a *Christian dog* should have engaged his sister's heart. Smith, who expected a cordial reception, had not been an hour in Timur's house when he had been beaten, stripped and shaved. They put an iron collar on him, covered him with a heavy horsehair cloak and sent him to work the land with the other Christian slaves of the pasha. Every day this barbarian master inspected the prisoner's work and flayed him with insults and blows.

Once when Smith was alone with him, and the pasha was berating him for the way he was threshing the grain, Smith killed him with a blow from the harrow, hid the body under the straw, and mounting the Ottoman's Arabic horse, fled at top speed. When he reached deserted country, he got his directions as best he could and after traveling for six days he arrived at Hexapolis on the Don River; there he met a Russian vanguard. The Russians received him generously; a charitable or merciful lady, the Princess or Baroness of Palamata, showered Smith with evidence of interest. After resting he set out for Transylvania where his friends wept for joy when they saw him, giving him generous help. From there he returned to England, passing through Germany, France, Spain, and the kingdom of Morocco.

He got to England just at the moment when an expedition was leaving for America to found a colony. Invited to participate, he accepted. Smith was then twenty-eight years old. The expedition left the Thames December 19, 1606, and entered Chesapeake Bay April 26, 1607. On May 13 he disembarked on a peninsula where the colony of Jamestown was founded. The traveler who goes up the James River today in a steamer will see on this peninsula a tower in ruins and the remains of a corner of a cemetery. That is all that is left of this first establishment.

As companions, Smith had mediocre men that could not forgive him his superiority; scarcely had they left the Thames when he was accused of plotting to have himself crowned in the colony. Under this absurd pretext he was put in prison during the crossing. After they disembarked, when they read the instructions given to the expedition, it was found that the government of the colony was entrusted to a council of seven persons, among whom was Smith. His companions excluded him under the pretext of his pretended aims. Smith asked for a trial, but he could not get one.

He armed himself with patience and went out to explore the areas around Jamestown, going up the rivers, getting acquainted with the Indian tribes, and paying visits to Powhatan, the most powerful of the Indian princes. During this time the colony was badly governed; nothing was planned in advance; no houses were built for winter which was approaching; there were little or no provisions, no military precautions against the savages, who because of some hostility had made known their dissatisfaction. One day the colony was suddenly attacked by Powhatan's warriors, a man was killed and seventeen wounded, there was discontent against the council and principally against President Wingfield. Smith took advantage of the occasion to insist upon his petition concerning the trial; he obtained it, was absolved of all charges, and Wingfield was condemned to pay him £200 sterling in damages, which Smith generously turned over for the benefit of the colony. At once there was a sort of reconciliation. All the colonists took communion the same day as a sign of forgetting what had happened, and Captain Newport, who had brought them from England, returned with his fleet, leaving the colony composed of 105 persons.

But then came scarcity and with it illnesses, and afterwards what is worse than the plague, discord. Fifty colonists perished miserably. In the midst of the general despair President Wingfield, in agreement with some of his companions, decided to take over secretly the only boat that the colony possessed and flee to England. The plot was discovered; Wingfield was deposed, and another president elected in his place. He had the good sense to be guided by Smith whose moment had come. Smith laid out a work plan and gave each one his task; he was obeyed. Houses were built, the colony was fortified and covered. He himself gave the example to the workers by working harder than they did.

It was not enough to have houses for the winter; it was necessary to have provisions also. Smith set about looking for these, and especially corn which the Indians cultivated. On one of these excursions he encountered a large tribe, took their idol, demanded as ransom for their god several bushels of corn as well as venison and hastened back to Jamestown with this food. He arrived just in time because Wingfield had again planned his flight, and this time it was necessary to fight to bring the conspirators to order. From that time on the authority remained firmly in Smith's hands.

Scarcely had he straightened things out in the colony when, allowing himself to be carried away by his enterprising imagination —perhaps more than was proper for a man upon whose shoulders the health of the colony depended—he set out to explore the Chicka-hominy River. He went up as far as he could in his boat, and leaving it with the greater part of the crew, hidden in a cove protected against all danger, he went even farther upstream in a canoe, taking with him two white men and two Indians. Unfortunately those that he had left behind forgot their orders as soon as he was out of sight. Against his command they disembarked and were attacked by a group of Indians under Opechancanough, brother of Powhatan, who was spying on Smith. One of them was taken prisoner and forced to tell where the captain had gone; the others were able to get back to the boat and save themselves.

During this time Smith had arrived at the swamps that were the source of the river. Opechancanough surprised him in the night and killed the two Englishmen. Smith was surrounded by two hundred barbarians; an arrow wounded him in the thigh, and he defended himself with the *wisdom of a serpent* and the *strength of a leopard*. He killed three of his enemies and tying one of his two Indians to his arm with thongs, he used him as a shield. His enemies were frightened and separated; he had gained ground and was going back to his boat, but as he crossed he fell into the midst of a swamp that he could not get through and sank with his Indian up to his waist. Such was the fear that he instilled in the savages that even under these circumstances none of them dared to approach him until he threw them his arms. He was half dead with cold. The Indians pulled him out of the swamp, put him by the fire and rubbed him down until he recovered the use of his limbs.

Smith considered himself lost. The bodies of his companions were lying to one side quartered. It occurred to him to take from his bag a compass and show it to Opechancanough. The savage could not get over his amazement caused by this needle that moved all the time. As he had no notion of transparency, he was even more surprised that it was impossible for him to take hold of the needle with his fingers although he could see it perfectly (it was covered with glass). Smith, in an effort to excite even more the wonder of the barbarian chief and his warriors, began to talk to them about the movement of the heavenly bodies, about the sun and the moon, all that he knew about astronomy. His listeners heard him in amazement. Savage instinct took over again. After Smith had finished his speech, they tied him to a tree. The savages made a circle around him and aimed their arrows at him. Smith was going to die.

When the time came to give the signal to let fly the arrows at his chest, Opechancanough ordered that he be pardoned. He wanted to show off his prize at the court of the neighboring princes, and especially at that of Powhatan, the lord and master of all, because all the chieftains had formed a confederation of the James River, as the German princes formed the Rhine Confederation some twenty years ago, and Powhatan was the protecting Napoleon.

Smith's bravery, his physical strength and active mind caused the savages to consider him as an extraordinary man, superhuman. His imprisonment was celebrated with endless ceremonies in which the savages heaped all manner of attentions upon him that they could imagine. So careful were they to furnish him with fresh food that Smith thought immediately that they were trying to get him fat in order to eat him later. Charlatans came to cast a spell upon him, the great spirit was consulted to know the depths of the captain's intentions. Powhatan brought out all his forest luxury to receive him. When Smith appeared before the first chief, a queen it was who washed his hands, and another presented him with a feather material as a sort of napkin. Smith was handed from tribe to tribe, and they wound up by proposing to him that he become a savage and direct the government of Jamestown. With this condition they offered him all the women and lands that he might want. At his negative reply there was a council of chieftains and kings in which it was decided that Smith should die, and that they should proceed immediately to the execution of the sentence.

This time everything was done. Two stones were brought to the feet of the great king, and the victim laid there. The chiefs took their places around him. The people were behind them in complete silence. Powhatan himself had wished to be the high priest. He approached with his mace and raised it to give the fatal blow. There was no hope!

Suddenly a woman—everywhere women were Smith's guardian angels—a woman had pushed through the crowd. She put her head between Smith's head and Powhatan's mace; she was the first-born daughter of the king, his most beloved daughter, the beautiful Pocahontas. Stretching out her arms to her father she begged him to pardon the captive. The king was angry at first, but he loved Pocahontas too much not to be moved by her tears. He looked around at his warriors, seeking in their eyes the resolve that he lacked; he saw that they were moved with compassion.

"Let him live," he said. The next day Smith was on his way to Jamestown with two guides. He was to send Powhatan as a peace testimonial two rifles and a grindstone.

Now that Smith was safe, he busied himself with the business of the colony, and when he had everything in order, he resumed his excursions. He ascended the Potomac and discovered in his course a thousand dangers—the small creeks, most of them backed up by the Chesapeake Bay. His presence of mind, the religious terror that he inspired in the savages, and especially the noble assistance of Pocahontas always saved him and the colony as if by a miracle.

Pocohontas, to be as famous as Atala, only needed to find a Chateaubriand. As young and as beautiful as the Muskogean daughter, she was more heroic, and it was not just one man that she saved. Weak as she was (she was fourteen or fifteen years old at the time), it happened many times that during the night she made long journeys through forests and across swamps, in the midst of hurricanes that are terrible in Virginia, to warn Smith and his colonists of the plottings of the savages. Other times when they were short of food, Pocohontas appeared as a kindly benefactor with a group loaded with provisions, and disappeared immediately after having supplied them.

Until that time no colony had been successfully founded on the American continent north of the Gulf of Mexico. Providence made use of the hands of that mysterious virgin to plant one at last. Greece would have erected altars to her or would have made her a goddess halfway between Diana, goddess of the forests, and Minerva, the wise and farseeing one. The colonists managed things differently. When Smith separated from them, they took control of Pocohontas, intending to hold her as a hostage against her father Powhatan. After holding her for some time and treating her with the greatest of care, they agreed to marry her with her consent and that of her father to one of them, to Mr. Rolfe, who took her to England.

Pocohontas—the beautiful, the modest, the heroic Pocohontas—thus became Madame Rolfe, a resident of London and Brentford. At the age of twenty-two she died of consumption in Gravesand, just when she was going to take a ship for America. It may be that had her end been more tragic, she would have become the heroine of twenty epic poems.

The great deeds of Captain John Smith are as numerous and as amazing as those of Hercules. According to what he relates simply (like Caesar he wrote his memoirs) about a festival that the women of the court of Powhatan gave for him, it would not be going too far to believe that not a one of the adventures of Jupiter's son were missing, even those that belong to the domain of the secret chronicle. Once he surpassed Antheus' destruction by garroting single-handed a chief of gigantic proportions, the king of the Pashipsays, who had laid an ambush for him; he carried the chief into Jamestown on his shoulders. Again Opechancanough had besieged him with seven hundred men, and Smith took the chief by the hair, dragged him trembling and humiliated into the midst of the Indians frozen with stupor and made them give up their arms.

The difficulties that he had to overcome were endless. Against him he had hunger and pestilence, the cleverness and the arrows of the savages, violence on the part of the colonists, and the complaints and feelings of the others who sighed afterwards for the *fleshpots of Egypt*, the laziness and ignorance of the adventurers who poured in on the colony in search of gold there, the treachery of some, Germans and Swiss, who had gone over to Powhatan's kingdom because there was better food there—everything was against him, even rebelllion and assassination by sword and poison.

There was no extremity to which he had not been reduced, and one day when his companions saw him in agony, they had already dug his grave. His perserverance and bravery triumphed over all else. Thanks to his tireless efforts the colony was established definitely; many towns were founded; and after remaining two years in Virginia, gravely wounded by the explosion of a barrel of powder, he left Jamestown never to return. After his departure, the colony still had much to suffer, but it had already put down its roots.

Such were the origins of Virginia. It was the most powerful state when the war for independence broke out. It would still be in the forefront without the institution of slavery, which holds it back like a great weight upon its feet. It is the one that gave the revolution Washington, Jefferson, Madison, Monroe and many less illustrious statesmen. It is evident that there are in the character of those men of Virginia generous and gentlemanly traits that like the example and lessons of Smith left a lasting mark upon the hearts of their companions.

If I recount thus in detail the life of John Smith, it is not because of the interest that is aroused by an extraordinary man, but it is indeed because of the analogy that our epoch presents with his.

142

It was a time of political and religious crisis, of civil war and revolution. It was the time of the reconstruction of Europe by the Treaty of Westphalia. It was then that Charles I lost his head; then another dynasty was on the eve of occupying the throne of England. It was the time when the Protestant party was trying to set up a republic in France. Imaginations were excited and unloosed; brains were working. Wise men believed then that the world was coming to an end. It was not, however, a world that was ending, but the new one that was being born, and the pains that the old one felt were the pangs of birth.

Let us suppose that men of the temperament of Smith had been obliged to remain in England. With that active imagination, that fiery energy, that determined will, inevitably they would have been launched into politics, at that time seething with interests and movements. And how many men of that temperament at the head of the parties would have been needed to turn the country upside down?

Let us say rather: England was indeed rocked upon her foundations then, and it may be said that it would not have been if two men, endowed as Smith was with a burning imagination and an iron will, had not been detained. Those two were John Hampden and Oliver Cromwell. They wanted to come to America; the king refused to let them. A few years later one of them struck down the royal power, at least as the Stuarts understood it; the other one killed the king.

VIAGE

A LOS

ESTADOS-UNIDOS.

DEL NORTE DE AMERICA.

CAPITULO I.

Salida del autor de la capital de Méjico y los motivos. — Llegada á Puebla, é indicaciones sobre el estado de los caminos. — Golpe de vista rápido acerca de las diferentes temperaturas. — Llegada á Vera-Cruz. — Salida precipitada de este puerto y los motivos. — Breves reflecsiones acerca de los sucesos de Méjico. — Llegada á la Baliza. — Descripcion de esta.—Continuacion en buque de vapor hasta Nueva-Orleans. — Periódico realista que publicaban unos Españoles. — Su objeto. — Clases de poblacion de Nueva-Orleans y descripcion rápida de la ciudad. — Su comercio. — Su rápido incremento.—Pintura hecha por M. Flint de esta ciudad. —Los lagos. — Mercado.

—

Despues de la caida del general Guerrero, en diciembre de 1829, arrojado de la silla presidencial por el general D. Anastasio Bustamante, yo habia permanecido en Méjico espuesto á todos los furores del partido dominante. Esta posicion era tanto mas peligrosa para mí, cuanto que uno de los pretestos

I

First page of Chapter 1 from Zavala's *Viage a los Estados-Unidos del Norte America.* (Courtesy Texas State Archives.)

CHAPTER XI.

Discussion concerning post offices on Sunday.—Decision of the commission.—Reasons on which they based it.—Petition of some citizens of Virginia against a project for religious schools.—Visit to General Jackson.—Celebrations in Washington for events in July.—A matter of tariffs.

In Washington in 1830 a question was being aired, the discussion of which and the decision of the commission of the House of Representatives, as well as the final resolution of Congress, are a new proof of the generous, liberal and independent policy of the United States of the North. A large number of groups, especially Presbyterians, sent general representations to Congress asking that on Sunday, a day set aside for rest and prayer, the post offices not be opened and that the post routes not be run. The commission's decision is worthy of being included in this work, the main purpose of which is that the Mexicans and all the republics of that part of America formerly Spanish may take examples and lessons from that practical school of free and independent politics, which is today the model of all civilized peoples.

Later on I shall also include another no less interesting document that is the representation of several citizens of Virginia, made by Mr. Madison in 1784 on a similar subject, and in which the same principles are developed. For these documents and many items that I have made use of in this book I am indebted to the most valuable work of Mr. James Stuart entitled *Three Years in North America*.

The Committee on Post-offices and Post-roads, to whom the memorials were referred, for prohibiting the transportation of mails, and the opening of Post-offices on Sunday, report:—

That the memorialists regard the first day of the week as a day set apart by the Creator for religious exercises, and consider the transportation of the mail, and the opening of the post-offices on that day, the violation of a religious duty, and call for a suppression of the practice. Others, by counter memorials, are known to entertain a different sentiment, believing that no one day of the week is holier than another. Others, holding the universality and immutability of the Jewish decalogue, believe in the sanctity of the seventh day of the week as a day of religious devotion; and by their memorial now before the committee, they also request that it may be set apart for religious purposes. Each has hitherto been left to the exercise of his own opinion; and it has been regarded as the proper business of government to protect all, and determine for none. But the attempt is now made to bring about a greater uniformity, at least in practice; and as argument has failed, the government has been called upon to interpose its authority to settle the controversy.

Congress acts under a constitution of delegated and limited powers. The Committee look in vain to that instrument for a delegation of power, authorizing this body to inquire and determine what part of time, or whether any, has been set apart by the Almighty for religious exercises. On the contrary, among the few prohibitions which it contains, is one that prohibits a religious test; and another, declares that Congress shall pass no law respecting an establishment of religion, or prohibiting the free exercise thereof. The Committee might here rest the argument, upon the ground that the question referred to them does not come within the cognizance of Congress; but the perserverance and zeal with which the memorialists pursue their object seems to require further elucidation of the subject. And, as the opposers of Sunday mails disclaim all intention to unite church and state, the committee do not feel disposed to impugn their motives; and whatever may be advanced in opposition to the measure, will arise from the fears entertained of its fatal tendency to the peace and happiness of the nation. The catastrophe of other nations furnished the framers of the constitution a beacon of awful warning, and they have evinced the greatest possible care in guarding against the same evil.

The law, as it now exists, makes no distinction as to the days of the week, but is imperative, that the post-masters shall attend at all reasonable hours in every day to perform the duties of their offices; and the post-master-general has given his instructions to all post-masters, that, at post-offices where the mail arrives on Sunday, the office is to be kept open one hour or more after the arrival and sorting of the mail; but in case that would interfere with the hours of public worship, the office is to be kept open for one hour after the usual time of dissolving the meeting. This liberal construction of the law does

146

not satisfy the memoralists. But the Committee believe that there is not just ground for complaint, unless it be conceded that they have a controlling power over the consciences of others. If Congress shall, by the authority of the law, sanction the measure recommended, it would constitute a legislative decision of a religious controversy, in which even Christians themselves are at issue. However suited such a decision may be to an ecclesiastical council, it is incompatible with a republican legislature, which is purely for political, and not religious purposes.

In our individual character we all entertain opinions, and pursue a corresponding practice, upon the subject of religion. However diversified these may be, we all harmonize as citizens, while each is willing that the other shall enjoy the same liberty which he claims for himself. But in our representative character our individual character is lost. The individual acts for himself,—the representative acts for his constituents. He is chosen to represent their religious views,—to guard the rights of man,—not to restrict the rights of conscience. Despots may regard their subjects as their property, and usurp the Divine prerogative of prescribing their religious faith; but the history of the world furnishes the melancholy demonstration, that the disposition of one man to coerce the religious homage of another, springs from an unchastened ambition rather than a sincere devotion to any religion. The principles of our government do not recognise in the majority any authority over the minority, except in matters which regard the conduct of man to his fellow-man. A Jewish monarch, by grasping the holy censer, lost both his sceptre and his freedom. A destiny as little to be envied may be the lot of the American people who hold the sovereignty of power, if they, in the person of their representatives shall attempt to unite, in the remotest degree, church and state.

From the earliest period of time, religious teachers have attained great ascendancy over the minds of the people; and in every nation, ancient or modern, whether Pagan, Mahomedan, or Christian, have succeeded in the incorporation of the religious tenets with the political institutions of their country. The Persian idols, the Grecian oracles, the Roman auguries, and the modern priesthood of Europe, have all in their turn been the subject of popular adulation, and the agents of political deception. If the measure recommended should be adopted, it would be difficult for human sagacity to foresee how rapid would be the succession, or how numerous the train of measures which might follow, involving the dearest rights of all,—the rights of conscience. It is perhaps fortunate for our country that the proposition should have been made at this early period, while the spirit of the revolution yet exists in full vigour. Religious zeal enlists the strongest prejudices of the human mind, and when misdirected, excites the worst passions of our nature under the delusive pretext of doing God service. Nothing so infuriates the heart to deeds of rapine and blood. Nothing is so incessant in its toils, so perservering in its determinations, so appalling in its course, or so dangerous in its consequences. The equality of rights secured by the constitution may bid defiance to mere political tyrants, but the robe of sanctity too often glitters to deceive. The constitution regards the conscience of the Jew as sacred as that of the Christian, and gives no more authority to adopt a measure affecting the conscience of a solitary individual, than that of a whole community. That representative who would violate this principle would lose his delegated character, and forfeit the confidence of his constituents. If Congress shall declare the first day of the week holy, it will not convince the Jew nor the Sabbatarian. It will dissatisfy both, and consequently, convert neither. Human power may extort vain sacrifices, but Deity alone can command the affections of the heart. It must be recollected, that, in the earliest settlement of this country, the spirit of persecution, which drove the pilgrims from their native homes, was brought with them to their new habitations; and that some Christians were scourged, and others put to death, for no other crime than dissenting from the dogmas of their rulers.

With these facts before us, it must be a subject of deep regret, that a question should be brought before Congress which involves the dearest privileges of the constitution, and even by those who enjoy its choicest blessings. We should all recollect that Cataline, a professed patriot, was a traitor to Rome; Arnold, a professed Whig, was a traitor to America; and Judas, a professed disciple, was a traitor to his Divine Master.

With the exception of the United States, the whole human race, consisting, it is supposed of 800,000,000 rational human beings, is in religious bondage; and in reviewing the scenes of persecution which history everywhere presented, unless the Committee could believe that the cries of the burning victim, and the flames by which he is consumed, bear to Heaven a grateful incense, the conclusion is inevitable, that the line cannot be too strongly drawn between church and state. If a solemn act of legislation shall in one point define the law of God, or point out to the citizen one religious duty, it may with equal propriety define every part of divine revelation and enforce every religious obligation, even to the forms of ceremonies of worship, the endowment of the church, and the support of the clergy.

It was with a kiss that Judas betrayed his Divine Master, and we should all be admonished, no matter what our faith may be, that the rights of conscience cannot be so successfully assailed as under the pretext of holiness. The Christian religion made its way into the world in opposition to all human governments. Banishment, tortures, and death, were inflicted in vain to stop its progress. But many of its professors, as soon as clothed with political power, lost the meek spirit which their creed inculcated and began to inflict on other religions, and on dissenting sects of their own religion, persecutions more aggravated than those which their own apostles had endured. The ten persecutions of Pagan emperors were exceeded in atrocity by the massacres and murders perpetrated by Christian hands; and in vain shall we examine the records of imperial tyranny for an engine of cruelty equal to the holy inquisition. Every religious sect, however meek in its origin, commenced the work of persecution as soon as it acquired political power. The framers of the constitution recognised the eternal principle, that man's relation with God is above human legislation, and his rights of conscience inalienable. Reasoning was not necessary to establish this truth: we are conscious of it in our own bosoms. It is this consciousness which, in defiance of human laws, has sustained so many martyrs in tortures and in flames. They felt that their duty to God was superior to human enactments, and that man could exercise no authority over their consciences; it is an inborn principle which nothing can eradicate.

The bigot, in the pride of his authority, may lose sight of it; but strip him of his power; prescribe a faith to him which his conscience rejects; threaten him in turn with the dungeon and the fagot; the spirit which God has implanted in him rises up in rebellion and defies you. Did the primitive Christians ask that government should recognise and observe their religious institutions? All they asked was toleration; all they complained of was persecution. What did Protestants in Germany, and the Huguenots of France, ask of their Catholic superiors? Toleration. What do the persecuted Catholics of Ireland ask of their oppressors? Toleration.

Do not all men in this country enjoy every religious right which martyrs and saints ever asked? Whence, then, the voice of complaint? Who is it that, in the full enjoyment of every principle which human laws can secure, wishes to wrest a portion of these principles from his neighbor? Do the petitioners allege that they cannot conscientiously participate in the profits of the mail contracts and post-offices, because the mail is carried on Sunday? If this be their motive, then it is worldly gain which stimulates to action, and not virtue and religion. Do they complain that men, less conscientious in relation to the Sabbath obtain advantages over them, by receiving their letters and attending to their contents? Still their motive is worldly and selfish. But if their motive be, to make Congress to sanction by law their religious opinions and observances, then their efforts are to be resisted, as in their tendency fatal both to religious and political freedom. Why have the petitioners confined their prayer to the mails? Why have they not requested that the government be required to suspend all its executive functions on that day? Why do they not require us to exact that our ships shall not sail,—that our armies shall not march,—that officers of justice shall not seize the suspected, or guard the convicted? They seem to forget that government is as necessary on Sunday as on any other day of the week. It is the government, ever active in its functions, which enables us all, even the petitioners, to worship in our churches in peace. Our government furnishes very few blessings like our mails. They bear, from the centre of our republic to its distant extremes, the acts of our legislative bodies, the decisions of the justiciary, and the orders of the executive. Their speed is often essential to the defence of the country, the suppression of crime, and the dearest interests of the people. Were they suppressed for one day of the week, their absence must often be supplied by public expresses, and, besides, while the mail-bags might rest, the mail-coaches would pursue their journey with the passengers. The mail bears, from one extreme of the union to the other, letters of relatives and friends, preserving a communion of heart between those far separated, and increasing the most pure and refined pleasures of our existence; also the letters of commercial men convey the state of markets, prevent ruinous speculations, and promote general as well as individual interest; they bear innumerable religious letters, news-papers, magazines, and tracts, which reach almost every house throughout this wide republic. Is the conveyance of these a violation of the Sabbath? The advance of the human race in intelligence, in virtue and religion itself, depends, in part, upon the speed with which knowledge of the past is disseminated. Without interchange between one country and another, and between different sections of the same country, every improvement in moral or political science, and the arts of life, would be confined to the neighborhood where it originated. The more rapid and the more frequent this interchange, the more rapid will be the march of the intellect, and the progress of im-provement. The mail is the chief means by which intellectual light irradiates to the extremes of the republic. Stop it one day in seven, and you retard one-seventh the improvement of our country. So far from stopping the mail on Sunday, the Committee would recommend the use of all reasonable means to give it a greater expedition and a greater extension. What would be the elevation of our country, if every new conception could be made to strike every mind in the union at the same time! It is not the distance of a province or state from the seat of government which endangers its separation, but it is the difficulty and unfrequency of intercourse between them. Our mails reach Missouri and Arkansas in less time than they reached Kentucky and Ohio in the infancy of their settlements; and now, when there are 3,000,000 people, extending 1,000 miles west of the Allegheny, we hear less of discontent than when there were a few thousands scattered along their western base.

To stop the mails one day in seven would be to thrust the whole western country, and other distant parts of this republic one day's journey from the seat of government. But were it expedient to put an end to the transmission of letters and newspapers on Sunday, because it violates the law of God, have not the petitioners begun wrong in their efforts? If the arm of government be necessary to compel man to respect and obey the laws of God, do not the state governments possess infinitely more power in this respect? Let the petitioners turn to them, and see if they can induce the passage of laws to respect the observance of the Sabbath; for if it be sinful for the mail to carry letters on Sunday, it must be equally sinful for individuals to write, carry, receive, or read them. It would seem to require that these acts should be made penal to complete the system. Traveling on business or recreation, except to and from church; all printing, carrying, receiving, and reading of newspapers; all conversations and social intercourse, except upon religious subjects, must necessarily be punished, to suppress the evil. Would it not also follow, as an inevitable consequence, that every man, woman, and child should be compelled to attend meeting; and, as only one sect, in the opinion of some, can be deemed orthodox, must the law not determine which that is, and compel all to hear these teachers, and contribute to their support? If minor punishments would not restrain the Jew, or the Sabbatarian, or the infidel, who believes Saturday to be the Sabbath, or disbelieves the whole, would not the system require that we should resort to imprisonment, banishment, the rack, and the fagot, to force men to violate their own consciences, or compel them to listen to doctrines which they abhor? When the state governments shall have yielded to these measures, it will be time enough for Congress to declare that the rattling of the mail-coaches shall no longer break the silence of this despotism. It is the duty of this government to affirm to all,—to Jew or gentile,—Pagan or Christian,—the protection and the advantages of our benignant institutions on Sunday as well as every day of the week. Although this government will not convert itself into an ecclesiastical tribunal, it will practice upon the maxim laid down by the founder of Christianity, that it is lawful to do good on the Sabbath Day.*

*Translator's note: Quoted directly from James Stuart, *Three Years in North America* (New York: J & J Harper, 1833), vol. 2, pp. 18-25, from which Zavala made his Spanish translation of this item.

This opinion filled with such brilliant principles, written with an irresistible logic and upon the basis of one of the freest and most philosophical of constitutions that is known, concludes by declaring the petition unconstitutional and was approved unanimously. Will not this be a useful lesson to the supporters of intolerance in Mexico, and other governments that make the pretense of being free? What was the Mexican congress thinking when it passed a law obliging ecclesiastical governments to provide parishes with property after having passed philosophical laws on monastic tithes and vows in which they limited themselves to withdrawing coercion? These are the great inconsistencies of our legislators. But even worse is what followed.

The second document that I am going to include is an exposition by several citizens of the state of Virginia made to the legislature of the state asking that it should suspend the project of establishing teachers of Christian religion as they considered doing in 1784. The author of this memorial [James Madison] was later president from 1808 to 1816.

TO THE HONORABLE GENERAL ASSEMBLY OF THE COMMONWEALTH OF VIRGINIA

We the subscribers, citizens of the said commonwealth, having taken into serious consideration a bill printed by the last session of the General Assembly, entitled ''A bill establishing a provision for teachers of the Christian religion,''—and conceiving that the same, if finally armed with the sanction of a law, will be a dangerous abuse of power, are bound, as faithful members of a free state, to remonstrate against it, and to declare the reasons by which we are determined. We remonstrate against the said bill,—

1st. Because, We hold it for a fundamental and undeniable truth, ''that religion, or the duty which we owe to our Creator, and the manner of discharging it, can be directed only by reason and conviction, not by force or violence.'' The religion, then, of every man must be left to the conviction and conscience of every man; and it is the right of every man to exercise it, as these may dictate. This right is in its nature an unalienable right. It is unalienable, because the opinion of men, depending only on the evidence contemplated in their own minds, cannot follow the dictates of other men. It is unalienable also, because what is here a right towards men is duty towards the Creator. It is the duty of every man to render to the Creator such homage, and such only, as he believes to be acceptable to Him. This duty is precedent, both in order of time and in degree of obligation, to the claims of civil society. Before any man can be considered a member of society, he must be considered as a subject of the Governor of the Universe: And if a member of civil society, who enters into any subordinate association, must always do it with a reservation of his duty to the general authority, much more must any man who becomes a member of any particular civil society do it, with a saving of his allegiance to the Universal Sovereign. We maintain, therefore, that in matters of religion, no man's right is abridged by the institution of civil society, and that religion is wholly exempt from its cognizance. True it is, that no other rule exists by which any question which may divide a society can be ultimately determined but by the will of a majority; but it is also true that the majority may trespass on the rights of the minority.

2nd. Because, If religion be exempt from the authority of the society at large, still less can it be subject to that of the legislative body. The latter are but the creatures and viceregents of the former. Their jurisdiction is both derivative and limited. It is limited with regard to the co-ordinate departments; more necessarily is it limited with regard to the constituents. The preservation of a free government requires not merely that the metes and bounds which separate each department of power be invariably maintained, but more especially that neither of them be suffered to overleap the great barrier which defends the rights of the people. The rulers who are guilty of such an encroachment exceed the commission from which they derive their authority, and are tyrants. The people who submit to it are governed by laws made neither by themselves nor by any authority derived from them, and are slaves.

3rd. Because, It is proper to take alarm at the first experiment of our liberties. We hold this prudent jealousy to be the first duty of citizens, and one of the noblest characteristics of the late revolution. The free of America did not wait till usurped power had strengthened itself by exercise, and entangled the question in precedents. They saw all the consequences in the principle, and they avoided the consequences by denying the principle. We revere this lesson too much soon to forget it. Who does not see the same authority which can establish Christianity, in exclusion of all other religions, may establish with the same case any particular sect of Christians in exclusion of all other sects? That the same authority which can force a citizen to contribute threepence only of his property for the support of any one establishment, may force him to conform to any other establishment, in all cases whatsoever.

4th. Because, The bill violates the equality which ought to be the basis of every law, and which is more indispensable in proportion as the validity or expediency of any law is more liable to be impeached. If "all men are by nature equally free and independent," all men are to be considered as entering into society on equal conditions,—as relinquishing no more, and therefore retaining no less

153

than another of their rights. Above all are they to be considered as retaining an "equal title to the free exercise of religion, according to the dictates of conscience." While we assert for ourselves a freedom to embrace, to profess, and to observe the religion which we believe to be of Divine origin, we cannot deny an equal freedom to those whose minds have not yet yielded to the evidence which has convinced us. If this freedom be abused, it is an offence against God, not against man: To God, therefore, not to man, must an account be rendered. As the bill violates equality, by subjecting some to peculiar burdens, so it violates the same principle by granting to others peculiar exemptions. Are the Quakers and Menonists the only sects who think a compulsive support of their religion unnecessary and unwarrantable? Can their piety alone be entrusted with the care of public worship? Ought their religions to be endowed, above all others, with extraordinary privileges, by which proselytes may be enticed from all others? We think too favourably of the justice and good sense of these denominations to believe that they either covet pre-eminence over their fellow-citizens, or that they will be seduced by them from the common opposition to the measure.

5th. Because, The bill implies either that the civil magistrate is a competent judge of religious truth, or that he may employ religion as an engine of civil policy. The first is an arrogant apprehension, falsified by the contradictory opinions of rulers in all ages, and throughout the world; the second an unhallowed perversion of the means of salvation.

6th. Because, The establishment proposed by the bill is not requisite for the support of the Christian religion. To say that it is, is a contradiction to the Christian religion itself; for every page of it disavows a dependence on the powers of this world. It is a contradiction to fact; for it is known that this religion both existed and flourished, not only without the support of human laws, but in spite of every opposition from them and not only during the period of miraculous aid, but long after it had been left to its own evidence, and the ordinary care of Providence. Nay, it is a contradiction in terms; for a religion not invented by human policy must have pre-existed and been supported before it was established by human policy. It is, moreover, to weaken in those who profess this religion pious confidence in its innate excellence, and the patronage of its author; and to foster in those who still reject it a suspicion, that its friends are too conscious of its fallacies to trust to its own merits.

7th. Because, Experience witnesseth that ecclesiastical establishments, instead of maintaining the purity and efficacy of religion, have had contrary operation. During almost fifteen centuries has the legal establishment of Christianity been on trial. What have been its fruits?

154

More or less, in all places, pride and indolence in the clergy; ignorance and servility in the laity; in both, superstition, bigotry, and persecution. Inquire of the teachers of Christianity for the ages in which it appeared in its greatest lustre, those of every sect point to the ages prior to its incorporation with civil policy. Propose a restoration of this primitive state, in which the teachers depended on the voluntary rewards of their flocks, many of them predict its downfall. On which side ought their testimony to have greatest weight, when for, or when against their interest?

8th. Because, The establishment in question is not necessary for the support of civil government. If it be urged as necessary for the support of civil government only, it is as a means of supporting religion; and if it be not necessary for the latter purpose, it cannot be necessary for the former. If religion be not within the cognizance of civil government, how can its legal establishment be said to be necessary to civil government? What influence, in fact, have ecclesiastical establishments had on civil society? In some instances, they have been seen to exert a spiritual tyranny on the ruins of the civil authority; in many instances, they have been seen upholding the thrones of political tyranny; in no instance have they been seen guarding the liberties of the people. Rulers, who wished to subvert the public liberty, may have found an established clergy convenient auxiliaries. A just government, instituted to secure and perpetuate it, needs them not. Such a government will be best supported by protecting every citizen in the enjoyment of his religion, with the same equal hand which protects his person and his property; by neither invading the equal rights of any sect, nor suffering any sect to invade those of another.

9th. Because, The proposed establishment is a departure from that generous policy which, offering an asylum to the persecuted and oppressed of every nation and religion, promised a lustre to our country, and an accession to the number of its citizens. What a melancholy mark is the bill, of sudden degeneracy! Instead of holding forth an asylum to the persecuted, it is itself a signal of persecution. It degrades from the equal rank of citizen, all those whose opinions in religion do not bend to those of the legislative authority. Distant as it may be in the present form from the inquisition, it differs from it only in degree. The one is the first step, the other the last, in the career of intolerance. The magnanimous sufferer under this cruel scourge in foreign regions must view this bill as a beacon on our coast, warning him to seek some other haven, where liberty and philanthropy, in their due extent, may offer a more certain repose from his troubles.

10th. Because, It will have a like tendency to banish our citizens. The allurements presented by other situations are every day thinning their number. To superadd a fresh motive to emigration, by revoking the liberty which they now enjoy, would be the same species of folly which has dishonoured and depopulated flourishing kingdoms.

11th. Because, It will destroy that moderation and harmony which the forbearance of our laws to intermeddle with our religion has produced amongst its several sects. Torrents of blood have been spilt in the Old World, by vain attempts of the secular arm to extinguish religious discord, by proscribing all difference in religious opinions. Time has at length revealed the true remedy. Every relaxation of narrow and rigorous policy, wherever it has been tried, has been found to assuage the disease. The American system has exhibited proofs, that equal and complete liberty, if it does not wholly eradicate it, sufficiently destroys its malignant influence on the health and prosperity of the state. If, with the salutary effects of this system under our eyes, we begin to contract the bonds of religious freedom, we know no name that will too severely reproach our folly. At least, let warning be taken at the first fruits of the threatened innovation. The very apperance of the bill has transformed "that Christian forbearance, love, and charity," which of late mutually prevailed, into animosities and jealousies, which may not soon be appeased. What mischiefs may not be dreaded, should this enemy to the public quiet be armed with the force of a law?

12th. Because, The policy of the bill is adverse to the diffusion of the light of Christianity. The first wish of those who enjoy this precious gift ought to be, that it may be imparted to the whole race of mankind. Compare the number of those who have as yet received it, with the number still remaining under the dominion of false religions, and how small is the former. Does the policy of the bill tend to lessen the disproportion? No: it at once discourages those who are strangers to the light of Revelation from coming into the region of it; and countenances, by example, the nations who continue in darkness, in shutting out those who might convey it to them. Instead of levelling, as far as possible, every obstacle to the victorious progress of truth, the bill, with an ignoble and unchristian timidity, would circumscribe it with a wall of defence against the encroachments of error.

13th. Because, Attempts to enforce by legal sanctions, acts obnoxious to so great a portion of citizens, tend to enervate the laws in general, and to slacken the bonds of society. If it be difficult to execute any law which is not generally deemed necessary or salutary, what must be the case where it is deemed invalid and dangerous? And what may be the effect of so striking an example of impotency in the government, on its general authority?

14th. Because, A measure of such singular magnitude and delicacy ought not to be imposed without the clearest evidence that it is called for by a majority of citizens. And no satisfactory method is yet proposed by which the voice of the majority in this case may be determined, or its influence secured. "The people of the respective counties are indeed requested to signify their opinion respecting the adoption of the bill to the next session of the Assembly." But the representation must be made equal, before the voice either of the representatives, or of the counties, will be that of the people. Our hope is, that neither of the former will, after due consideration, espouse the dangerous principle of the bill. Should the event disappoint us, it will still leave us in full confidence that a fair appeal to the latter will reverse the sentence against our liberties.

15th. Because, finally, "The equal right of every citizen to the free exercise of his religion, according to the dictates of conscience," is held by the same tenure with all our other rights. If we refer to its origin, it is equally the gift of nature;—if we weigh its importance, it cannot be less dear to us;—if we consult the "declaration of those rights which pertain to the good people of Virginia as the basis and foundation of government," it is enumerated with equal solemnity, or rather studied emphasis. Either, then, we must say, that the will of the legislature is the only measure of their authority, and that, in the plenitude of this authority, they may sweep away all our fundamental rights; or that they are bound to leave this particular right untouched and sacred. Either we must say, that they may control the freedom of the press,—may abolish the trial by jury,—may swallow up the executive and judiciary powers of the state,—nay, that they may despoil us of our very right of suffrage, and erect themselves into an independent and hereditary assembly; or we must say, that they have no authority to enact into law the bill under consideration. We, the subscribers, say, that the general assembly of this commonwealth has no such authority. And, that no effort may be omitted on our part against so dangerous an usurpation, we oppose to it this remonstrance, earnestly praying, as we are in duty bound, that the Supreme Lawgiver of the Universe, by illuminating those to whom it is addressed, may, on the one hand, turn their counsels from every act which would affront his holy prerogative, or violate the trust which may be worthy of his blessing, may redound to their own praise, and may establish more firmly the liberties, the prosperity, and the happiness of the commonwealth.*

Mr. Van Buren was kind enough to accompany me on my visit to President Jackson, whom I saw for a second time since I had seen him before in Cincinnati as I have said. The famous chief invited me to

*Translator's note: Quoted directly from Stuart, vol. 2, pp. 26-32, from which Zavala made his Spanish translation of this item.

GENERAL ANDREW JACKSON
The Hero, the Sage, and the Patriot

dinner, and I had the satisfaction of sitting beside one of the great historical personages of the Anglo-American republic, and hearing from his mouth the account of some important events. Our conversation turned particularly to events in Mexico, and the honorable old man expressed himself with a tact and discernment that gave me a good idea of his mental ability and of his correct judgments.

"You have to pass through many tests," he said to me, "before ridding yourselves of the vices and prejudices of your earlier education and form of government. For a long time after a political change nations follow the impulses and direction of their former habits, and to change them training and popular education are needed more than laws."

When I was there, they were celebrating in Washington the triumphs of the liberals in the three days of July in Paris. After a long and gala procession in which artisans and other classes of society were divided with their respective banners, the crowd made its way to the home of the president of the United States; he came out and accompanied them to the Capitol (more than a mile) where he made a speech. That night there was a ball which was very well attended and very popular.

The question of the Tariff of 1828 began to heat up from 1830 on, and ended happily in 1833 after heated discussions between the supporters of South Carolina and the states of the North. The former claimed that it was not fair that import taxes on goods manufactured in Europe should be placed at high levels only to increase their prices for the purpose of protecting the processors and manufacturers of the states of New England while a portion of luxury items were subject to extremely low rates. The result of this was, said the *nullificationists* (a name adopted by those of South Carolina), that in attempting to protect the manufacturing companies of the states of the North, our working classes who raise sugar and cotton have to pay higher prices for goods to clothe their families. This tariff had been put into effect under the administration of Mr. Adams while Mr. Clay was secretary of state.

The defenders of the tariff said that the Northern states consumed the cotton, sugar, and other products of the states of the South and the West, and that these should contribute to promoting their manufacturing, which within a few years would have no need of this extra tax upon foreign goods. The question became very heated as always happens in matters of large interests, to the point that a dreadful collision was feared in that happy republic.

In November of 1832 the convention of South Carolina published a decree nullifying the tariffs of the general congress, a curious document that should not be omitted from this book. It reads as follows:

Whereas the Congress of the United States, by various acts, purporting to be acts laying duties and imposts on foreign imports, but in reality intended for the protection of domestic manufactures, and the giving of bounties to classes and individuals engaged in particular employments, at the expense and to the injury and oppression of other classes and individuals, and by wholly exempting from taxation certain foreign commodities, such as are not produced or manufactured in the United States, to afford a pretext for imposing higher and excessive duties on articles similar to those intended to be protected, hath exceeded its just powers under the Constitution, which confers on it no authority to afford such protection, and has violated the true meaning and intent of the Constitution, which provides for equality in imposing the burthens of taxation upon the several States and portions of the Confederacy: And whereas the said Congress, exceeding its just power to impose taxes and collect revenue for the purpose of effecting and accomplishing the specific objects and purposes which the Constitution of the United States authorizes it to effect and accomplish, hath raised and collected unnecessary revenue for objects unauthorized by the Constitution:—

We, therefore, the people of the State of South Carolina in Convention assembled, do declare and ordain, . . . that the several acts and parts of acts of the Congress of the United States, purporting to be laws for the imposing of duties and imposts on the importation of foreign commodities, . . . and, more especially . . . the tariff acts of 1828 and 1832 . . . , are unauthorized by the Constitution of the United States, and violate the true meaning and intent thereof, and are null, void, and no law nor binding upon this State, its officers or citizens; and all promises, contracts, and obligations, made or entered into, or to be made or entered into, with purpose to secure the duties imposed by the said acts, and all judicial proceedings which shall be hereafter had in affirmance thereof, are and shall be utterly null and void.

And it is further Ordained, That it shall not be lawful for any of the constituted authorities, whether of this State or of the United States, to enforce the payment of duties imposed by the said acts within the limits of this State; but it shall be the duty of the Legislature to adopt such measures and pass such acts as may be necessary to give full effect to this Ordinance, and to prevent the enforcement and arrest the operation of the said acts and parts of acts of the Congress of the United States within the limits of this State, from and after the 1st day of February next . . . .

And it is further Ordained, That in no case of law or equity, decided in the courts of this State, wherein shall be drawn in question the authority of this ordinance, or the validity of such act or acts of the Legislature as may be passed for the purpose of giving effect thereto, or the validity of the aforesaid acts of Congress, imposing duties, shall any appeal be taken or allowed to the Supreme Court of the United States, nor shall any copy of the record be printed or allowed for that purpose; and if any such appeal shall be attempted to be taken, the courts of this State shall proceed to execute and enforce their judgments, according to the laws and usages of the State, without reference to such attempted appeal, and the person or persons attempting to take such an appeal may be dealt with as for a contempt of the court.

And it is further Ordained, That all persons now holding any office of honor, profit, or trust, civil or military, under this state, members of the Legislature excepted, shall, within such time, and in such manner as the Legislature shall prescribe, take an oath well and truly to obey, execute, and enforce this Ordinance, and such act or acts of the Legislature as may be passed in pursuance thereof, according to the true intent and meaning of the same; and on the neglect or omission of any such person or persons so to do, his or their office or offices shall be forthwith vacated . . . and no person hereafter elected to any office of honor, profit, or trust, civil or military, (members of the Legislature excepted), shall, until the Legislature shall otherwise provide and direct enter on the execution of his office, . . . until he shall, in like manner, have taken a similar oath; and no juror shall be empanelled in any of the courts of this State, in any cause in which shall be in question this Ordinance, or any act of the Legislature passed in pursuance thereof, unless he shall first, in addition to the usual oath, have taken an oath that he will well and truly obey, execute, and enforce this Ordinance, and such act or acts of the Legislature as may be passed to carry the same into operation and effect, according to the true intent and meaning thereof.

And we, the People of South Carolina, to the end that it may be fully understood by the Government of the United States, and the people of the co-States, that we are determined to maintain this, our Ordinance and Declaration, at every hazard, Do further Declare that we will not submit to the application on the part of the Federal Government, to reduce this State to obedience; but that we will consider the passage, by the Congress, or any act . . . to coerce the State, shut up her ports, destroy or harass her commerce, or to enforce the acts hereby declared to be null and void, otherwise than through the civil tribunals of the country, as inconsistent with the longer continuance of South Carolina in the Union; and that the people of this State will thenceforth hold themselves absolved from all further obligation to maintain or preserve their political connexion with the people of the other States, and will forthwith proceed to

161

organize a separate Government, and do all other acts and things which sovereign and independent States may of right to do.*

Here we have a *pronunciamiento*, or uprising, which resembles those that take place on a monthly basis in the Mexican republic. Fortunately this act found no echo in any one of the other states as they did not consider the claims as having foundation and much less the manner of making them. There is, however, more openness and frankness than in those absurd plans of the revolutionaries of Mexico, who always begin by pleading and end up killing or banishing.

November 14 of the same year 180 citizens met in the capital of the same state (Columbia), and signed a declaration in contradiction to the previous resolution, and it was stated in these terms:

The supporters of the Union and of the rights of the State of South Carolina set forth and protest solemnly against the resolution passed by the convention of the same State on November 24, last.

1st. Because the people of South Carolina elected their delegates to said convention with the solemn assurances that these delegates would not propose other than peaceful and constitutional remedies and measures in order to avoid the evils of the tariffs without compromising the union of these States. Instead of acting in this manner, the convention has published an *ordinance that directly violates all these principles*.

2nd. Because the above mentioned *ordinance* has attacked one of the inalienable rights of man by attempting to shackle all freedom of conscience by the tyrannical intervention of the power of the *oath*.

3rd. Because the resolution that those who do not wish to swear such an oath *shall be deprived of their civil and military* posts has *attacked and proscribed* about half the free men of South Carolina only because they hold an honest and legal opinion that is different.

4th. Because it has trampled upon the *great principles of liberty guaranteed to the citizens* by the constitution of this State, *depriving free men of this country of the right of impartial trial by jury,* thus violating the clause of the constitution which is to be *perpetual* that declares that *trial by jury as has been done in this State, as well as freedom of the press, shall be forever preserved inviolate*.

5th. Because it has violated the independence of the *judicial* power by ordaining that all judges shall swear the absurd oath, or that they shall be *removed arbitrarily from their positions,* thus depriving them of the

---

*Translator's note: Quoted directly from *Statutes at Large of South Carolina,* vol. 1, p. 329 ff., "Ordinance of Nullification," from which Zavala made his translation into Spanish.

privilege of trial by proper accusation, which by the constitution of the State is the safeguard for the security of these positions.

6th. Because by prohibiting the payment of imposts within the boundaries of the State the ordinance *has directly violated the constitution of the United States* which authorizes the Congress to impose taxes.

7th. Because it *has violated the constitution of the United States* itself in the article which ordains that it shall not give preference to one port over another, when the ordinance declares that goods that are brought into the ports of South Carolina shall pay no duty whatsoever.

8th. Because it *violates the constitution itself* and attacks the rights of the citizen by denying him the right of appeal in cases of *law and equity* that are granted by *the constitution and laws of the Union*.

9th. Because *it has virtually destroyed the Union* by opposing the decisions of the general government being put into effect by placing obstacles in the way of the execution of the laws by means of the courts of the States and proclaiming that if the government uses means of repression then it will separate therefrom.

10th. Because *tyranny and oppression,* effects of the ordinance, are of a character so repulsive and ruinous that they have already weakened the *trade* and *credit* of the State, which will lead these areas to their destruction since industrous and peaceful citizens will find themselves obliged to seek peace and tranquility in other states.

The Union supporters of South Carolina meeting in convention protest solemnly, furthermore, against the plan for a *permanent army* proposed by the party in power as dangerous to the *liberties of the people*. They respectfully ask their fellow citizens whether, if such an army is not capable by their confession of protecting the *nullification party* against the people of the United States, they will resolve to restrain it. What other purpose if it cannot hold back that force but to serve as an instrument of tyranny against its fellow citizens?

This *convention protests* also against all efforts made to put into effect a system of *conscription* which will oblige citizens to abandon their homes and occupations to take up *arms* under penalty of *treason*, in order to uphold doctrines that the people were sure did not need the aid of force and whose triumph could and should be obtained by constitutional means.

Solemnly declaring, as at the present it does declare, against the aforesaid resolutions the *Union Party* can do no less than to set forth its firm determination to support the same principles of conduct which have directed it thus far, and while on the one hand they will continue in forceful opposition to the vicious tariff act, on the other they will never separate themselves from the joys of those inalienable rights which by inheritance belong to every *American citizen*. Disavowing consequently all intention of revolutionary and extra-legal violence, *they proclaim* here and now their resolution to protect their rights by all constitutional means, and in so doing they wish to continue to maintain the character of peaceful citizens unless they be compelled to rise up against an intolerable oppression.

Thomas Taylor, president.—Henry Middleton.—David Johnson.—Richard I. Manning.—Starling Tuckec.—Vice-presidents (180 signatures follow). Given in Columbia Friday December 14, 1832, in the year fifty-five of the independence of the United States of America.—Authorized.—Franklin J. Moses.—James Edward Henry. —Secretaries of the Convention.

This dispute which brought fear of ill-fated results for the cause of liberty and the republic was brought to an end by the prudent and moderate conduct of President Jackson and the enlightened and patriotic agents whom he chose for so delicate an undertaking. He pointed out to the general congress the propriety and even the necessity that existed to moderate the tariffs, which was carried out upon the bases proposed by the excellent Mr. MacLane and with the cooperation of Mr. Livingston, secretary of state, and Mr. Poinsett, member of the legislature of South Carolina.

Those who know the distance that exists between the manner of handling matters in the United States of North America and in the United Mexican States will look in vain for the causes of the different organization of powers. In their ways, in the enormous distance that exists between material and mental capacities of the two countries, in their customs, in their interests, in their very beliefs, is where the legislator-philosopher must find the origins and the divergent directions that negotiations take with respect to the descendants of the English and the descendants of the Spanish.

CHAPTER XII.

Washington is a new city in the District of Columbia ceded to the
general government by the State of Maryland. Its area is two square
leagues as is that of Mexico City. The city has a sad appearance
although it has some very pleasant views. But the streets are too wide,
and there is a great distance between the houses. A town has grown
into isolated groups of buildings so that it does not yet present that
combination of houses and people that gives one at once the aspect of a
city. There is a small theater in Washington and several hotels. The
Gadsby, which is the one where I stayed and surely considered the best,
is rather expensive and does not offer the comforts of those of
Baltimore, Philadelphia, and Boston.

The principal street which is called Pennsylvania Avenue extends
through the center of the city from the president's home to the Capitol.
It is more than a mile and a half long. The president, as I have said, has
no guards, nor halbardiers nor other trappings. He goes to the Presbyterian Church on Sunday as any other citizen and takes his seat among
the others without any distinction. When in the first months of the
year 1833 we in Mexico saw Señor Pedraza and later Señor Farias in
their roles as presidents present themselves with the same simplicity in
public places and live their private lives in the same manner, we
thought that there was being introduced the informality of our
neighbors in their first magistrates, and that never again would we see
the pompous ways of the vice-royalty. Sweet but vain illusion!!

A mile from Washington is a place called Georgetown, where there is a convent named the Sisters of the Visitation. There are probably sixty nuns whose principal occupations are to give free education to the young girls intrusted to their care. The free school is under the instruction of the youngest nuns who have more than four hundred little girls in attendance. The most important establishment consists of a pension or boarding place which is in a rather flourishing condition. These convents are not like those of Spain where the victims of an ill-considered and premature vow are shut up for their whole life. When their inclinations have changed, or their interests require it, the law does not force them to remain cloistered, living in perpetual torment which the Divinity cannot accept. They leave to better their conditions and to live in society as mothers or in some other respectable manner. Two daughters of General Iturbide were in this convent when I visited his widow.

Each year there is held in Washington a convention of the famous society founded about thirty years ago with the philosophical object of redeeming slaves and sending them to Liberia, the name given to a colony established on the coast of Africa to receive these unfortunate beings. In the memorial presented by Mr. Clay in December of 1829 one reads that one of the first acts of the society was to dispatch an agent to explore the coast of Africa and find a place that was suitable for the colony. The selection fell upon a person capable of carrying out so weighty a commission. The purchase of good fertile land was made in 1822, and more was added later.

The land bought from the authorities extends as far as two hundred miles inland from the coast, in some places advantageous for trade, and the climate is analogous to the complexion of the blacks. The society founded this colony under the name of Liberia; it established towns, farmed lands, and built fortresses in order to defend them from the natives. Each year, or more often if the financial circumstances of the society permitted, ships were sent from the United States loaded with emigrant slaves with the tools of agriculture or of some trades for their work, as well as things necessary for their establishment. There has never been any difficulty in transporting colonists when the funds of the society have permitted it. Rather there have not been sufficient funds to take care of all who sought aid so eagerly. The travel expenses were greater in the first years; today the cost is only twenty dollars per person, and it is likely that it will be even less.

During the first period of their existence the colonists had to struggle with the native tribes even to open warfare. It all had a happy ending as soon as the natives were convinced of the greater ability, bravery, and discipline of the colonists.

The colonists have a government adequate to protect their rights, their persons and property, as well as for maintaining good order. The society's agent is governor, commanding general and supreme judicial chief. The colonists participate in the government through the election of various officials and minor employees. Annually they select commissions for public works, agriculture, health and sanitation, which are charged with overseeing these important areas.

The colony has established schools for the instruction of the youth and built churches for public worship which is held with great regularity. Finally they have a public library with more than twelve thousand volumes and their printshop where they publish the regular newspaper. The colonists work in trade, agriculture or mechanical trades according to their knowledge and inclination. The lands produce rice, corn, yucca, coffee, potatoes and all kinds of vegetables. In a short while they will have sugar, indigo, and other tropical products. Trading is carried on effectively by exchanging their goods with the natives of the country who have ivory, gums, ink plants, medicinal drugs and other articles which account for the sum of seventy thousand dollars; this amount is increasing year by year.

This society has branches in many of the states of the American union where there is a truly philosophical enthusiasm for the gradual abolition of slavery and the formation of a nation of civilized blacks on the coast of Africa.

"It is impossible longer to maintain the abuse of slavery in some of our states," said Mr. North, president of Union College of New York.

It will not take a domestic revolution nor foreign intervention to bring down an institution that is so repulsive to our sentiments and so contrary to our institutions. Public opinion has already declared itself on this issue, and the moral energy of the nation will sooner or later carry out its abolition. But the question that arises then is what will be the situation of this class restored to liberty? In other nations the races have blended with each other forming a general mass. Here we do not have the same situation. Our freed slaves in the third, fourth, and ever so many generations would still be what they are today—that is a distinct, degraded and unfortunate class.

Consequently when their chains have been broken, and this will happen evidently, either all at once or by degrees, it is clear that this country will find itself covered with a population as useless as it is miserable, a population which with its increase will lessen our strength, and its numbers will only bring crime and poverty. Slave or free it will always be for us a calamity. Why then must we hesitate one moment in promoting their departure from the country? It is prudent and praiseworthy to restore to Africa as citizens the children of that region, who as slaves and bound in chains we have brought here with grave affront to their humanity.

Such is the general feeling of the people of the United States concerning this class as different in color as they are in moral qualities from the others. It is not certain that once the castes were mixed the natural stigma would never disappear. The quadroons in Louisiana and Carolina give the lie to the assertion. But how many centuries would be needed for this to take place? And in the meantime the difficulties of the permanent residence of the black people in the United States are a matter of too much concern for a farsighted people that look well to their interests to fail to make provisions to free themselves from the ills or at least to lessen them. Recent events in New York and Philadelphia between whites and blacks are forerunners of what that nation may fear in the future.

I returned to New York by the same road that I had taken to Washington. Before my arrival in the United States a group known as the Temperance Society had begun to spread. Every establishment that has for its purpose the promoting of a principle, some particular virtue, or of some doctrine, always winds up by going to the extremes and often to the extravagant and the ridiculous. Seldom does it fail to gain the enthusiasm of its members and followers, and the consequences are sometimes harmful.

What is apparently more reasonable and useful than the establishment of societies whose purpose will be to preach and set examples of sobriety and temperance? However, the first ones professed to renounce all spirituous liquors; the second ones then added wine, beer, cider and other fermented liquors; the third group proscribed the use of coffee, tea, chocolate and all types of stimulants. Heaven knows where we will be led by this new sect that happily until now is not associated with any mysteries of religious dogma. In one of the sermons that Dr. Beecher of Boston has published on this new doctrine we read the following remarkable advice:

> I know that many defend the moderate use of spirituous liquors, but this is the same thing as speaking of the prudent use that may be made of the plague. Others have recommended beer as a cordial that can be a substitute for those in the habit of drinking spirituous liquors, but although beer may not nurture habits of intemperance so quickly, it does not have the power to dislodge them. In the end it produces the same effects with the sole difference that it does not weaken the vital organs with the same harshness and swiftness as does

whiskey and only leads its victims to the grave more slowly, gradually making them stupid idiots, without the frenzied fury of the former. Some have proposed wine as an innocent thing for distracting the habits of intemperance and to maintain the health, but habits cannot be gotten rid of, just as a voracious appetite is not satisfied with a sober and temperate table. Useless precautions that are successful one time in a thousand! They are the efforts of a child against a giant—the efforts of a lap dog against a lion.

Evidently habits of intemperancce have visibly decreased. But there have been many harmful results from that absolute abandonment of spirituous and fermented liquors. There have been very frequent sudden deaths of people who in the heat of summer, after some exercise, drink pure cold water straight from the pump, and all the doctors are agreed that if this were mixed with a little brandy, it would not cause such dire effects. What would those of the societies say if they were to see our pulque shops on fiesta days, and even more the Indians of Yucatan fallen here and there along the public roads, in the streets and in the plazas? Such scenes are never found in the United States, nor in the civilized cities of Europe.

Often in the course of my travels I come upon travelers' descriptions concerning the same places and persons that I have visited. Such is the one that I am going to deal with at this time, and it is the visit that I made to Hyde Park, which belonged to Dr. Hosack on the Hudson River. This is a country home built on the high hills on the left bank of the beautiful river, and from where one can look out upon picturesque views. Dr. Hosack is a learned American educated in Scotland and married to a very rich landowner of the state of New York. He has beautified that spot with man-made groves, gardens and plantings of trees and Scottish fruit trees. I must make mention of the friendliness, of the pleasant treatment at the hands of the entire family of Dr. Hosack. There I met the daughter of the famous Fulton, a young girl of eighteen at the time, full of charm, and one of the beauties of the state of New York.

A short time later I left with Mr. Poinsett for New England, going by way of the Hudson River. I shall speak later of various points along this river that deserve special mention when I relate my trip to West Point with Señor Salgado.

Albany on the right bank of the river is 148 miles from New York, and the trip takes ten hours by steamboat. The cost is two dollars, although this varies up to four dollars. We stopped at the Cittendew Hotel, one of the most popular in the city, frequented by both working people and great merchants. It is located on one of the highest hills in the city and dominates a greater part of it. Mr. Poinsett introduced me to Mr. Cambreleng, a member of Congress, one of the most learned and eloquent of men. At that time he was busy laying out the project of the decree concerning tariffs—the project that was later adopted in the noisy question of the nullificationists.

The Statehouse, where the two bodies meet, is a newly constructed building and has two chambers for the two assemblies of senators and representatives with their corresponding offices, all very well laid out and arranged. The view from the cupola of this building is picturesque. The river dominates the whole city, and in the distance can be seen the high Catskill Mountains, of which I shall speak later.

The constitution of the state of New York was written in 1821. The executive power rests with the governor, who is elected by the people every two years at the same time as the lieutenant governor who presides over the senate and performs the duties of the governor in case of death, or separation for any reason. The legislative power is exercised by the two chambers—the senate which is made up of thirty-two members elected every four years, and the assembly of twenty-eight representatives, and they meet annually. The members of this body are elected by divisions called counties, in numbers proportionate to the population. For the election of senators the state is divided into eight districts, each one of which elects four senators, of whom one is chosen each year.

The election of the governor, lieutenant governor, senators, and members of the assembly is held the first Monday of the month of November, and continues for three days. The legislature can vary these days by legal arrangements. The political year begins with the New Year, and the legislature meets annually the first Tuesday in January. The constitution gives the right of suffrage for political offices to all white male citizens above the age of twenty-one that have lived one year prior in the state and six months in the county where the election is held. Citizens of African descent must have real property in the value of at least $250 free of lien in order to have the right to vote. The governor names the chancellor and judges with the approval of the senate. The judges and the chancellor remain in office during good behavior, but only to the age of sixty years. The other county judges hold office for five years.

I have already spoken elsewhere about the famous canal that starts from this city and for a distance of more than 120 leagues runs to Lake Erie; it gets its water from there and from several streams that it crosses. It is worth noting that in this part of the state of New York one finds the names of ancient Greek or Roman cities, such as Rome, which is a small town on the canal, Troy, a town near Albany, Utica. There are a number of waterfalls on this road. The one at Genesee is about 160 feet high, the one at Trenton, the one at Mohawk, or Little Falls, and others. At the first one a maniac named Sam Patch died; he amused himself jumping from waterfalls. On another occasion he jumped from the one at Leucade easily; on the second occasion he fell and was never heard from again. I remember hearing of a certain Rodriguez, also crazy, from Merida, Yucatan, who was continually climbing on church steeples and the highest buildings, jumping with great agility, and he died in one of his undertakings.

For the most part the people of Albany are of Dutch descent. One of the most outstanding persons of this city is General Van Rensselaer, known as the "Patroon" of Albany. I made the acquaintance of him and his family through Mr. Poinsett. His daughter, seventeen years of age (1830), spoke Spanish, French, Italian and her own language perfectly. General Rensselaer is extremely wealthy, and his fortune consists principally of real estate inherited from his grandfather, to whom the legislature of the state had given full possession of the lands which the king of England had granted him for colonization. He has done many good things for the state, and there is a town that bears the name of the family. My wife's birthplace is in the vicinity of this town.

We left Albany in a stagecoach which in order to cross the river went aboard a vessel called a *ferry boat*, a general name given to those boats designed to go from one side of a river to the other in the United States, sometimes propelled by steam and sometimes by horses. We were going towards Lebanon, a town of the same state about twenty-five miles from Albany where there are mineral waters and baths; consequently it is quite crowded in the summer, as are the baths of Ems, Wiesbaden, and others in Europe. On the way there is nothing of note other than some lands called Greenbush, where the general congress has decreed the cultivation of mulberry trees for silkworm culture, which has gotten under way with success.

We arrived at Lebanon on the same day, and we lodged in one of the large hotels of that small town. Lebanon is located in a gorge surrounded by hills and woods that give it a somber aspect, in addition to the fact that the poor and meager population have done nothing to beautify it. The hotels are all of wood and very large. The thermal waters are not good to drink, and their temperature is constantly 75° F. The town overlooks a small valley, which gives it a pleasant view in that direction. One league from Lebanon there is a community of the Shakers, an unusual sect which I shall describe briefly.

This new religion had its beginnings in Manchester, England, in 1747. A woman by the name of Anna Lee came to be received as the mother of the Society in Christ as its prophetess, teacher and director. Consequently she received revelations from the spirit of

Christ, of whom she was a second representation, and she conversed with them frequently, as did many others, with which our legends are filled. Because of persecutions by the authorities and other sects Anna Lee emigrated to the United States with her disciples in 1774 sixty years ago, and there she was joined by others from New York and New England. They bought lands in order to live as a community, and there they founded their first establishment. Anna Lee died ten years later, giving with her last breath testimony of the firmness of her faith and the sanctity of her doctrine.

The group is called the Millennial Society; its first religious principle is the Unity of God. Jesus Christ, according to them was not the son of God, nor coeternal with the Divinity, but an outflowing of that Divinity in time through the operation of divine power. They say that religion consists rather of the practice of virtue than of faith or of speculative doctrines; that man was created innocent, although free to choose between good and evil; but that having lost his original uprightness, no one can be saved until the coming of Christ; that Christ took upon himself the burden of lifting fallen human nature and overruling the power of death—which indeed he did; but that the Church departed from the true spirit of Christ, involving itself in worldly interests, and then the Anti-Christ placed himself at the head of it; that the manifestations of the second coming of Christ began again in the person of Anna Lee, and that through her the same divine spirit that had dwelled in Christ announced itself. The confession of sins is one of the principle articles of faith, following the gospel text,. ''He who hides his sins shall not prosper, but he who confesses and abandons them shall have mercy.''

Its principal commandments are:

1. Duties to God. ''Thou shalt love the Lord with all thy heart and all thy faculties.''

2. Duties to man. ''Thou shalt love thy neighbor as thyself.'' In this rule are included all the obligations of man to his fellow beings.

3. Separation from the world. ''My kingdom is not of this world.'' Hence the obligation to abstain from all participation in politics and the renunciation of any worldly honor or pomp.

4. Peace. Christ is the prince of peace; therefore, his disciples must maintain this spirit. ''If my kingdom were of this world, then my followers should fight.''

5. Simplicity of speech. ''Guard your tongue from evil and your lips from deceit.'' All kinds of profane language, idle and false conversation, are to be avoided. ''Flee from all titles of honor or distinction. Do not call yourself Doctor (learned).''

172

6. The legitimate use of property. Christ asked that his disciples be one with him. This unity should be understood with regards to temporal and spiritual things. The primitive church was established upon these principles—the apostles lived in common.

7. A virgin life. They invoke the example of our Saviour. "Married persons take care for the things of the world and the manner of pleasing their husbands and wives, but the unmarried person takes care for the things of the Lord and the way in which he can be holy in body and in soul.—The children of this world marry and are given in marriage, but those who are counted as worthy of the other world and the resurrection from the dead neither marry nor are given in marriage." The Shakers consider marriage as a purely civil institution with which true Christians have nothing to do.

They believe that freedom of conscience is the most sacred right that God has given to man. They recommend that everyone should live according to the dictates of his conscience as the only means of making himself acceptable in the eyes of God. Their worship is quite different and must seem very unusual to those who judge only by what they have seen in their own country. One Sunday on August 15, 1830, I attended their church, which is a square building without any sort of decoration, altar, or pulpit, and only in the form of a large room with a number of benches for strangers or spectators. Their worship began with a brief talk made by one of their ministers to the spectators, which was simply to ask them to maintain the composure and decorum due the assembly of a religious people who were worshiping the Supreme Being in the way that they thought would be most pleasing to him.

"Reason and the sacred scriptures support our manner of praising God," said the Millennial pastor.

The Israelites danced after crossing the Red Sea; David danced, and likewise the people of Israel, before the holy ark; and Jeremiah says let the virgins rejoice in the dance, and that the young and the old shall dance together. Jesus Christ in the parable of the prodigal son says that on his return home there was music and dance. Therefore, we have the scriptures on our side. Reason dictates likewise that both the body and the soul exercise themselves in acts of devotion before the Creator; and that since God has created all the active powers of man for his honor and glory, let not the tongue alone pay him homage. The hands and the feet which are useful to man in their proper utilization and service should also offer their worship to the Divinity. In other rites people sing; others have made use of the dance; we use the one and the other.

After this discourse the service began. The men and women, separated on two different sides and in line, began a dance reduced to a few simple and easy movements, at the same time singing in unison to not unpleasant music. All the while they moved their hands as in a gesture of beckoning to some one, and thus they were dancing and singing for the space of an hour and a half. The sermon came next and was simply an attempt to prove the truth and the divinity of the sect and of their dogma.

As for the dress of the Shakers, the women wear a tunic of fine wool held in at the waist with a leather belt, wool or cotton stockings, a cape, or else a cap, all very well fitted and very neat. I saw these people eating together—the farmers under the trees, the craftsmen in their workshops, and the women in charge of the storerooms in their large refectories or dining halls. They have about five hundred acres of land which they cultivate and harvest the seed, which they sell throughout the United States. I bought some and sent them to Veracruz to Don Alejandro Troncoso of that city, to send to President Santa Anna in 1830. They also sell brushes, baskets, feather fans, brooms, handbags and a number of domestic utensils. The funds that they have left over they deposit in the banks of the United States and now have more than half a million. The men and women live separately and maintain the strictest chastity—evidently stricter than that of our friars. Generally they are pale and do not appear to be in very robust health. It seems that they must thus be going contrary to the strongest inclination of human nature.

The authorities do not bother about their affairs, nor do they avail themselves of their political rights to vote or to be elected. They live under their own rules without any other policing or authority. Later we shall see a manufacturing town, which without following a religious sect and only under the control of the manufacturing companies, lives in almost the same manner—although more naturally. Agriculture and horticulture are the principal occupations of the members of this sect. The visible head of their church is a ministry composed of four pastors, two men and two women, selected from among them.

174

CHAPTER XIII.

Departure from New Lebanon.—Northampton.—Mt. Holyoke.—Arrival in Boston.—Origins of the State of Massachusetts.—City of Boston.—Penitentiary at Charleston.—Anecdote concerning Charleston.—Anecdote about a prisoner.—Arsenal.—Visit with Mr. Adams.—Home of Mr. Perkins.—Factories in Lowell.

From New Lebanon, Mr. Poinsett and I continued along a road that was mountainous but rather good. After twelve hours we arrived at Northampton at eight o'clock at night. This is a town in the state of Massachusetts in New England on the Connecticut River, where there are some cotton factories, and where they raise excellent crops of wheat, barley, potatoes, green beans and other vegetables and grains. About a mile away, on a hill called Round Hill, is the literary establishment of Mr. Codswell, where I had placed my son, and at the same time another Yucatecan named Don Juan Cano had sent his son. This boy's talent, application and conduct will within a few years make him one of the leading men of Mexico. The Connecticut River is navigable from this point for steamboats, and they go as far as Hartford, a port and the capital of the state of the same name.

During the morning we visited Mt. Holyoke which is on the other side about a thousand feet above the level of the river. The views from here extend to the boundaries of the states of Connecticut, New Hampshire and New York. Beautiful valleys, rivers and springs, meadows, and towns recently started among the forests—all present a surprising spectacle.

From the moment that one enters New England one notes an improvement in the roads, inns, agriculture, beauty of houses and gardens, in short in everything that surrounds the traveler and that can be perfected with the aid of hard work. All these small towns—North-

SHAKERS NEAR LEBANON

N. Currier, undated

ampton, Worcester, Belcherton, and others up to the outskirts of Boston—appear to be country homes built expressly for recreation and pleasure. Such is the cleanliness, the beauty, and such the charm of these small towns. The roads for the most part are macadamized.

Boston, today the capital of the state of Massachusetts, was before independence the capital of New England, which was composed of the states of New Hampshire, Vermont, Maine, Rhode Island, Connecticut and Massachusetts. The diversity of sects in England and the intolerance of the predominant ones obliged a portion of the English in 1620 to come to colonize this part of North America in search of liberty. This purpose and not the spirit of commerce nor of material advantages prompted the first settlers to abandon their native land and to seek refuge in the inhospitable forests of the new continent. Their great sufferings, the endless tasks that they underwent in a harsh climate, in a country without resources, beset by hostile savage Indians, and obliged to live at first in their boats while they constructed their first houses—all this caused them to be called Pilgrims. A few years later the famous Cromwell tried to come to this colony with all of his followers the Puritans, but Charles I opposed that emigration because of the large numbers, holding back in this manner, without dreaming of it, the very man who some years later would cause him to lose his throne and to be led to the scaffold.

The city of Boston is located on a peninsula in the great Massachusetts Bay. It has two suburbs which are Charleston and South Boston. In Charleston, which is reached by a wooden bridge about half a mile long, there is a great glass factory which competes with the best of England, although the product is more expensive and can only meet the competition from Europe because of the import duties. In Charleston also is the penitentiary, where when I was there they had three hundred prisoners and only fourteen jailers, without there having been any case of an escape or an attempt, although as is to be presumed the greater part of them are daring people with very intemperate habits. But the rigorous discipline and the constant watchfulness of the guards is sufficient to keep them quiet and docile while hoping for an end to their confinement. During the day they are busy at their trades, lining up at mealtime to go to the kitchen to get their plates which they take to their rooms where they eat. Twice a day they pray or listen to a religious and moral exhortation, and at night they are locked up in their small cells. A melancholy example for humanity is the following anecdote taken from the work of Mr. Hamilton to whom it was told by the prison warden.

Many years ago before the establishment of the present state prison or penitentiary, a man with honorable connections but of rough character and unbridled habits was convicted of the crime of robbery at night and sentenced to life imprisonment in the Charleston jail in the state of Massachusetts. His pride was not taken down with the disgrace and the punishment—his conduct was arrogant and insubordinate with his jailers, so that it was necessary to separate him from the other prisoners and subject him to harsh discipline. The first year he remained silent and scowling; the clergyman who visited him found him unteachable and unbelieving. But during the following months he changed gradually in manners and ideas. His disposition was more friendly; he was seen reading the scriptures regularly; and the chaplain and the jailer congratulated themselves on such a healthy change in the prisoner. He would talk of his past life and of the terrible offenses that he had committed against God and men, full of grief and repentance; and he gave thanks to the Creator for having preserved his life so that he might have time to ask for his mercy. Now the prisoner's conduct was edifying, and his conversation evangelical; all who saw him became interested in the fate of so good a Christian, so that a number of well-known people interceded with the governor of the state to pardon him. This magistrate was inclined to do so, when one day with the greatest trust the jailer and other persons were talking with the prisoner, and he threw himself upon the jailer, wounded him several times, and tried to flee, although without success.

He was taken to a solitary cell with bars where he remained for some years without the slightest hope of getting out. Finally a brother-in-law of his, a person of influence and wealth in South Carolina, went to Boston and accepted responsibility for the prisoner if he were pardoned. They granted his request, and to remove from him all temptation to commit the same crimes they provided him with everything necessary in the city of Charleston, South Carolina.

The prisoner got out after twenty years, during which time he had not breathed the pure free air of the heavens nor seen the splendor of the sun. During this time Boston, which was a small town when he was locked up, had changed into a rich and beautiful city. At every step he took he had to marvel at some new thing that he saw. The physical and moral appearance, the customs, clothing, thoughts, worries and opinions of the generation that he saw were very different from those of the generation that he had known. The wooden houses that he had seen standing alone and unadorned had been replaced by magnificent buildings of marble, granite or brick; he saw plazas and promenades in places that had been wooded and sylvan when he left them. In short he felt like the inhabitant of another planet that had come to an unknown world. At the sight of such new things, of a spectacle so alive and interesting, surrounded by so many strange and unknown objects, this man dissolved into tears thinking that he had been transported to an unknown land.

178

He arrived in Charleston, South Carolina, where his brother-in-law found him good lodgings and the comforts of life. The first year his conduct was above reproach, but the evil hour induced him to visit New York. There he ran into people of evil ways, associated with them, again robbed by night and was condemned to life imprisonment in Sing Sing, the penitentiary of the state of New York, from where he will go forth as a corpse. Can human nature be so incorrigible as is shown by this sad example? Are there in the physical makeup of man irresistible tendencies? These are questions that concern phrenologists and their adversaries. There is no doubt that our material composition has much to do with our moral character.

Commodore Morris, an old friend of Mr. Poinsett, was good enough to go with us to the arsenal where they are building a granite dry dock for constructing and repairing war ships. It is three hundred feet long, twenty-five feet deep, and fifty feet wide. It is elliptical in form, and the water comes and goes at discretion as it is needed. The cost is figured to be five hundred thousand dollars.

The next day we went to visit Mr. Adams at his home in Quincy. This illustrious American is the son of the president who followed Washington, and he himself was president for the four-year term of 1824 to 1828. He had been secretary of state in Mr. Monroe's administration, and minister to the English government. I never saw a man so cold and circumspect of character. During the visit which lasted more than half an hour we scarcely said more than what would in other circumstances take five minutes. "What do you hear from Mexico?" he asked me. After some silence I related to him briefly the series of revolutions that had occurred.

"You won't be at peace," he said to me, "for any period of time until you adopt institutions fitting to the circumstances. These circumstances must be created also."

We said goodbye and left this strange man in his lonely house seven miles distant from Boston. We went to see Mr. Perkins, one of the richest persons in New England, the owner of rich granite quarries which furnish this valuable stone for buildings, docks, stone pavements, columns, etc., of the nearby towns. We had tea in his famous country home which is enhanced by a great number of exotic plants and fruit trees, flowers and vegetables. Mr. Perkins has the particular pleasure of eating pineapples from his garden, pears and peaches in the winter time, by means of conservatories kept at various temperatures.

As one of the richest manufacturing impresarios of Lowell, Mr. Perkins invited us to go with him to see that remarkable town which had sprung up among the trees in the short space of seven years. Nowhere does the power of hard work and liberty make one feel so forcefully its beneficial effects as in the United States of America. I shall give a description of this amazing progress with the aid of the able pen of a young man named M. Chevalier, who when he visited this place felt himself inspired at the sight of the order, prosperity and good customs of the workers of Lowell.

It is not war, that last rationale of kings, that can lift a people or a nation up to prosperity. A battlefield will excite horror, or feverish enthusiasm, or piety and fear. The strength of man applied to production is more majestic than human strength applied to killing. The pyramids and the temples of colossal dimensions of Thebes, the Coliseum, or St. Peter's Church in Rome, disclose more grandeur than a battlefield covered with dead men and ashes, even when there were three hundred thousand corpses lying about as in those battles in which Napoleon carried fear to the world and covered France with glory. The power of man is thus like that of God, visible in small things as in large ones. There is nothing in the material order of which our species has more right to boast than the mechanical inventions by means of which man curbs the unordered vigor of nature or develops its hidden energy. By means of mechanics man, weak and wretched in appearance, by extending his hand over the immensity of the world, takes possession of its floods, of its unleashed winds, of the ebb and flow of the sea, of metals and combustibles scattered about over the surface of the earth, or hidden in its depths, of the liquids that are converted into steam to be the most powerful agent in the hands of man.

Is there indeed anything that gives a more exalted idea of the power of man than the steam machinery in the forms that have been given to him for application to transport, either in ships upon the sea and the rivers, or in trains across the surface of the earth. It is a living being rather than a machine. It goes by itself, runs like a horse; more than that, it breathes. In fact the steam that comes out of the stacks regularly and that condenses into white smoke truly looks like breath, the violent respiration of a horse running a race.

Anyone in the midst of these forests a short time ago when they were inhabited by a few wandering tribes, and today dotted here and there by a few recently built houses—anyone who with no knowledge of these prodigious machines—that happened one night to see a body moving along showering millions of sparks, breathing loudly and frequently running with an unknown speed without a horse or other animal to move it, would no doubt think that he was seeing one of those dragons or fabulous monsters that spew flames out of their mouths and threaten to devour the unfortunate mortal that happens to get in their way. A few years ago when the Brahmans saw a steamboat struggling and conquering the currents of the sacred Ganges, in good faith those fathers of ancient knowledge believed that it was an unknown animal recently discovered by the English in a distant land.

In modern societies mechanical progress has produced factories that promise to be for the human race an inexhaustible source of prosperity and well-being. English factories produce today about eight hundred million yards of cotton textiles that are equivalent to one yard for every individual upon the earth. If all the men living were to set to work on these products with only the help of their fingers, it is probable that in a year they would produce only a part of what Great Britain does. Thus the labors of the human race would be engaged in a work which, thanks to mechanization and factories, employs at the most a million and a half in that nation.

We must infer from this that when manufacturing is developed and well planned, the moderate work of a portion of the human race will be sufficient to provide for all the comforts of material life. There seems to be no doubt that that day will come, but up until this time it has not been possible to set up this wonderful order of things, and a long time will pass before it is accomplished. The system of manufacturing is a new discovery; it is developing more every day, and as it develops it will improve. Here is an example. The cotton imported into England for manufacturing in 1785 weighed 11 million English pounds. In 1816 it amounted to 90 million and in 1831 to 245 million. These three numbers are in this ratio: 1:9.5:22.25. However, this progress is slow, and in those countries where these skills are just beginning it must be much slower still.

In this North America the development of manufacturing is, however, surprising. Who is not amazed at the sight of the town of Lowell, a forest village ten years ago, and today a town of seven thousand people with factories that are competing with those of Europe.

''I had scarcely recovered from the sight of this improvised city,'' says M. Chevalier,

> scarcely had I seen and touched it to assure myself that it was not a cardboard city like those that Potemkin had had built on Catherine's dressing table, in order to find out to what extent the factories in this place had stirred up, with respect to the wellbeing and morality of the working class with relation to the security of the rich and that of public order, the dangers that had been experienced in Europe. Thanks to the supervising agents of the two principal companies (Merrimack Corporation and Lawrence Corporation) I have been able to satisfy my curiosity.

The cotton factories alone employ six thousand persons in Lowell. Of this number about five thousand are young single women from seventeen to twenty-four years of age, daughters of tenant farmers from the different states of New England, particularly Massachusetts, New Hampshire and Vermont. There they are far from their families and on their own. As I saw them in the morning or in the afternoon in the streets dressed neatly and cleanly, leaving the shops and taking from the hangers covered with flowers their hats, caps, shawls and kerchiefs, I said to myself, "This is not like Manchester." Here are the average general salaries such as were paid during the recent month of May per week—that is, for six days of work:

	$3.00 ⎤
Preparatory operations (ginning and cleaning)	3.12
	2.50 ⎦
Spinning	3.25
Weaving of various types	3.25
Dyeing and sizing	3.75 ⎤
	4.00 ⎦
Measuring and packing	3.25

The salaries of skilled workers are notably higher and are as much as $6.00 per week.

Let us now compare the situation of these workers with those of Europe, and an enormous difference will be noted in favor of those of the United States of the North. There are few women in Europe of that class who earn more than eighteen or nineteen cents per day, or $1.08 to $1.14 per week. Bear in mind also that articles of prime necessity such as bread, meat, sugar, coffee, rice, etc, are much cheaper in the United States. Thus, a large number of the women workers of Lowell can save up to $1.50 per week. At the end of four years they will have $300, and that is the dowry with which they go out to establish themselves by marrying a young man who has an equal amount, and they apply themselves to the exercise of a profession.

In France, and much less in Mexico, one cannot even imagine the position of pretty young girls, most of them twenty to thirty leagues from their parents' homes, with only their virtue. In spite of this one does not notice deplorable effects in Lowell, with the exception of a very limited number of cases which do not break down the general rule. The English race has customs very different from the Spanish and the French. Other habits, other ideas. Protestant education draws around each individual a circle much more difficult to penetrate than that drawn by Catholic education. For one thing there is, indeed, more coldness, less communication in social relations, more or less an absolute absence of free expression and confidence. But on the other hand, one finds more respect, more consideration for the personality of others. What among us would be considered as a bit of mischief, an insignificant adventure, would be reproached severely in England or in the United States of the North. Let no one be surprised then in this country to see the daughters of farmers and landowners leave their parents to go to a city where they know no one and remain there in their work for three or four years until they have made a small fortune. They are under the safeguard of public faith.

This presupposes in customs an extreme reserve, and in public opinion a watchful and unrelenting sternness and this reserve give society a certain coloring of sadness and tedious monotony which wearies those who are not used to it, but when one reflects upon the perils to which the opposite system exposes unwitting young girls who rush into pleasure, when one counts the victims that have resulted from that ease of communication and that abandon in other countries, it is difficult not to agree that the coldness and the Anglo-American incommunicative manner are a great deal better than the friendly and easygoing sociability of the French and the Mexicans.

The manufacturing companies watch over the habits of these young working women. Each company has constructed a building that has a number of rooms sufficient to house the women in what they call *boardinghouses.* There they are under the protection and sponsorship of the landladies who run the places, for which the women pay each week only one dollar for their board and room. The landladies keep the company informed of the conduct of the young women in their care, and they live by rules that are laid down for them. Here is an excerpt from these rules:

1st. All persons employed by the company must be busy at their tasks during the hours of work. They must also be capable of doing the job to which they are assigned or to make efforts to be so. On all occasions and under all circumstances either in speech or by conduct they are to demonstrate a love of temperance and all the virtues, and to be motivated by a feeling for their moral and social obligations. The company's agent will strive to set for all a good example. Any person who is notoriously lazy, dissolute or intemperate, or who is in the habit of missing divine worship, who violates Sunday rest, or who is given over to gambling, will be dismissed from the company.

2nd. No spirituous liquor is allowed on the premises of the company unless it be by a doctor's orders. Nor is any game of chance or of cards allowed. Article 13 requires that all workers must live in the boardinghouses.

Since Lowell is a workers' town where everybody is subject to company rules, it is evident that it is like a vast monastery where civil authority is little concerned. They are like large families or school groups under special constitutions, whose object is to stimulate work and maintain good habits as the basis of every social establishment. Just as at the end of ten or twelve years young people come out of literary institutes with a wealth of knowledge and learning, so the working men and women leave these shops after some years with the monetary capital which is the fruit of their savings, and furthermore with the habits of love of work, respect for virtue, and horror towards vice. Sunday, which among us is a day of pleasure and fiesta, in these places is dedicated to prayer, meditation and rest. This is one of the many aspects in which the Anglo-American and the Mexican peoples are different. In the moral and religious aspect among South Americans there is a relaxation and contempt that is in direct contradiction with our religious profession and the hypocritical zeal which we manifest in support of our exclusive worship. This reflection leads to very sad consequences for the new republics, but it is no less the truth. These consequences are that since the source of political authority among us could not be found, as it should have been in a republic, in that severe restraint of North American customs, in the inflexibility of life habits, and in the religious sternness of the people, alongside a multiplicity of sects, we have found ourselves obliged to find such source in material force, in terror on the same basis as before independence, in open conflict with the institutions and openly incompatible with republican principles.

So certain is it that the need for order and for liberty is essential to human nature, and that it is impossible to found a society with only one of these elements. If you give one portion of social institutions over to liberty, be assured that the principle of order will play a part no less exclusive on another point. Unfortunately among us the laws of equilibrium between order and liberty have not yet been established.

The company rules are religiously observed in Lowell. In the factories which are buildings of great extent there are bells to call the people to work so that they resemble the convents of one of our cities. But in Lowell there are no supplicants with saints, there are no beggars, there are no ragged and poverty stricken people. These nineteenth-century nuns, instead of keeping busy making relicaries, scapularies and shrouds, are employed in spinning cotton and weaving textiles of all qualities. In Lowell there are no pastimes nor entertainment, but a peaceful town inhabited by people dressed with charm, neatness and decency.

184

CHAPTER XIV.

On the way from Boston to Lowell we went by Lexington, the town where the first action between Americans and English occurred in the War of Independence. General Gage had sent eight hundred soldiers to occupy the warehouses of war materials that the Massachusetts assembly had ordered to be set up, and as the British troops passsed through Lexington they were attacked by civilian troops there, and eight men were killed. They continued their march, but on their return they encountered a large number of militiamen, and there was a hard fought action in which 273 Englishmen and 88 North Americans died. The first blood was shed between the two nations. In the public square of that small town there is a monument erected in 1799 in granite with the following inscription:

Sacred to the liberty and rights of mankind; the freedom and independence of America, sealed and defended by the blood of her sons.

This monument is erected by the inhabitants of Lexington, under the patronage and at the expense of the commonwealth of Massachusetts, to the memory of their fellow citizens, Ensign Robert Munroe, Messrs. Jonas Parker, Samuel Hadley, Jonathan Harrington, junior, Isaac Muzzey, Caleb Harrington, and John Brown of Lexington, and Asahel Porter of Woburn, who fell on this field, the first victims to the sword of British tyranny and oppression, on the morning of the ever-memorable 19th of April, 1775.

The die was cast. The blood of these martyrs, in the cause of God and their country, was the cement of these states, their colonies, and gave the spring to the spirit, firmness and resolution of their fellow citizens. They rose, as one man, to revenge their brethren's blood, and at the point of the sword to assert and defend their native rights. They nobly dared to be free. The contest was long, bloody, and affecting. Righteous Heaven approved the solemn appeal. Victory crowned their arms, and the peace, liberty, and the independence of the United States of America were their glorious reward.*

After the Battle of Lexington the English general fortified Boston, and both parties prepared for war. The Americans immediately occupied the heights around the city where they set up fortifications. The English dislodged them after a fierce battle in which they lost a third of their troops. The theater of this action was Bunker's Hill, famous in these parts since that day. On this hill there is a monument 220 feet high which was erected in 1825.

The inn where I stayed in Boston is the best there is in the United States. It is called Tremont House, in front of the theater. The building is of that beautiful micah-granite which is so plentiful in the northern states, especially in New England. There is room for four hundred persons to stay in this hotel, and there were at least three hundred of both sexes when I was there. Everyone eats at a common table, or else privately if one wishes to pay a little more. The service is prompt; the food is very well seasoned; the beds comfortable and clean; that large house is lighted with gas, and in all the hallways there is sufficient light to get around. The charge is thirteen dollars per week with wine extra.

Boston streets are mostly crooked, and most of them rather narrow; some are stone paved, others are beautiful and comfortable with Macadam's method. There are very notable buildings of white marble and granite. The State House built on a small hill rises up to a height so that one looks out from the cupola over all parts of the city and the bay. The two chambers that make up the legislative body meet there.

The constitution of this state was written in 1780 and revised in 1821. The legislative power rests in the senate and house of representatives, and both are called the General Court of Massachusetts. The members of the house of representatives are elected each year the second Monday in November. Each town that has 150 voters listed

*Translator's note: Quoted directly from James Stuart, *Three Years in North America* (New York: J & J Harper, 1833), vol. 1, pp. 202-203, from which Zavala made his Spanish translation.

186

names a representative, above that, another one for each 225 increase. The senate has forty members elected by the districts annually the second Monday in November. The governor is also elected annually by the people the second Monday in November, and likewise the lieutenant governor. There is a governor's council composed of nine members taken from among the senators and selected by both houses. The legislative body meets in Boston the first Wednesday in January each year.

All citizens twenty-one years of age or older can vote, provided they have lived for one year in the state and six months preceding the time of the election, and that they have paid taxes to the state for two years, unless the law makes an exception.

The judicial power rests in judges named by the governor in agreement with the council. Their term of office is *ad vitam aut culpam* ("for life during good behavior").

Boston is one of the best-educated cities in the United States, and the State of Massachusetts is one that has produced a large number of learned men, eloquent orators, well-educated lawyers and famous statesmen. The Adams, Franklins, Hancocks, Ticknors, Quincys, Everetts and other similar names occupy a distinguished place in the literary and political annals of that area. The last of these is the principal editor of a tri-monthly review known as the *North American Review*, comparable to the most classical reviews of Europe. When I arrived in the United States in 1830, I found discussed in that review events of Mexico of December 1828, in which unfortunately I had a part under the colors that Mr. Ward had pictured them in his writings in a supplement on his trip to Mexico. The same subject, although from a very different point of view, had been treated by the skillful hand of Mr. Walsh in his *Quarterly Review*.

The editors of these periodicals imitate the English reviews, and they prefer more extensive articles and analytical discussions to a greater number of superficial items or simple accounts. In one of the numbers of this review, when analyzing the work of Father Guasi on the United States, there are, he says, a Jesuit college in Georgetown near Washington, and a literary institution of the same order in New York, a college for priests of St. Sulpice in Baltimore, and a school in Emmetsburg. In Kentucky the English Dominicans have a school and a church under the tutelage of Santa Rosa of Lima. In the western states there are missionaries of St. Francis of Paula and a convent of Carmelite nuns of Santa Teresa. In Georgetown another one of the Visitant Sisters.

The abbott Dubois founded another convent in Emmetsburg for the education of young women, and himself started another in Philadelphia, in which he had the double purpose of education and caring for the sick. This establishment is supported not only by the charity of the Catholics but of the Protestants as well. The abbott Nerina has founded in Kentucky a convent for nuns who go under the name of Sisters of Mary at the Foot of the Cross, and finally a Protestant minister converted to the Catholic faith has brought to Boston, his birthplace, the Ursulines and has left them sufficient funds for their establishment.

Although this progress of Catholicism caused some alarm to the friends of religious independence, the editor of the *Review* sets forth his own alarm with the expression of a sincere tolerance as religious as it is philosophical. In a country where the force of law does not come to the support of an exclusive religion there is nothing to fear.

In Boston there are sixty-eight free schools besides twenty-three Sunday schools. It is true that in this state and in Connecticut education is most advanced. According to figures compiled by official reports coming to the capital in 1830, among 60,000 persons there were only 400 who did not know how to read or write, and of 131 towns that sent in reports on education there were 12,393 children of both sexes learning to read and write, do arithmetic and algebra, the principles of geography, history, drawing, and religion, and there were only fifty-eight who did not know how to read and write among all the children between fourteen and twenty years of age. The annual sum of public funds dedicated to this sacred object in the city of Boston is from $50,000 to $70,000.

The method of arranging these establishments in the United States deserves the attention of Mexicans. Each year the representatives of the respective wards meet and name ten or twelve commissioners that are called Trustees, who are charged with the collection of funds, their distribution, the examination of the state of the schools, the conduct of the teachers, the number of children, instruments, books, etc. They collect the income from legacies, donations, legislative grants and others set aside for education. When the year has ended, they make a report in which they give an accounting to the public of all that they have observed, the improvement that they think should be made, the expenses, number of children, etc. As I write this I have before me the twenty-fourth annual report of the Trustees of the public society of New York, *Twenty-fourth Annual Report of the Public School Society of New York*.

It can be stated on very approximate calculations that a third of the inhabitants of the states of Massachusetts and Connecticut attend schools, and that with the exception of two thousand persons in a population of two million of these states, all know how to read and write at least. Compare this moral situation of the people of the

United States with one or two of our states, and it will be clear as to the true reason why it is impossible at the present time to bring our institutions up to the level of those of our neighbors, *particularly in some states*. Of those of the state of Mexico, for example, and of Yucatan, which I know best, it may be said that among 1,200,000 inhabitants in the first and 700,000 in the second, there will probably be at the most one in twenty [who can read]. And something more—among the five in a thousand that know how to read and write two fifths do not know arithmetic, and three fifths do not even know the meaning of the words geography, history, astronomy, etc. Four fifths do not know what the Bible is, and the names of Genesis, Paralipomenon, Gospel, Apocalipsis are entirely unknown. Add to this that in Yucatan there are at least a third of the people who do not speak Spanish, and in the state of Mexico one fifth. Those who consider the degree of civilization of the masses as no reason to give institutions to the people are either dismally ignorant or they are extremely perverse.

This state of public education in the United States can well justify the call made to all classes of citizens to take part in the elections and other governmental functions. I remember having read that one of the big arguments that were made for extending the electoral census in France and England was the ignorance of a large part of the people in some provinces. In the county of Wales, for example, one in twenty knows how to read and write; in Scotland one in ten. In the southern departments of France there are some where one out of twenty-five knows how to read and write. But in these places there are many persons who compensate in some degree for the roughness or ignorance of the masses by their learning, experience and general knowledge.

Mr. Otis was the mayor when I was in Boston. I had the honor of being invited to his table where there were several people well known for their knowledge and long services. Mr. Otis has made sacrifices for the cause of liberty, although he did not belong to the democratic party. His connections with Adams, Webster, Everett and other men of the former Federalist group cause him to be placed in their lineage.

Cambridge College is one of the most famous in the United States. On the visit which I made to this establishment under the guidance of Mr. Quincy I had reason to be satisfied with the intelligence of the rector, the beauty of the place, the elegance of the building, the literary wealth of its library and museum of antiquities. At Cambridge College they teach the humanities, physical sciences, mathematics, history, the Greek, Latin, French, Spanish and German languages, ideology and political economy.

In the same town I visited Mr. Gros, a man who has made a great fortune in the tannery trade. He uses a considerable part of it to acquire beautiful pictures and original paintings or good copies of the best artists. The Atheneum in Boston is an establishment that attracts the attention of the educated traveler because of the great number of well-chosen books and curious monuments. Mr. Everett, junior, did me the honor of introducing me to this society.

In Boston there is a beautiful marble statue of General Washington made by Mr. Chantry, and in a cemetery near the public park is the tomb of Franklin and his family. The park is a beautiful grove on a level spot in front of the State House, and the only adornment, if such it can be called, is a pool 120 feet long and half as wide, No statues, no fountains, no pavilions, etc. In the United States they look for the necessary and the useful. There are not even any establishments of pleasure and luxury.

Boston society is generally educated and one might say has good taste. In the winter there are dances and tea parties where the people of different classes of society get together according to their different tastes, inclinations, and professions.

Eight miles from Boston there is an island in the very mouth of the bay known as Nahant, very popular in the summer for sea bathing. The views are magnificent over the sea, the coasts, small towns and towers of Boston. On the island, which is about a mile long, there are two or three good hotels, baths and places of entertainment.

From Boston I went to the state of Rhode Island, taking a seat on a stagecoach. As in the state of Massachusetts, this is one of those with the least navigation because of the lack of rivers. It is also the one where there are more carriages proportionally, and in which the roads are kept up better and railroad lines are undertaken with the most enthusiasm. The roads generally are much better than in the other states of the Union. From Boston to Providence is about forty-five miles; we had dinner in Dedham and got to Providence, the capital of the state of Rhode Island on the Providence River. This is a manufacturing city as are all those of New England. It has fifteen tò sixteen thousand people, and a college where they teach physics, geometry, history, Greek and Latin, ideology and penmanship.

The government of the state is based on the charter granted by Charles II at the time of the establishment of the colony in 1683, and this is the only state in the Union which does not have a written constitution. The legislative power is exercised by the General Assembly which consists of a senate and a house of representatives. The latter is composed of seventy-two members taken six from New Port, four from each of the cities of Providence, Portsmouth, and Warewich, and two from each of the towns of the state. They are elected every six months in April and August. The senate is composed of ten members elected annually in April.

There is a governor, popularly elected each year in April, and a lieutenant governor elected at the same time who stands in for the governor when necessary. The assembly meets four times a year—in New Port the first Wednesday in May, which is the beginning of the civil year, and is the first session, until the first Wednesday in June; the first Wednesday in October in Providence, until the first Wednesday in November; those of January and March in the towns of South Kingston, East Greenwich, and Binsol.

From New Providence to New York the distance is 180 miles by the maritime canal the Sound. The first colonization of Providence recalls one of those sad effects of the intolerance of religious sects that wish the exclusive dominion of their beliefs. The *Puritans*, pursued in England under the government of Charles I, leaving their native land under the name of the Pilgrim Fathers, came to the New World in search of the liberty that they did not find in the Old World. But scarcely were these victims of persecution settled in New England than, contradicting not only their former principles, but even those of universal morality, and especially that of the gospels which is the most tolerant, they in turn became *persecutors*. The Socinians, the Quakers, in a word all those who did not hold to their religious opinions and beliefs were run out of the colony violently with offense against their property. Among these was Roger Williams, a Puritan clergyman, who was bold enough to expose what he considered evidence of apostasy in the churches of Massachusetts.

At first the clergy proposed to fight him with theological arguments and demonstrations. Since they were not able to make him or the others disappear, they had recourse to civil authority so that by force they might throw out of the midst of the *true believers* so able and learned an enemy. Roger Williams was banished, and accompanied by his followers he wandered through the wilderness until he came to a place called Moohausic by the Indians, and here he placed his settlement and named it Providence.

When nature made the people of New England, according to Mr. Hamilton, it seemed to be her wish to give them *twice the amount of brains* and *half a heart*. Indeed, they are perhaps the most intelligent and astute people known. When one says *Yankee*, which is what they are commonly called, it is understood that one means a man who knows his business; that the odds of his being cheated or cheating are nineteen to one in favor of the latter. The character of

AMERICAN FOREST SCENE
Maple Sugaring

N. Currier, 1855

192

these people, says the same writer, is not friendly, does not inspire confidence; but it is also far from being scornful. They have a degree of energy, strength and independence that does not allow one to look down upon them.

Wealth is better distributed in New England than in any other part of the globe. Although there are great capitalists, there are no huge fortunes. There are no poor, and it is very rare to find families in poverty. Regularly beside great palaces there is the unfortunate fellow who is begging for bread for his children. Although there are some beggars, they are always foreigners, especially Irishmen who have recently arrived and are looking for a way to get along.

The state of Connecticut has three hundred thousand inhabitants and lies between the maritime canal called the Sound, the states of Rhode Island, Massachusetts, and New York. The capital is Hartford, a city of about nine thousand inhabitants on the Connecticut River, and it has a very busy port. The constitution of Connecticut was granted by Charles II in 1662 and revised in 1818 by the General Assembly. There are a senate and a house of representatives. The latter is composed of 208 members who receive no pay. There are thirty-four senators, and both groups are elected for one year. The governor is elected by the people annually. He receives three hundred dollars per year. The assembly meets one year in Hartford and the other in New Haven. There is universal suffrage for whites among those citizens aged twenty-one years or over.

New Haven is one of the beautiful cities of the United States, because of its location and the elegance of its buildings. The population is nine thousand, it is built on an extensive bank, and extends about two miles from north to south and three from west to east. The children's academy run by Mr. Dwight is notable for its size and would surprise anyone who did not know that in that small state the whole attention of the people is directed to the education of the young. Yale College is another educational institution that competes with the University of Cambridge in the state of Massachusetts. The number of students is about five hundred. The cemetery of this city is the best in the United States because of its size, symmetry, beauty of monuments, trees and location.

Before leaving the state of Connecticut I shall include an interesting document which is the manifesto of the famous Hartford Convention held in 1814, when Mr. Madison was president of the United States and during the critical moments of the second war with England, when the states suffered great bankruptcies because of the interruption of trade, and the general congress passed some laws that did not meet with the approval of many. The delegates to the convention were from the legislatures of Massachusetts, Connecticut and Rhode Island, from the counties of Grafton and Cheshire in the state of New Hampshire, from Winthrop County in the state of Vermont. The total number was twenty-five. Here is the manifesto.*

The convention ended its long declaration with propositions that subsequent events and the rising prosperity of that fortunate nation have shown not to have been in conformity with the spirit of its wise institutions, and this noisy happening had no further consequences, with the brilliant victory in Louisiana one month later. This changed the political and mercantile aspect of the United States of the North and brought an advantageous peace with Great Britain.

*Translator's note: Since the Hartford Convention Manifesto is well known in United States history, the lengthy document has not been included here. The text is available from various sources, including James M. Banner, Jr., *To the Hartford Convention* (New York: Alfred A. Knopf, 1970).

CHAPTER XV.

Return to New York.—Colonel Burr.—General Santander.—Elections.—Popular meetings,—Reflections.—Trip to West Point.—Idea of the military college.—Reflections.—Shelters for juvenile delinquents, deaf and dumb and the insane in New York.—Prisons.

Since my return to New York after my trip to New England was followed by the one that I made to Europe, in the account I shall continue of the United States I shall not follow the order of dates, but will talk about New York, which I also visited in 1832 on my return from Europe. During this time I met the famous Colonel Burr, a lawyer of great knowledge in his profession, an enterprising and remarkable man in the United States in the first years following independence.

Colonel Burr was introduced to me by Dr. Johns who had been for some time in the state of Tabasco. One day I saw this doctor come into my living room with a small man about seventy years old, with a very spiritual countenance, and in whom, in spite of the fact that he was half-paralyzed, there could be seen mental strength and vigorous character. Colonel Burr speaks French after a fashion and likes to use this language in conversation. He was vice-president of the United States during the administration of the elder Mr. Adams,* and at the time of the election of Mr. Jefferson as president he was tied twenty-three times in the voting by the chamber. Aaron Burr lost the esteem of his fellow citizens because of a noisy duel with the virtuous General Hamilton which resulted in the death of the latter. After that Mr. Burr went to Europe to give his fellow citizens time to forget the bloody catastrophe.

*Translator's note: Zavala is mistaken as Burr was vice-president during Jefferson's first term, not during Adams' term.

The British government did not allow him to remain in England long, because he became greatly involved with the *radicals* and maintained close communication with the French revolutionaries. Later he tried to gain possession of the province of Texas; *some say* that he had the idea of proclaiming himself emperor. What is certain is that there was a scandalous trial, and although he was absolved by successive juries, public opinion did not consider that he was proven not guilty. Today he makes his living as a lawyer, and his forensic ability would give him sufficient to live on even if he had not acquired a fortune to which he has recently added by his marriage to a rich lady of New York.

In New York at this time was Don Francisco de Paula Santander, the present president of New Granada. He had been banished from Colombia under the dictatorship of Bolívar, who had had him sentenced to death for a conspiracy against the life of the dictator, in which he was supposed to have taken part. Bolívar, out of mercy, commuted the death sentence to banishment for six years. From the trial, of which General Santander gave me a copy, it was brought out only that some one had revealed to him confidentially the secret of the conspiracy against the usurper. On such a charge Santander was condemned to death because he had not denounced the plot. This general was feted by the leading people of New York, and I recall that they gave him a public dinner at which there were at least one hundred fifty present.

I had occasion to be with him considerably in France, during the voyage and in the United States. At his hotel in Philadelphia I met General Don Manuel G. Pedraza, who had not been allowed to land on the coast of Mexico for reasons of state. General Santander is an honorable man who loves liberty and is able to discern the true road to happiness for his fellow citizens. Perhaps he is a little more fond of his own judgment than is good. But his moderation and tact in business correct this fault.

During this time the election of the president of the United States was going on. General Jackson had been elected in 1828 against Mr. Adams, in whose reelection the old Federalist Party was quite active in opposition to the Democratic Party. Quite worthy of note are two public documents of that time among a thousand others because they give an idea of the character of the parties in the United States. The first is the one that supported the election of General Jackson, and the second that of Mr. Adams. It should be kept in mind, as I have said before in this work, that anyone can announce through the newspapers that there is going to be a *Convention* or a meeting on this subject or that when public opinion is divided.

REPUBLICAN CONVENTION IN EDINBURG
(State of New York)

In a well-attended and respectable convention of Republicans of the town of Edinburg, held in the restaurant of Mayor Weeks Copeland in said town, September 13, 1828, to name the delegates that would go to the county convention for the purpose of dealing with the nomination of a president for the following year, John Rhodes was named to preside over the meeting, and Martin Butler was named secretary. The committee appointed for the purpose reported the followed resolutions, which were indeed approved unanimously.

We Resolve: That it is not only the right but the duty of Republicans to investigate the conduct of those who are placed at the head of the government, to discover and put an end to their arbitrary acts, and to repress examples of corruption and disorder. The convention is of the opinion that in the present crisis it is urgently called to make this investigation.

We Resolve: That we cannot support the conduct of the present administration with our future votes because of their disorderly handling of affairs, their lack of respect for many of our more distinguished citizens, the profusion of rewards showered upon their favorites, the abandonment of their obligations because of involvement in the elections, the very unbecoming means that they have employed to maintain themselves in power and assure their reelection.

We Resolve: That we are persuaded that General Andrew Jackson is the man that has covered his country with glory, and that his services to the nation cause him to be due the highest recompense, that because of his solid principles, his ardent love for his country manifested in the days of greatest danger, his devotion to democracy, his simple life free of all pomp, his incomparable services to the nation, he is a citizen fitted to check the progress of prodigality, halt the march of corruption, and reinstate the government in the purity of its former principles.

We Resolve: That for these and other considerations we approve the nomination of Andrew Jackson for the presidency, and that we shall employ our efforts to secure his election.

We Resolve: That this confidence is increased because we believe that he wishes to rise to this elevated post by the voice of the people, without the aid of public funds, the influence of the cabinet, or by intrigue, begging, or threats.

We Resolve: That we approve the nomination of John C. Calhoun for the office of vice-president, persuaded that during the course of his public life he has conducted himself in a manner that makes him worthy of our votes.

We Resolve: That we should not thank any of our representatives or senators for having abused in a bastardly manner their franking privilege to send throughout all the states innumerable printed pamphlets and papers that contain absurd declarations to support an election that is disapproved by civilized men and even more so by knowledgeable Republicans.

We Resolve: That we are not in agreement with the opinion set forth in Utica which supports the party of the present administration and proposes for governor and lieutenant governor persons of that party.

We Resolve: That these resolutions shall be signed by the president and the secretary and be published in the newspaper in Saratoga.

John Rhodes, president.
M. H. Butler, secretary.

THE AMERICAN SYSTEM
Convention of the Republican Admninistration

In this convention of delegates supporting the administration of the present national government, gathered from all the towns of the County of Saratoga, held in the Town Hall of the town of Ballston Spa, on Wednesday, October 22, 1828, General John Prior was called to the chair, and John House and James McCrea were named secretaries.

It Was Resolved that the outstanding and patriotic present administration of our national government is worthy of our most ardent votes and that we shall use all honorable means in order to procure the reelection of John Quincy Adams to the presidency, and the election of Richard Bush for the office of vice-president.

It Was Resolved that we cordially approve the nomination of Smith Thompson for the position of governor of the state, and of Francis Granger for lieutenant governor, and we are ready to support their nominations by our votes.

It Was Resolved that we have complete confidence in the talents and integrity of John McLean, junior, of Washington, and heartily united with the Republican convention of this district we recommend him for senator.

It Was Resolved that the delegates from each town shall name one from among their group to compose a committee chosen with

198

instructions to inform the convention about the persons that should be the candidates for the county offices.

The said committee having withdrawn and then returned to the convention hall, they reported that they had unanimously agreed to recommend the following candidates: for elector John Child, for deputy John Taylor, for sheriff John Dunning, for county clerk Thomas Palmer, for members of the legislature Gilbert Waring, Joshua Mandeville and Calvin Wheeler, for coroner Herman Rockwell, Dirck L. Palmer, Hugh Alexander and Nathan D. Sherwood. After which, having read and approved each recommendation individually and unanimously, it was resolved that Salmon Child, Samuel Treeman, Edward Watrous, James McCrea, Amon Brown, Increase W. Child and Moses Williams shall be the ones to compose the central committee for the coming year, and that the delegates elected by the people to this convention shall be the ones who compose a watch committee in their respective places to carry out the elections referred to above; finally *it was resolved* that these minutes be signed by the president and the secretaries.

The proclamation is as follows:

Citizens: in a government such as ours in which each of the citizens has in his hands a portion of the sovereign power, it is all important that he make use of the authority with which he is vested with clear judgment. The coming presidential election is of the most vital importance for the happiness and the progress of the United States, and consequently it will determine whether a virtuous and illustrious administration shall remain or be overthrown, and whether measures that profoundly affect the interests of this vast majority of our fellow citizens are to be promoted or abandoned.

The present administration of the general government is at the head of a great political system that promises to put into effect undertakings that will extend the resources, increase the wealth, and promote all those principles that will assure the independence of the country. For many years now Great Britain has refused to receive into her ports goods produced in the states of the North and the South while this country receives annually from that nation the value of many millions of dollars of her manufactured goods; from this has come the result that all our gold and silver have taken that road to pay for her merchandise. From this has resulted the fact that our workers have not found a market for their surplus products, and all classes of society have found themselves in dire straits because of this slowing down of circulation. Our government has provided for a remedy for these ills—while American industry continues in the competition which it offers to foreigners—by means of a law of the country concerning the maxim of buying from them only the equivalent of what they buy from us, putting into effect Jefferson's doctrine of setting the manufacturer and the worker opposite each other, and thus creating a domestic market for the surplus at our ports. The adoption of this economic system, so fitting for our situation, so inseparable from our prosperity, and so honorable for our character, is the reason that the present administration has been attacked. Our fellow citizens of the South have abandoned themselves to factious and illegal threats to dissolve the Union in the event that Mr. Adams should be reelected. We trust that our fellow citizens are not ready to abandon their interests by abandoning the present government in order to please an ill-starred faction. If you are all prepared to assert your own rights against the violent Southern faction, unite your votes in the upcoming elections and support the cause of the principles of your country. The candidates that we have presented to be elected have been well known to you. They are staunch friends of the administration, and no one doubts their qualities and capacity for carrying out the duties of the respective offices for which we have chosen them.

John Prior, president
John House, James McCrea, secretaries.

The latter part of this proclamation makes reference to the noisy question of tariffs, concerning which I have had enough to say to my readers by including the documents in their proper places. This is the way they treat elections in the United States, but the saving principle of the country is that when the election has been carried by the majority, then all are silent before the law. Much of this is due to the fact that the election of the president comes directly from the people, and consequently is not subject to the intrigues and maneuvering which take place where the election is carried out by the legislatures in a country in which the elections are indirect. When done in this manner, the president is far from his legitimate origins, which should be the will of the majority of the citizens.

In New York at this same time was Don José Salgado, banished from Mexico for political reasons. With him I made a trip to West Point, one of the most picturesque spots in the world.

West Point is the place where the military school is located, on a vast plateau that is a part of the Allegheny chain, and at its foot runs the majestic Hudson River. The level area is more than three hundred feet above the river, and consequently the air is fresh, and the students enjoy good health. The very isolated location of this institute gives them protection against the corruption of the city, and at the same time obliges them to give themselves over to their studies without distractions. Teaching and habits both gain by this. There are 220 students, and they attend without charge since the secretary of war of the United States transmits the order of the president. The qualifications that the young men must have are that they be from fifteen to eighteen years of age, have a good education and a perfect knowledge of the English language and possess the first principles of arithmetic. The course of study is four years, in which period they learn mathematics, astronomy, experimental physics, military science, natural history, geography, French, history, drawing, moral philosophy and the laws of the Union. At the same time they are taught the handling of arms, field exercise, and the practice of military art in general. With this in mind they devote two months out of the year to making excursions into the surrounding areas, where the students make surveys, take positions and become accustomed to the fatigues of the campaign.

The mathematical sciences are the ones that they are most actively involved with. The students are expected to show a very broad knowledge much superior to what is required in Europe to make a good infantry or cavalry officer. Great importance is given to mathematics in the United States certainly because there is still and will be for a long time to come a great amount of territory to explore and develop, for which purpose knowledge of mathematics is very useful.

The staff of the school consists of a commander in chief of the institution, which must have an officer of artillery or engineering, a professor of natural history and physics with an assistant, a professor of mathematics with a second, a professor of engineering with a second, an ecclesiastical professor of eloquence and literature, a teacher of drawing, a professor of French, a fencing master and a physician.

The library is well chosen. It is composed of works on statistics, natural history, civil and military history. Among the latter are all the letters from the French campaigns, enhanced by very rich engravings. Also included are the campaigns of Frederick the Great and the plans of the fortifications of Vauban. The collection of maps, which is very valuable, contains among others the Baltic and North Sea ports by Beautemps and Beaupré.

West Point was during the revolution an important point which the English tried to get control of several times. Still to be seen are the ruins of some of the fortifications of that period. There travelers see the place where the tents of Washington were pitched, Kosciuzko's gardens cultivated by his own hands, and the cenotaph of this famous Pole. It would be difficult to select a place richer in memories, more appropriate for bringing out in the hearts of the young the love of patriotic virtues and a noble desire for studies that contribute to maintaining national glory and independence. The views across the Hudson River are romantic, filled with natural beauties and capable of firing the imagination.

Throughout the whole institution things are orderly and clean, and the instruction is rather advanced. A few years ago a young Indian from the Creek tribe named Moniac held a distinguished place among the students. I have heard praises of his mathematical knowledge from persons that saw him solve varied questions of geometry and analysis with great ease. This example and many that I could cite of Mexican Indians who do honor to their country give the lie to the statement by Buffon and Reynal that the natives of the Americas cannot attain the degree of intelligence of the inhabitants of the Old World.

The students in this institute are divided into companies, and they perform military service under the orders and direction of an army officer who gives them lessons in tactics. Each one receives a degree according to the merits and progress of his studies in accordance with the special rules of each class. The cadets are in camp during two months each year, during which time they are only concerned with military exercises. Then they receive rations twice a day and sixteen dollars per month, which amounts to about twenty-eight dollars. When he leaves school each student receives a commission or place in one of the military branches according to his ability and merit. Some come out to continue their studies and receive broader instruction in the great colleges of Europe, with their same salary.

A great part of the prime policy of governments is to favor a literary, scientific, and industrial direction suitable to impress the natural movement of the human mind. The activity, the very ferment of the minds of our new republics, favor the progress of civilization, and that abundance of life that produces long and violent political and military shakeups which have stirred up the social structure in the new states, have had, from some points of view, salutary effects like the flooding of the Nile that spreads fertility over the lands that its waters have covered. This activity, which cannot appear dangerous, except to those who have plans of tyranny and oppression, who wish to do away with superior men of sound character and capable of thoughts and plans of general interest, will become useful and advantageous when it receives proper direction. Its effects will be beneficial to public morality, the free development of intellectual faculties, the stability of philanthropic institutions, bringing glory to the directors.

In New York there is a house of refuge for delinquent youths of both sexes where they are taught trades suitable to their dispositions, and they are not exposed to being corrupted by the bad examples of the criminals in the other jails. There is also a school for the deaf and dumb and an asylum for the insane. In these establishments there is the best order, and nothing is lacking for the unfortunate ones whom fate has condemned to suffer. The interest which those in charge take in watching over the direction of these institutions and the perfect cooperation that they meet with in all their agents are truly laudable and worthy of being proposed as models. Those who may compare this establishment with our San Hipólito in Mexico will note in the Mexican hospice the magnificence of the buildings, great staffs of employees and administrators, a spacious temple, many rules and ample incomes, by the side of the lack of cleanliness and little attention for the troubled ones. In the North American institution the building is proportionate to the need, there is a chapel, the care and attention for the insane are admirable, and the neatness and cleanliness of beds and clothing leaves nothing to be desired, and the salaries are very moderate.

In the state of New York there are two large prisons more or less on the model of those of the states of Massachusetts and Pennsylvania of which I have already spoken. These are Sing Sing on the Hudson River and Auburn on the Oswego. The latter has 550 cells with a prisoner in each one. Their imprisonment is not such as to keep them solitary for the whole time of confinement as is true at the penitentiary at Philadelphia.

Since the state legislature has felt that physical exercise is necessary to maintain health, they are put to work during the day under the strictest of rules. As soon as the convict comes in he is given prison clothing, they read him the rules and instruct him as to his duties. These consist solely of obeying orders and working diligently and silently, speaking respectfully to the prison guards, not speaking except when necessary even to the guards, not dancing or singing or making any sort of noise whatsoever, not going away from the area where they are assigned without permission, not becoming distracted from their work nor resting for a moment. Nor are they permitted to receive letters, nor have any sort of communication with the outside. Anything of this nature must be through their custodians. Each prisoner has a Bible furnished by the state.

Any infractions against the rules or verbal admonitions are immediately punished by the penalty of lashing with a leather whip. Punishment is so swift and immediate for breaking the rules that there are very few cases of this. Early in the morning a bell rings, and the jailers open the cells of the prisoners. These come out into a common courtyard in the summertime or into a great hall in the winter; they wash their hands and faces in basins provided, and then continue in line like soldiers to their respective jobs. The new prisoners, if they have a trade, work at it; if not, they are taught one that they choose. They regularly work twelve hours. They eat in a refectory and always with their backs to each other in the greatest silence. When they need something, they raise their hands and are served what they want. The time allotted for each meal is regularly half an hour. When they retire for the night they wash their hands and faces again. Their clothes are always kept clean.

On Sunday, after washing, instead of working they go to the chapel where the chaplain has the divine service. Those who know how to read and write, who are very few, go to Sunday School where they receive suitable instruction.

The daily rations for each prisoner are ten ounces of pork or sixteen of beef, ten ounces of wheat flour, twelve of cooked corn-meal, hot potatoes and half a quart of barley made in the form of coffee and sweeted with molasses. At noon they are served soup made with beef broth thickened with cornmeal bread, potatoes and cold water. For supper there is a sort of cornmeal porridge, that they call *mush,* and cold water. This amount of food has been considered as sufficient for keeping the prisoners in perfect health.

The daily earnings of each prisoner are calculated at twenty-five to thirty-five cents. From this fund come the expenses of the prison, which is so neat and clean that one could not ask more. Before the prisoners leave, they are obliged to relate their lives, and tell what trade they have followed and intend to follow. This will make an interesting collection of case histories from which may be drawn useful observations concerning the national character, and even about human nature. Of 170 who have gone forth, 112 have straightened up completely, and 26 have continued in their evil ways; the others were indifferent. The prisoners say that the greatest penalty is not to be able to talk or to have news of what is going on outside. One must confess that these precautions are necessary and weep over the fate of the man condemned to suffer such great priva-tions. Here one cannot say with Dante: *Qui vive la pieta quand' e ben morta.* ("Here mercy dwells when it is quite dead").

CONCLUSION

"The United States," Mr. Hamilton says very well, "is perhaps the people least exposed to revolutions today. But its stability," he adds, "consists of the unique circumstances that the great majority of the inhabitants are property owners."

There is no doubt that it is one, but not the only cause for the unchanging tranquility of that fortunate people. In social systems a question cannot be resolved by the explanation of a single circumstance. Spain, for example, remained peaceful until the year 1808 under the tyrannical yoke of monarchy, inquisition and military government. And this peace of the tomb could not be explained solely by one single cause, to wit, the *terror inspired* by the established forms. There were in addition ignorance, superstition, the tremendous influence of friars and clergy, support of the grandees, in short an order of things established and coordinated in such a manner that they upheld each other. Set up in that same Spain or in Mexico *the agrarian law,* distribute properties equally, and the result will be to throw all classes into confusion, debase values, nourish and foster laziness and multiply disorders.

It is true that one of the principal causes of the stability of the institutions of the United States of North America is the fortunate situation of the great majority of the people. But side by side with those material enjoyments the people place the sacred right of taking part in all transactions that have as their purpose the organizing of public powers, individual guarantees that assure them their laws, freedom to write and publish their opinions, freedom that they have to worship God according to their own consciences, and the deep and indestructible conviction of all the citizens that the law is equal for all, and that there are no institutions set up to favor one class, nor a hierarchy of privilege.

As he casts a rapid glance over this gigantic nation which was born yesterday and today extends its arms from the Atlantic to the Pacific and the China Sea, the observer stands in deep thought and naturally asks himself the question, "What will be the final outcome of its greatness and prosperity?" It is not the power of conquests nor the force of arms; nor is it the illusions of a cult that unites the rules of morality with the mysteries of dogma; it is a new social order, brilliant, positive; a political system that has excluded all privilege, all distinctions consecrated by previous centuries, that has produced this prodigious creation. Standing before this political phenomenon statesmen of all countries, philosophers, economists have stopped to contemplate the rapid march of this amazing people, and agreeing with one accord on the never before seen prosperity of its inhabitants side by side with sobriety, love of work, unlimited liberty, domestic virtues, a creative activity, and an almost fanatical religious feeling, they have made an effort to explain the causes of these great results.

What have the ancient republics, the anarchies of the Middle Ages, or the European confederations been in comparison with this extraordinary nation? Athens was a turbulent democracy, four leagues in extent, dominated by skillful orators who knew how to exploit it to their own advantage. Sparta, a vast community subject to rules rather than laws, a family rather than a society, without individual independence, without stimulation for the arts, the sciences, or virtues, a religious order similar to the Templars, that cannot serve as a model to any modern people.

Rome! In what period did that proud republic ever do anything for the well-being of the masses? The Roman people were oppressors of others and oppressed themselves by their patricians, even in their days of greatest liberty. Turbulent tribunals, often victims of their demagogic furies and of the hatreds of the patricians, they kept in ferment the common people who were content with a lessening of their debts, with occasional distributions of wheat, or with an apologue told with wisdom. Miserable attempts, although useful lessons, in order one day to arrive at the establishment of the American system!

Indeed, the political school of the United States is a complete system, a classic work, unique, a discovery such as that of printing, the compass, steam power, but a discovery that applies moral force to individual intelligences to move the great social machine, which until our day has been dragged rather than directed, driven by factious springs composed of heterogenous combinations, a monstrous mosaic of gathered bits of feudalism, superstition, caste privilege, legitimacies, sanctities, and other elements against nature, and ruins of that flood of shadows that inundated the world for twelve centuries.

Political experts of Europe may well turn to interpretations, prophecies, conjectures, and doleful commentaries upon the constitutions, future, stability, and laws of the United States. What they cannot deny is that there is not nor ever has been a people where the rights of the citizens were more respected, where individuals had more participation in government, where the masses were more perfectly equal in all social pleasures. What sort of argument against its institutions is it to announce to a nation an unhappy future, melancholy catastrophes, when the present is filled with life, happiness, and good fortune?

Those who cannot resist the conviction of obvious facts of daily experience resort to doleful prophecies and predict now the dissolution of the great republic. We shall answer them that the present good is better than hopes unrealized; that there is probably no man or people who would prefer living under oppression or in poverty to the happy and independent existence of that republic; only because some dyspeptic politicians tell them that that prosperous situation will not last two hundred years. No, never will the strength of that living and perservering example of social Utopia be weakened by such arguments. Be welcome to spy out their small and fleeting mob scenes; exaggerate the heat of their public debates, the turmoil of their elections, their most curious aberrations of Presbyterian fanaticism, their aversion to the black caste, their difficulties because of their system of slavery, their questions of tariffs, momentary difficulties with their banks, make the most unfavorable comments concerning these political and economic crises; a positive solution, a happy and quick insight comes forward to answer all your arguments. That nation, full of life and movement continues its course towards a goal, and from the frontiers of Nova Scotia to New Mexico the North American labors only upon these principles: *work and the rights of the citizen*. His code is concise, but clear, pure and easily perceived. Complicated questions, which they cannot decide since they are beyond the grasp of the less-educated classes, they refer entirely to that part of the people that has seemed to them to have best deserved their confidence because of a series of upright actions and decisions with beneficial results.

All those who are trying to make social improvements in the peoples that are marching towards progress look to Great Britain or the United States of the North, true and original types of social organizations that are solid and progressive. But the first one, a great nation, mistress of the seas, the depository of great wealth, with an abundance of outstanding and profound men, still has many steps to take in the direction of an order that is more liberal, more economical, in short more independent of the ancient feudal shackles; and her *Whigs* and *radicals,* after their triumphs of the Catholic emancipation, their bill of parliamentary reform, of ministerial organization, demand new improvements to put themselves in some degree at the same level as the latter. Still pending are questions of high political interest that were resolved in the United States since its birth. The tithes, the privileges of the nobles, the absolute separation of worship and administrative functions, primogeniture and others less essential, consequences of the former, are points that have been tossed about for a long time in the newspapers, in the tribunals, in the clubs and in the cabinet. What sort of shake-up will the colossal Albion have to undergo before seeing a definite end to these matters! Her great political experts, her ministers, have said so recently. "Much has been done," one of them was saying not long ago to his fellow citizens who were flattering him, "but we still have much left to do." Words filled with good sense and great hopes.

After the struggle that took place in the United States of the North a few years after independence between aristocratic and democratic parties, the latter came out victorious, to the point that the former disappeared completely, which is another phenomenon in the history of peoples; since then all the questions that have been aired on the rostrum, in the newspapers, and popular meetings have been purely economic. The Hartford Convention, which in 1814 attempted to revive the old Federalist principles, found no support anywhere, and since then there has been no single statesman who has dared to come forth to defend the system of Hamilton and Adams. Popular power in all its fullness, governing a nation powerful and of vast extent, taking its course with wisdom, moderation, and care, seeing the elements of a great territorial, industrial, and commercial prosperity develop under its administration, is perhaps the most powerful argument that can be put up against the eternal declamations of the absolutists and aristocrats.

In such a state of affairs two hundred thousand Europeans come to the United States every year seeking refuge in their wretchedness, and recompense for their work and weariness, free from the deductions to which the taxes of the Old World subject them, and from the shackles placed upon them by their systems more or less arbitrarily; with active and robust arms they find work immediately, and within a few months, owners of land made fertile by their sweat,

208

they found towns in spots a short time before inhabited only by wolves, bears and other wild animals.

Populous cities spring up overnight, steamboats ply rivers and lakes thousands of leagues from the sea in lands just discovered and unknown to the civilized world, manufactured goods are transported by skilful craftsmen from Europe, flying printing presses that multiply thoughts and ideas spreading education, missionaries of sects that from Italy, Germany, France, England, and other places come to preach their gospel beliefs, each one as he understands and professes it, and that agree completely in moral principles. The love of God and a fellow man is the basis of all religions. Immigrants from Ireland, France, Mexico, Colombia, Spain, Italy, from both hemispheres, who in the political upheavals in their own countries, obliged to leave their fatherland, come to find out what the enviable tranquility of that people consists of. Here you have the spectacle that the United States of the North presents. Add its maritime cities; that of New York, third port in the world, receiving in its bay three thousand boats each year that come loaded with products from the four corners of the world; that of New Orleans, the depot for a hundred cities that send to it their fruits by the boundless Mississippi, and by means of which a thousand communities are provided with foreign articles. Philadelphia, the city of peace, brotherhood and monotony, surrounded by country houses as beautiful as its daughters, founded upon the pleasant Delaware and the delightful Schuylkill, occupies a distinguished place on the commercial ladder. Baltimore, Charleston, Boston, remarkable cities because of the education of their inhabitants, their trade activity, the advantageous situation of their ports, the hospitality of their people, in short that openness, that assuredness, that liberty that all men enjoy, without the hindrances of passports, without the apparatus of soldiers, without the troublesome police, are circumstances that cannot fail to lead to prosperity and progress in all areas.

Those who accuse the North American people of being rude and unsociable fail to think about the elements that have gone into the makeup of that unusual nation. Persecuted families who came to seek liberty and a living in the frozen and uncivilized forests of northern America were forced to devote themselves to harsh and difficult tasks, to suffer painful privations, and to accustom themselves to a monotony of foods, words and communication, to which the needs of their continual work condemned them. So here you have the forefathers of the North Americans. To these have been added the farmers and artists that have come later from Holland, Germany, and Ireland, people who are generally hard working, economical, taciturn, dedicated exclusively to their undertakings;

and think then how there have come the Washingtons, the Jeffersons, the Franklins, the Adams, the Clintons, the Madisons, the Clays, the Websters, the Livingstons, the Hamiltons, the Monroes, the Jacksons, the Van Burens, the Dwights, and many other statesmen, famous writers, profound sages, distinguished literary men, economists, and illustrious generals who have lifted the country to its high degree of prosperity and glory.

The people of the United States are wise, economical and fond of accumulating capital for the future. That is the way it should be naturally. Because, in addition to their origins from which they inherit these qualities, in a climate like that, where man is obliged to work half the year for a severe season that confines him to his hearth and home, he cannot abandon himself to chance, confident in the fertility of the land and the cooperation of the seasons. The peoples of the south of Europe and of Asia were always the *least industrious,* and in Spain one notes that the Galicians, the Catalans, and the Basques are better farmers than the peoples of Andalucia and Castilla; besides, they have a more serious and less communicative and less flexible character. The progress of primary education, to which Americans give a great deal of interest, and the ease of their communications will with time make the manners of that people better and more sociable.

Before bringing this book to a close, I must not overlook the political relations that should progressively increase between the United States of the North and the United Mexican States, and the influences that the first undoubtedly exercises over the second. There is not a more seductive example for a nation that does not enjoy complete liberty than that of a neighbor where are found in all public acts, in all writings, lessons and practices of an unlimited liberty, and in which instead of the disastrous *cataclysms* that have overwhelmed some peoples in their anarchial revolutions, or in their bloody despotic systems, one sees the spectacle of the peaceful joys of a numerous segment of the human race, lifted up by the simultaneous energy of its popular intelligence to an eminently free and happy social rank. Could the legislators of the Mexican nation resist so strong an influence when they had in their hands the arranging of the destinies of their constituents? The model was sublime, but not to be imitated. Those who set themselves to copy a painting of Raphael or of Michael Angelo at times succeed in imitating some of the shadows, some of the characteristics that bring them somewhere within range of the original. However, they never manage to equal those sublime concepts. Original artists do not copy or imitate others; they invent, they create upon the models of nature, and they study her secrets and divine mysteries.

One of the political plagues that have brought many ills to some peoples has been the false persuasion of their legislators that such an organization or such laws would have their effect, and would be put into practice only because the majority of their representatives favored them. A similar error was fought against by the doctrines of all the great writers and by the experience of the centuries. But the example of thirteen republics born at the end of the last century in the New Continent, that have not only maintained themselves but by growing progressively have become twenty-four, thus forming a great confederation, produced so great and universal a sensation in minds that forthwith ancient doctrines were considered to have been destroyed by such an event. The reasoning appeared to be conclusive. English *colonies* with which at that time the political and commercial world little concerned itself, which with just the name of *colonies* were supposed to be degraded, ignorant and enslaved, suddenly elevated to the rank of free nations, in consequence of a well-written declaration of the rights of man and of peoples. "Why should we not do the same thing," said many writers, politicians and philosophers of the Old World, "we the depositories of the sciences, masters of the human race, proprietors of the commerce of nations, heirs to the glory of the Greeks and the Romans, fathers of those emancipated peoples?" Great events that have come to pass subsequently in both hemispheres have provided sufficient proof of the irresistible impulse given to the social movement by the appearance of that bright star in the firmament of nations.

What should be then the consequences of the constant example near at hand presented by the United States of the North to the Mexican nation, young and inexperienced, full of life and desirous of shaking off the remains of its ancient chains? In the narrow circle of continental Europe public right is that of the conservation of certain monarchial principles, the basis of all European political activity. Upon this code, sketched out for the first time in Pilnitz forty years ago, modified several times according to the diverse interests of the high contracting parties, European governments model themselves and change in different ways. In America things are different. Although the monarchial principle is not proscribed, it is evident that the opinion as it can be applied to the emerging republics is almost exclusively democratic. There one finds no interventions nor alliances, no diplomatic maneuvering, no money bags, not a single element with sufficient influence to determine the monarchial form. The only one that exists to some degree is ecclesiastical power, whose weakness is demonstrated by the experience of its fruitless endeavors up to now.

Consequently the influence of the United States upon Mexico will with time be a power of opinion, of teaching by guidance, all the stronger because it is purely moral, founded upon its doctrines and lessons. But there is more. Ten thousand citizens of the United States settle each year in the territory of the Mexican republic, especially in the states of Chihuahua, Coahuila and Texas, Tamaulipas, Nuevo Leon, San Luis Potosi, Durango, Zacatecas, Sonora, Sinaloa, and the Territories of New Mexico and the Californias.

These colonists and businessmen along with their hard work carry with them habits of freedom, economy, industry, their austere and religious ways, their individual independence and their republicanism. What change must these enterprising guests not make in the moral and material existence of the former inhabitants? Carthage was a Carthaginian people, Cadiz a Phonician people, Marseilles a Greek people for many centuries, because their colonists were from those nations. The Mexican republic then within a few years will come to be molded to a combined regimen of the American system and Spanish customs and traditions.

But it is necessary to distinguish in the Mexican nation that part populated, disciplined, founded, to put it thusly, in the mold of its former mother country, from that part bare of inhabitants, and consequently susceptible to a new population, completely different from the other one. In the first there will exist for many years yet the struggle of opposing principles that have been planted in their institutions, and civil war will be inevitable, while in the second the American, German, Irish, and English colonies are establishing completely free settlements that will prosper peacefully under the influence of their democratic institutions, and even more of their work habits, their ideas and convictions concerning the dignity of man and the respect that is due the law. Thus, while the states of Puebla, Chiapas, Oaxaca, Mexico, Queretaro, Michoacan, and Guanajuato continue in the grip of the military and ecclesiastical arm as a penalty for their prejudices, their ignorance, and their superstition; while in the bosom of these states a few generous and enlightened patriots will make efforts to lift their fellow citizens up to the level of the adopted institutions and will seek to give them lessons in liberty and tolerance; while these opposing elements light the fires of combat among an ardent youth that loves progress and civilization and an ignorant clergy strongly attached to their privileges and income, supported by a few generals and officers of the former Spanish army, without faith, without honor, without patriotism, possessed of a sordid greed and given over to degrading vices; while this is happening in these states, the others will be populated, will become rich, striving to avoid being contaminated by the disastrous things happening to their brothers in the south.

The net result, however, will be the triumph of liberty in these states, and upon the Gothic ashes and the remains of untenable privileges there will be raised up a glorious and enlightened generation that will put into motion all the sources of wealth that abound and will bring into association with the civilized family that indigenous group, until today debased and vilified, and will teach them to think and to hold in esteem their dignity by lifting their thoughts to a higher level.

What barrier can oppose this torrent that was born twenty-four years ago in a small town in the Bagio, obscure in its origins, without direction or channel, destroying everything in its path, today a majestic river that receives pure crystalline waters from other countries that will make fertile the entire Mexican territory? Unsuccessful efforts will oppose a debased generation, heir to Castilian traditions and beliefs and defender without great results of their antisocial doctrines. The American system will obtain a complete though bloody victory.

INDEX

215

DATE DUE

HIGHSMITH 45-102   PRINTED IN U.S.A